Economics, Ethics, and Ancient Thought

T0270766

It is argued that the normative and ethical presuppositions of standard economics render the discipline incapable of addressing an important class of problems involving human choices. Economics adopts too thin an account both of human motivation and of "the good" for individuals and for society. It is recommended that economists and policy-makers look back to ancient philosophy for guidance on the good life and good society considered in terms of eudaimonism, or human flourishing.

Economics, Ethics, and Ancient Thought begins by outlining the limitations of the normative and ethical presuppositions that underpin standard economic theory, before going on to suggest alternative normative and ethical traditions that can supplement or replace those associated with standard economic thinking. In particular, this book considers the ethical thought of ancient thinkers, particularly the ancient Greeks and their concept of *eudaimonia*, arguing that within those traditions better alternatives can be found to the rational choice utilitarianism characteristic of modern economic theory and policy.

This volume is of great interest to those who study economic theory and philosophy, history of economic thought and philosophy of social science, as well as public policy professionals.

Donald G. Richards is Professor of Economics at Indiana State University. His research interests have focused on international economics and international political economy, writing on intellectual property rights and welfare. In recent years his research has concentrated on sustainability and the environment.

Routledge Studies in the History of Economics

For a full list of titles in this series, please visit www.routledge.com/series/SE0341

185 On Abstract and Historical Hypotheses and on Value-Judgments in Economic Sciences
Critical Edition, with an Introduction and Afterword by Paolo Silvestri
Luigi Einaudi
Edited by Paolo Silvestri

186 The Origins of Neoliberalism
Insights from economics and philosophy
Giandomenica Becchio and Giovanni Leghissa

187 The Political Economy of Latin American Independence
Edited by Alexandre Mendes Cunha and Carlos Eduardo Suprinyak

188 Jean-Baptiste Say and Political Economy
Jean-Baptiste Say
Gilles Jacoud

189 Economists and War
A heterodox perspective
Edited by Fabrizio Bientinesi and Rosario Patalano

190 Great Economic Thinkers from the Classicals to the Moderns
Translations from the series *Klassiker der Nationalökonomie*
Bertram Schefold

191 Business Cycles in Economic Thought
A History
Edited by Alain Alcouffe, Monika Poettinger and Bertram Schefold

192 Economics, Ethics, and Ancient Thought
Towards a virtuous public policy
Donald G. Richards

Economics, Ethics, and Ancient Thought

Towards a virtuous public policy

Donald G. Richards

Routledge
Taylor & Francis Group

LONDON AND NEW YORK

First published 2017
by Routledge

2 Park Square, Milton Park, Abingdon, Oxfordshire OX14 4RN

52 Vanderbilt Avenue, New York, NY 10017

Routledge is an imprint of the Taylor & Francis Group, an informa business

First issued in paperback 2019

British Library Cataloguing in Publication Data
A catalogue record for this book is available from the British Library

Library of Congress Cataloging in Publication Data
A catalog record for this book has been requested

ISBN: 978-1-138-84026-3 (hbk)
ISBN: 978-0-367-87174-1 (pbk)

Typeset in Times New Roman
by Taylor & Francis Books

Of the things which wisdom provides for the blessedness of one's whole life, by far the greatest is the possession of friendship.
Epicurus

For,

EKR
ECR
GSR
JMR
JCS
(A)PA
RHL

Contents

Preface and acknowledgments   viii

PART I
Ethics and economics   **1**

1   Introduction   3

2   *Eudaimonia*: the ancients and the good life   13

3   The impact of the ancients   34

4   Conceptions of rationality: thin, thick, and ancient   67

PART II
Ethics and public policy   **93**

5   The problem of pathological consumption   95

6   Economics, ethics, and the environment   123

7   Reason, ethics, and the end of life   142

8   Towards a virtuous public finance   160

9   Final thoughts on virtue, the market, and policy   178

Index   183

Preface and acknowledgments

Books are often very personal statements. That much is widely recognized and non-controversial. What may be somewhat more controversial is a book about public affairs and policy that is also highly personal. This is just such a book. Its genesis resides in notions I developed many years ago about the importance of economics as an academic and policy-oriented discipline, combined with what I felt then, and continue to believe today, are its severe limitations as a guide to human behavior. My early career as a "rogue" economist was aided by my (non-assigned) reading of John Kenneth Galbraith's *The Affluent Society* and Tibor Scitovsky's *The Joyless Economy*. These books, and many other since, taught me that economists can and should be advocates for a vision of "the good life" even when that vision is motivated by a highly critical view of mainstream economics and its most prominent proponents. That is, they taught me that polemics in the service of a vision is not a fault. Thus I began, and have operated ever since, however anonymously, under the cover of heterodoxy. A second source of inspiration for this work came to me during a period of personal crisis when I sought succor from Marcus Aurelius's *Meditations*. To say the least, Aurelius's words of wisdom gave me valuable perspective on my circumstances, and it sparked my curiosity about his life and times. One thing led to another, and I began my self-education in Hellenistic ethics, the deficiencies of which will probably be obvious to the professional philosophers who bother to read on. These deficiencies begin with the fact that I read neither Greek nor Latin. I have depended naturally then on English translations of the ancient works. I realize from my reading of the secondary literature that there are frequently competing interpretations of these works among classicists. I shamelessly admit that I have chosen among these according to the support they provide to my argument. As the notes and references will make clear, I have also relied very heavily indeed on the secondary literature. I apologize in advance for whatever short-comings in my understanding of this body of scholarship are revealed in this work, and I thank the many authors who provided so many well-spent hours of instruction to a very imperfect student.

There are others I wish to thank. Versions of Chapters 6 and 7 were previously published in *Ethics & the Environment* and *Review of Social Economy*, respectively. I am grateful to (respectively) Routledge and Indiana University Press for permission to reprint portions of those articles here. Several of the chapters were presented at academic conferences. I thank participants in sessions at the Eastern Economics Association, Midwest Economics Association, and the Indiana Academy of the Social Sciences for their comments and suggestions. The following individuals helped me to come to a better understanding of many of the ideas expressed in this book: Greg Peterson, Rick Lotspeich, Paul Burkett, Julia Annas, Julia Wildberger, Spencer Pack, and Jean Kristeller. None of them bear any responsibility for any errors that remain. Finally, I wish to thank the staff at Cunningham Memorial Library (CML) at Indiana State University for their support. The collections at CML are small, but its inter-library loan department is "dynamic."

Part I
Ethics and economics

1 Introduction

This is a book about economics. It is also a book about ethics. The combination of economics and ethics may seem a bit strange to some readers. After all, economics is a social science and science is about *what is*. Ethics, on the other hand, is about *what should be*. How can we reconcile the two? We might start by recognizing that in the beginning economics was considered to be a part of the study of moral philosophy. The beginning of economics, at least modern economics, occurred with the publication of *The Wealth of Nations* by Adam Smith. As most students of Smith are aware, however, the original modern economist was originally a moral philosopher. Before he published *The Wealth of Nations* he published *A Theory of Moral Sentiments*.

We can go back much further than Smith to find that perhaps the very first thinker on economics questions was the ancient Greek philosopher, Aristotle. To find Aristotle's thoughts on such matters as exchange, price and currency, however, we would have to dig fairly deep into Book 5 of his *Nicomachean Ethics*. For Aristotle these seemingly objective scientific economic concepts were inseparable from a consideration of justice. If we move a few decades forward in time from Smith we encounter John Stuart Mill. Mill was also both a moral philosopher as well as an economist. The basis for Mill's moral philosophy was utilitarianism, an approach he literally learned at the knee of his father James Mill and family friend Jeremy Bentham. Utilitarianism is the philosophic belief that the best decision is the one that creates the greatest amount of happiness, or utility, for the greatest number of people. In a revised form this remains an important normative principle underpinning contemporary economic theory.

These three figures by no means exhaust the list of important thinkers who developed important economic theories as well as moral systems. Thomas Aquinas and Karl Marx provide additional examples. So the question arises as to how, when, and why did the discipline of economics become separated from its close relationship with moral philosophy? The answer that most historians of economic doctrine give to the "how" and "when" questions cite a movement termed the Marginalist Revolution during the 1870s. The Marginalist Revolution consisted of the simultaneous development among a variety of economists of an approach to the discipline that impressed it with a firm scientific stamp.

The leading figures of this movement were Stanley Jevons, Leon Walras, and Carl Menger. These economists along with some others made economics "scientific" by making it mathematical. Jevons and Walras in particular expressed economic relationships in such a way as to make analysis amenable to differentiable calculus. The emphasis in the kinds of questions asked was less concerned with the causes and consequences of economic growth and distribution, but rather with the conditions for equilibrium.

So, what happened to the normative/ethical content of economics that seemed to preoccupy so many over the preceding hundreds of years? The answer is the Marginal Revolutionists believed that utilitarianism had provided all the answers needed to these sorts of questions and concerns. That is, they shared the view of Bentham and his followers that the "good" is best understood as that which delivers maximum utility. For the Revolutionists the important remaining task was to describe in rigorous, mathematical terms the conditions, or assumptions, under which this goal could be achieved and the equilibrium rules that assure its realization. The assumptions that drove their models are ones familiar to anyone who has ever taken a basic economics course that appoints pride of place to the notion of perfect competition. The theory or model of perfect competition makes a number of assumptions including:

1   There are a large number of buyers and producer-sellers of a good or service.
2   No market participant (buyer or seller) is large enough to unilaterally affect the market outcome.
3   Producer-sellers sell a homogeneous output.
4   Market participants possess perfect information.
5   There are no obstacles to market entry or exit.
6   There are no side effects, or externalities, of consumption or production activities that befall third parties.
7   Market participants are rational, self-interested utility (or profit) maximizers.

Under this set of assumptions the Revolutionists' models demonstrated that unfettered market prices were able to allocate scarce resources to their most highly valued uses. Moreover, these same market prices ensured that the welfare of any particular individual could not be improved without reducing that of some other individual. In other words, the system of market prices guaranteed efficiency in the allocation of goods and resources, and at the same time it maximized welfare understood in utility terms. Furthermore, the models demonstrated that perfectly competitive factor markets also worked efficiently so that factor market prices reflect the (marginal) productivity of their corresponding productive factors including capital, land, and various skill grades of labor, thus guaranteeing an efficient distribution of income. In the minds of the Revolutionists this was tantamount to distributive justice. And there wasn't much more that needed to be said about ethics where economic matters were concerned.

As I've already noted, the result of the Marginal Revolution was that economics was transformed into a much more "scientific" discipline. This is true at least to the extent that one equates the term "scientific" with a tendency to express theories in terms of formal, quantitative models. This scientific transformation came at the cost of the discipline's development on the basis of a highly truncated set of normative presuppositions. In particular, the assumption that human behavior can be adequately described in terms of utility maximization has in recent years come under increasing scrutiny and criticism. Additionally, the implicit assumption that the value of any and all economic choices can be perfectly encapsulated in terms of the relative price attached to any choice(s) has also been subject to critical examination.

This book makes a contribution to this critical literature. Its main contention is that there is an important class of public policy concerns for which the standard model of economic behavior, typically referred to as neoclassical economics, fails to provide adequate guidance due to the inadequacy of its guiding normative presuppositions as well as its assumptions respecting human motivations and behavior. The question which I pose is this: Where shall we look to find replacement, or at least supplemental, normative presuppositions? The answer I give is that we should look back to ancient thought. This is not a very original suggestion. After all, the source of much of our moral philosophy derives from ancient sources. In fact, as I shall argue in the next chapter, the source of the normative presuppositions that have guided modern economic thought is inspired by ancient thought, and in particular by ancient Greek philosophy.

In particular, I wish to focus on the ethical thought of an epoch of the ancient Greek world called the Hellenistic period. Historians of economic thought often cite Aristotle as the ancient thinker who had most to say about economics. In fact the origins of the word economics are traced to the ancient Greek term *oikonomikè*, which is translated as household management. In this book, however, the focus is not on Classical Greek thought, a period that would include Plato as well as Aristotle, but rather the philosophy of a later period called the Hellenistic age. The Hellenistic age is said to commence around the time of death of Alexander the Great in 323 BCE and end around the time of the defeat of Marc Antony in 31 BCE. The period includes the ideas of both Greek philosophers and Roman philosopher/statesmen. I hope to show that the ideas of several of the important thinkers of this period have direct relevance to the ethical-normative basis of modern economics and that they were an important source of inspiration for several important modern economic thinkers.

Why should we believe that the ancient Hellenistic period might have some relevance for contemporary political economy? This is not the first time this question has been posed. Consider the opening words of Michael I. Rostovtzeff in his 1935 (p231) address to the American Historical Association:

In these days of unsettled and chaotic economic conditions, of an acute economic crisis which prevails over all the civilized world, when all sorts of remedies are suggested for healing the wounds, and among them, under the label of the last word in economic science, some old-age and many times tried devices, it is perhaps not inappropriate for a student of ancient economic history to recall to mind the remote past of Greece and Rome where similar crises were not infrequent and where many devices were tried in the hope of solving them.

It is clear that Rostovtzeff sees a certain parallelism in the economic trauma of the Great Depression and the political economic upheaval of the Hellenistic age. There are good reasons for this. The spread of Alexander's empire had profound consequences for the global economy of the time just as did the spread of international economic relations and imperialist adventures in the decades leading to World War I. These expanding political and economic entanglements reverberated on the established centers of power and control. Thus, for example, the prevailing mode of political, social, and economic organization of ancient Greece, the city-state, fell into decline. Economic self-sufficiency was replaced by a growing dependence on foreign sources of new goods and on foreign markets for domestic output. Overall the Greek economies found themselves in a position of trade deficit relative to the oriental regions of the new empire compounded by rising prices, and dramatic shifts in land-ownership that accompanied the rise of new prosperous elites, (Sibley 1970: 107). An overall result of this globalization process was a much more unequal distribution of income and a tendency to economic stagnation. Moreover, money wages were stagnant and, in the face of rising prices, this meant a decline in real wages. The condition of the masses had declined to such a great extent that calls for debt forgiveness and land redistribution increased. The propertied classes were in turn alarmed by this as well as by a growing fear of revolution (Erskine 1990: 35–36).

Politically, Greek democratic institutions of governance found themselves displaced by "kingship" rule. As a Macedonian, Alexander was predisposed to concentrating political power in his own imperial hands and he took encouragement from the oriental despotism he encountered in his travels. After his death the empire was divided up into a variety of kingdoms. The Greek city-states sought greater autonomy by forming alliances to oppose foreign domination and were often successful but at the cost of entering into a state of almost perpetual war against non-Greeks and with one another. A long period of military and political turbulence lasted until the Greek city-states were subdued by the Roman Empire in 146 BCE, (Sibley 1970: 109). Hellenistic philosophy quite naturally reflects the political economic instability of its era. The various schools of thought that emerge might be said to express a "siege mentality" in the face of tremendous turbulence and change.

Chapter 2 provides an overview of the Hellenistic schools paying particular attention to their views on ethics. Notable is the contrast between the

Hellenistic philosophers and their classical era predecessors, Aristotle and Plato. By and large the latter two were systems builders. Their ethics had definite implications for the way they believed political and social institutions should be structured. As far as that is concerned, Aristotle and Plato probably had more to say about topics that we would today identify as "economics" in their substance. The Hellenistic philosophers might be said to lay greater stress on how "the good life" should be pursued as a personal matter. But there are good reasons to focus on the implications of Hellenistic ethics for the meaning of "the good society" as well. The first is that at least one school of Hellenistic thought, the Stoics, believed that a well-lived life could not be separated from a concern with how the individual related to society as a whole. That is, the individual had a eudaimonistic concern that led her to be engaged with society and this concern could extend itself to mean an engagement with political life. Second there are good reasons to believe that a belief in equality was a value that attaches itself more to Hellenistic ethics than it does to the classical Greek ethical outlooks. Hellenistic thought is for this reason more likely to suggest the democratic norms and values and provide the context for contemporary public policy questions and challenges. A third reason to focus on Hellenistic ethics is its greater cosmopolitanism as compared to their Aristotelian and Platonic predecessors. This tendency may be a reflection of the "globalization" process at work during the period of Alexander and, later, the Roman Empire. Certainly there was an acceleration in the spread of ideas and cross-cultural influence that caused the Greeks to reconsider their localism and associated chauvinism. Once having been exposed to the wider world, it was much harder to dismiss its inhabitants as "barbarians." Just as the comparative egalitarianism of the Hellenistic philosophers renders them more relevant to contemporary concerns, so does their relative cosmopolitanism.

The classical Greek philosophers, of course, bequeathed to the Hellenistic schools many important elements of their own thought that persisted in the ideas of the latter. First among these is the central organizing concept for this book, *eudaimonia*. It could be said that much of our present-day economic and social policy is driven by a concern with utility, or pleasure. It is hedonic in its orientation.[1] Utilitarian social policy is that which is concerned with increasing, even maximizing, society's welfare, where "welfare" is understood in hedonic terms. Now, there is nothing necessarily wrong with this as an object of policy and it seems entirely appropriate that policy ought to aim to increase our hedonic welfare. But the ancient Greeks going back to Socrates knew that there is more to the well-lived life than just pleasure.

This brings us to a second ethical notion held in common by the classical and Hellenistic thinkers, virtue. Virtually all the ancient Greek philosophers considered that virtue was a necessary component to *eudaimonia*. Where they differed among themselves was in their understandings of the specific content of virtue. Notwithstanding these differences, nearly all schools of Greek ethics cite Socrates as the paradigmatic virtuous man. What made Socrates a model of virtue? Primary was his unceasing commitment to the search for truth via the application of reasoned debate and the critical examination of assumptions. The "Socratic method" is today a widely employed pedagogical approach that encourages interlocutors to examine their assumptions and define their terms in rigorous dialog. Socrates was also well known for his humility. Famously, he claimed that the only thing that he knew was that he knew nothing. His personal lifestyle was equally humble as he was said to own few possessions and to walk about shoeless even in the dead of winter. Perhaps, however, Socrates is most revered in the history of philosophy for his physical, intellectual and moral courage. In terms of the first of these he was an acclaimed soldier who was fearless in battle. In terms of the latter two his lasting legacy was a refusal to flee in the face of imminent death by execution despite the urgings of his followers who loved him. Each of these virtues is reflected in the outlooks of one or the other of the main schools of Hellenistic ethics, and it isn't surprising that they each attempt to claim Socrates as a source and a model. The model of Socrates is also an appropriate one in relation to the comparatively more democratic outlook of the Hellenistic philosophy as compared to the class-based views of Plato and Aristotle. As Gottlieb (1999) notes, for example, for Socrates the search for truth was open to anyone who was willing to engage in a critical examination of their own life and assumptions. It was not, as it was for Plato, an activity reserved for an intellectual elite.

It is important to understand that the various schools of Hellenistic philosophy competed with one another for disciples and influence. While they have some commonalities they also oppose one another on points of particular doctrine and emphasis. No attempt is made in this book to reconcile them where they differ. Rather, I shall choose a more eclectic path and select those teachings that are especially useful in support of examining particular contemporary social and economic problems and their possible policy solutions. There is plenty of precedent in modern thought for this approach. Even the development of Hellenistic philosophy itself in the form of the Stoic school, as we shall see, has been selective in the particular doctrines it has chosen to reject and retain and in the amount of emphasis it has afforded to others.

In Chapter 3 I trace the impact that the Hellenistic philosophers had upon the development of economic thought. The focus here, as mentioned above, is on the ethical presuppositions of economics, rather than on economic theory itself. The influence of the ancients worked its greatest effects on those latter modern economists who also thought deeply about ethics. This includes most prominently Adam Smith whose Stoic influence is most obvious in his *The Theory of Moral Sentiments*. Like most Enlightenment Age thinkers, Smith was intimately familiar with ancient philosophy and could assume that this same familiarity would be found among his readers such that he would freely quote ancient sources without attribution or citation. Mid-nineteenth-century philosopher/economist John Stuart Mill is a key figure of discussion in the development of modern value theory. As we shall show, while Mill was trained in the utilitarian tradition developed by Bentham, he also broke with it. "Better to be a dissatisfied Socrates than a fool satisfied," he wrote. Not coincidentally, J. S. Mill was introduced at a very early age by his father to the ancient Greek texts. J. S. Mill would later cite these ancient sources in his qualification of the utilitarianism championed by James Mill and Bentham. The influence of Epicurean materialism on Marx's thought is taken up as is Aristotle's insights on his value theory. The question is raised about Marx as a moral philosopher and what we might say about his own ethical requirements for human flourishing.

Reason is a motivating principle in Hellenistic and in Greek philosophy generally. As it turns out, reason, or rationality, is a motivating assumption in modern economics as well. And yet, the term is understood to mean substantially different things in the two contexts. The primary purpose of Chapter 4 is to compare the eudaimonistic understanding of "reason" and "rational" to similar notions as they are employed in modern social sciences, and especially neoclassical economics. The important point is made that while the latter concept is descriptive of human behavior, the former is prescriptive of the would-be wise. Put another way, rational choice utilitarianism (RCU) describes rational human behavior in terms of a set of consistent decision rules, or algorithm. By contrast the eudaimonistic account sees the concepts of "rational" or "reasonable" as ethical aspirations. They are characteristics of the sage. The status of sage in turn requires a developmental commitment on the part of the individual. It is not one automatically conferred on us as human beings.

I argue in this chapter that while the RCU approach has its place in policy-making, the approach also has some serious limitations which I detail. Despite these limitations RCU is the standard, effective basis for a large and growing number of social and economic policy decisions ranging from health care to environmental protection. Economics has become so influential in policy circles that there seem to be no limits to the effort to extend its methods and applications well beyond the sort of concerns that we traditionally associate with the discipline.[2] My argument boils down to the position that some important issues or concerns require that we appeal to individuals, including policy makers, on the basis of their impulses toward such motivations as duty and commitment rather than on the basis of utility maximization. Further, I hope to demonstrate that an enlarged ethical/normative world-view informed by a eudaimonistic understanding of the good and valuable will improve policy-making in several important areas of social concern. These specific areas are taken up in Chapters 5 to 8.

"Rational addiction" and human flourishing

Some neoclassical economists have argued that addictive behavior is merely a variant of normal consumption behavior and that the addict acts from a fully informed information set pertaining to the costs and benefits of the activity in question. The choices made by the addict are in no important way then different than other results of utility maximizing choice-making. This perspective, I argue, is a logical extension of an exceedingly narrow understanding of both human behavior and an equally narrow understanding of the requirements for human flourishing. It considers that human well-being is the aggregation of the episodic moments in which hedonic pleasure is realized. It is a perspective that runs counter to the Stoic injunction that we exercise moderation and temperance and that we ascertain in a very deliberate fashion our natures and the discipline required to live "according to our natures" as the Stoics urged.

A eudaimonistic approach to environmental protection

The standard tools of economic analysis and policy-making are typically employed in decisions on environmental protection and natural resource use. Environmental ethicists have raised some cogent objections to these methods that are supported, I believe, from what I have described here as a eudaimonistic perspective. Standard (neoclassical) economic accounts of environmental use and protection tend to view the environment as a set of useful commodities to be appropriated for human use, rather than as a larger life system within which humans must live and that impose constraints on our behavior. Thus, while standard economics emphasizes substitution possibilities between and among natural resources, and between natural resources and manufactured goods, other (biocentric) critics emphasize the imperative that human beings face in reducing their impact on the larger natural system of which they are but a part. Economists are also often criticized as being too anthropocentric in their advocacy of particular environmental and natural resource management. Inspired by Hellenistic philosophy the position I take in Chapter 5 is also undeniably anthropocentric. It differs from the standard neoclassical view however in the broader understanding of what it sees as falling within the scope of human concerns as they relate to nature. It is certainly one that understands the economic system as a subordinate component to a larger natural system. Epicurean notions of pleasure, it is argued, actually point in the direction of consumption minimalism and, as such, are quite useful to a workable sustainability ethic. This eudaimonic approach also recruits the Stoic concept of *oikeiōsis*, or familiarity, to support the requisite inter-generational obligation essential to any meaningful concept of environmental sustainability.

Eudaimonism and the end of life

Another area fraught with important personal and public choice implications is concerned with the decisions we make toward the end of our lives. Economists have not paid a great deal of attention to such matters. Of the few who have, one has suggested that "rational denial" is an appropriate attitude to adopt considering the disutility we experience when we recognize our mortality. I argue that this attitude, while consistent with a narrow application of the hedonic calculus familiar to neoclassical economics, is not conducive to a well-lived life. At the core of the problem of "rational denial" resides an abiding fear of death that the mainstream approach accepts as part of the information set from which utility maximizers make their decisions. By contrast, Epicurus urges us not to fear death. The Stoic philosophers likewise enjoin us to consider the arc of our lives which includes its termination. To the extent that people take up this challenge from the ancients, they are likely to make much different decisions than they are if they adopt a standard pleasure seeking-pain avoidance rule. End of life healthcare choices are especially susceptible to re-evaluation. Decisions relating to organ donation, bequests, and life insurance may also come in for more careful examination. Public policies that support careful consideration of such issues will be examined in this chapter. The controversy over physician-assisted suicide is also given attention.

Virtue and public finance

Increasingly, government has shown a growing preference for financing its operations that are politically expedient. At the national level this has meant a preference to bond-finance rather than tax-finance expenditures. At the state and local levels it has resulted in a preference for schemes that rely on the voluntary choices of the public. In particular excise taxes and gambling have taken on increasing roles in funding state and local government. In this chapter I raise the question of how a "virtuous state" can expect to operate on the basis of public finance mechanisms that appeal to the "vicious" choices of its constituencies. The chapter will also raise questions related to "justice" and "community" as it was understood by Roman Stoic philosopher-statesmen. It will further explore whether or not this same understanding of justice has contemporary application and, if it does, how it might properly inform our choice of public finance instruments.

The overall message of this book points in two directions. The first is a call for a greater degree of ethical pluralism than presently appears to exist in our economic policy-making. The present excessive focus on the utilitarian consequences of our policy choices needs to be supplemented with, and in some cases replaced by, a greater concern for "doing the right thing," or for policies that encourage people to make better choices. This presupposes that such "right choices" exist and can be agreed upon. The position I take in this book is that right choices do exist. My position then might be identified as moral *objectivist* and contrasted to the moral relativism or subjectivism that has characterized many late twentieth-century social science arguments. It is sometimes observed that "morality can't be legislated." There is a sense in which this is true. We cannot expect that people will find a new disposition toward virtuous behavior simply by passing laws that reward some behaviors and punish others. At the same time, however, it is clear that our ethical predispositions do not develop in a social vacuum. For most of us they are the result of the experiences and opportunities we have early in life. They are also the result of the social and economic milieu in which we grow and reach maturity. Public policy can and does importantly contribute to this environment. To paraphrase John Maynard Keynes, good policies are not those that make people *feel* good; they are policies that *make* people good.

The second direction reveals the need for a "practical philosophy" which I take to mean a philosophy that can serve our needs for day-to-day decision-making both in our private and public lives.[3] Companion to the need for practical philosophy is a corresponding tolerance for philosophical eclecticism. It is not my goal in this book to suggest that we adopt an Epicurean outlook or to formulate a Stoic policy course of action. It is rather to take from these schools of thought ideas and inspiration for private and public economic decision-making that might improve our lives. The Hellenistic philosophers were not interested in philosophical speculation for its own sake. The goal of practical philosophy is well-served by a study of the Hellenistic schools inasmuch as their common goal was to provide a practical guide to life. I submit that this guide to life has a great deal of contemporary usefulness.

Notes

1 Hedonic is an adjective derived from the noun "hedonism," meaning concerned with pleasure.
2 This influence has been aided and abetted by publications such as *Freakonomics* whose authors (Levitt and Dubner 2005) claim "the aim of this book is to explore the hidden side of ... everything."
3 I take the expression from Bryan Norton (2005) as he applies it to an environmental ethics that both respects the wider concerns of so-called "biocentrists" while providing workable policies consistent with other needs of people and their communities.

References

Erskine, Andrew. 1990. *The Hellenistic Stoa*, Ithaca, NY: Cornell University Press.
Gottlieb, Anthony. 1999. *Socrates*, New York: Routledge.
Levitt, Steven D. and Stephen J. Dubner. 2005. *Freakonomics: A Rogue Economist Explores the Hidden Side of Everything*, New York: Harper Collins.
Norton, Bryan. 2005. *Sustainability*, Chicago, IL: University of Chicago Press.
Rostovtzeff, Michael I. 1936. "The Hellenistic world and its economic development," *The American Historical Review*, 41, 2 (January): 231–252.
Sibley, Mulford D. 1970. *Political Ideas and Ideologies*, New York: Harper & Row.

2   *Eudaimonia*: the ancients and the good life

A primary thesis of this book is that utilitarianism is too narrow a basis upon which to formulate our economic decisions and to conduct public policy. The notion that hedonistic pleasure is, or ought to be, the one and only motivation for our choices has come under critical examination in recent years. Increasingly, thoughtful people are asking the question if the single-minded pursuit of income, and the goods and services it will purchase, is justified.[1] Certainly, recent empirical research casts doubt on the standard economic assumption that more is necessarily better than less. Part of the problem as some have noted is that where income is concerned relative income plays a more important role in self-reported levels of happiness than does absolute income. If all levels of income increase simultaneously then it is evident that relative income position will remain unchanged and happiness will not increase even as absolute consumption increases.

The question presents itself then: are income and consumption, and the narrowly considered pleasure they purport to deliver, all they are cracked up to be? Or, is there more to a well-lived life? This, of course, is not a new question. It was addressed by philosophers dating back to the earliest recorded history, including by the ancient Greeks.[2] The Greeks were certainly aware of the potential for wealth and consumption as sources of pleasure. They did not typically equate these, however, with the goal of a well-lived life, or *eudaimonia*. The latter concept is translated to human happiness, or even better, human flourishing. How would we differentiate *eudaimonia* from utility? There are several important ways that they are distinct from one another. The first is that whereas utility tends to be a matter of sensory perception; *eudaimonia* is considered to include a broader array of goods including those associated with human relationships, especially friendship, as well as the exercise of virtue. Now one might ask, as some have, are not human relationships, including friendship, and virtue a source of utility just as are income and wealth? The answer to this question, I believe, is "no, they are not." One reason is that these sources of *eudaimonia* make demands on us that the enjoyments of sensory goods do not. In fact, they may often entail considerable disutility. Human relationships and virtue-oriented choices typically entail considerations such as commitment and duty that are altogether absent in the ordinary sense of utility. A second way that *eudaimonia* differs from utility is that while the latter tends to be delimited and episodic, the former is experienced over the arc of one's life. To illustrate, I may derive utility from a good meal. But once that meal is consumed, its associated utility is also over and complete. To realize additional utility of this sort I must consume an additional and similarly satisfying meal. The eudaimonistic experience is characteristically different. Rather than providing discrete payoffs, it is more properly understood as a permanent state of mind attendant on a correspondingly appropriate apprehension of the world. As such *eudaimonia* might probably be better described as a goal to which we aspire rather than as an experience to be indulged in.[3] Still, a third way to distinguish between utility and *eudaimonia* as the object of our choices concerns how we understand the overall objective of our choice-making. It is routinely assumed that an economic agent is a "utility maximizer." This characterization makes no sense if applied to a eudaimonistic perspective. Again, *eudaimonia* is a state to achieve rather than a thing to maximize.

The ancient Greek philosophers did not all understand *eudaimonia* in precisely the same way. All, however, were concerned with ethics and propounded a view of the well-lived life. In the following sections I will trace the outlines of the major ethical systems of Classical Greek ethics and of the Hellenistic schools. While I am mostly concerned with the later of these in the remainder of this book, an acquaintance with the Classical thinkers will help us to appreciate the contribution they made to the Hellenistic systems and in the important ways they differed.

Socrates

The widely acknowledged difficulty in describing the philosophy of Socrates is that he left no written record of his views. What we know of him and his thinking comes to us either via his contemporaries or those who lived well after his death. Among these is Plato who refers to Socrates in several of his works. The difficulty here is that Plato was himself a philosopher with his own agenda. Separating out the views of Plato from those authentically Socratic presents us with additional difficulties. The scholarly consensus, however, seems to be that the most genuine representation of Socrates ethics is given in the early dialogs of Plato (Hulse 1995: 11, White 2002: 173). These include the *Apology* and the *Crito*, which provide an account of his trial and of his death by execution at the hands of an Athenian jury. These works also provide what probably amount to the clearest expression of Socrates ethical outlook.

Socrates was variously and metaphorically characterized as a mid-wife, a gadfly, and a physician. The mid-wife metaphor applies to his belief that knowledge resides in every individual and only requires the help of a skilled interlocutor (presumably Socrates himself) to be revealed to the light of day. The image then applies to Socrates method of dialog by which he examines the assertions of another and (usually) finds them inadequate. In this manner he is very effective in helping others to discover their errors, though somewhat less successful in helping them to arrive at the truth of the matter. This essentially negative approach to inquiry is where the "gadfly" image becomes most applicable. While Socrates unapologetically proclaimed that he knew nothing, he further proclaimed himself superior to others who had no knowledge of their own ignorance.[4]

About the closest Socrates comes to a positive assertions are the propositions that "Virtue is knowledge" and "No man does wrong knowingly." The particular sort of knowledge that Socrates has in mind here is knowledge of good and evil. Evil, or vice, said Socrates, is to the soul as a disease is to the body. Knowledge of virtue and vice is necessary to keep the soul in good condition. This is the sense that Socrates considered himself to be a physician in as much as he strove to help others to maintain the health of their souls. Virtue in this sense is a state of the soul more than it is a matter of engaging in virtuous acts.

Socrates himself was said to exemplify virtue in his manner of living and displayed the cardinal virtues of wisdom, courage, temperance, justice and piety. He was a poor man who showed no concern for his poverty. He refused to take payment from his student followers. He was temperate in his consumption and just in his dealings with others. He distinguished himself on the battlefield and is attested by Plato in the *Symposium* to have saved the life of Alcibiades in the battle of Potidaea. Socrates's alleged asceticism is part and parcel of his ethics. He argued that externals, e.g. material goods, are unnecessary for virtue and that virtue alone is sufficient for *eudaimonia*. In fact, he argued further that the proper up-keep of the soul required that it be kept free from contamination by bodily desires (Huby 1967: 24).

Plato

As a student of Socrates Plato's ethical views bear a close similarity to those of the master. At the same time what we know of Socrates comes mostly, and most reliably, from Plato. Disentangling the two individuals thinking is therefore no easy task. As already noted, however, there seems to be a consensus among classics scholars that the early dialogs of Plato are a likely faithful rendering of the thoughts of Socrates while Plato's later works reflect his own particular views.

One of the ways in which Plato is often said to differ from the historical Socrates was in his willingness to draw conclusions about the good society from his ethical assumptions about the good, or wise, man. The connection between these conceptions of the good are derived from Plato's notion of justice which is understood as a state of the soul. The soul according to Plato is tripartite consisting of reason, a "spirited element," and the passions. Reason, the most supreme of the parts, allies itself with the spirited element to control the passions. When the three parts are in accord justice prevails in the individual. When this occurs the individual is happy; otherwise, the unjust man is miserable.

The just society is constructed along analogous lines with the three parts of the soul corresponding to three classes. At the apex of the social structure sit the guardians, or rulers. This elite rule by virtue of their outstanding reasoning abilities, particularly as concerns the ability to identify good and evil. The auxiliary class of police and military personnel work with the guardians to provide protection against outside threats and to maintain domestic tranquility. The largest class is the producing class of free working people as well as slaves. Plato describes in detail the characteristic virtues of the members of each of these classes and prescribes prerogatives and responsibilities for each. A defining characteristic of the guardian class is said by Plato to be "self-command." Given the tripartite nature of the individual's soul it is clear that there is potential for conflict, particularly between the passions (or appetites) and reason. It is expected that for philosopher-kings, another way to refer to the guardian class, the passions must be subordinated by reason, the most divine of the soul's parts. This self-command of the guardians parallels the command by the guardians of the class of producers for whom it cannot be presumed that similar such self-discipline is possible.

Education assumes an important function in Plato's state, and therefore in his moral system. Once again this is most important for the ruling class of guardians so that they are able to obtain the harmony of the soul's parts required for justice. Plato also followed Socrates closely in the belief that virtue depended on knowledge. Plato's theory of knowledge held that ideas, which he called forms, were the ultimate reality, while the visible phenomena that we observe are mere shadows. Knowledge of the forms, and these included forms that pertain to such cardinal virtues as temperance, courage, prudence, etc., required intense training in philosophy and mathematics. Understanding of them constitutes wisdom and, as only the elite could ever obtain wisdom, only these same elite were capable of ruling.

It should be evident that Plato's state is far from democratic. In fact Plato was hostile to the idea of democracy and believed that it had a corrupting influence on society. He believed that while the masses could hold opinions, these were likely to be formed under the influence of the passions and susceptible to the rhetoric of the sophists:

> The sophists, Socrates adds, only teach the opinions of the masses, and dignify it with the title of wisdom. They are like keepers learning to manage a large and powerful animal by studying its likes and dislikes: good is what pleases it, bad what displeases it. The masses, we are told, have utterly no conception of goodness and beauty, and are unfitted to judge anything – hence their low opinion of philosophers.
>
> (Rowe 1976: 70)

One of the principle issues that concern Plato, and others, begins with the question, what is the ultimate nature of the good? The typical answers are "virtue" and "pleasure." Support for each of these answers can be found in

Plato's dialogues. What Plato says in support for pleasure hardly places him in the camp of ethical hedonists, however. One reason is that he considered there to exist a hierarchy of pleasures. Higher order pleasures are those associated with the pursuit of knowledge, wisdom, virtue, etc. Lower order pleasures are those associated with wealth, consumption, prestige, etc. A second reason is that unlike modern ethical hedonism such as the sort we associate with modern economic theory, Plato urges moderation in the pursuit of lower order pleasures rather than the maximization of pleasures. Moreover, some pleasures are to be avoided altogether as false pleasures. These are the type of pleasures that are likely to involve more than compensating future pains. And violent pleasures that interfere with activity of thought are to be avoided altogether.

Aristotle

Just as Plato's ethical outlook was informed by his relationship with Socrates, so too was Aristotle's ethics in many ways an extension of Plato's vision. This is inevitable given that Aristotle studied in Plato's Academy. Like Plato, Aristotle argued that the good life consists in an accord of the soul with virtue. He also agrees with Plato in his view that the soul consists of more than one part and that each of these parts has corresponding virtues. Further, he agrees with his teacher in the belief that for man the preeminent virtue is his rationality. All this said, it is also true that Aristotle's conception of "the good" differs in some important ways from that of Plato. To begin with, Aristotle rejected Plato's theory of forms. Aristotle was a thorough-going empiricist who studied the world in its particulars. He recognized that the concept of the good could and should apply to these particulars. There could be such a thing as a good horse, or a good hammer, for example, that has nothing whatsoever to do with the good friend or the good life. No single notion of "the good" could possibly apply to all the sorts of different things which might be characterized by the word. This does not stop Aristotle from formulating a more general understanding of "the good" for man, however.

   Aristotle's general definition of the good is the things at which men aim – that is, their *telos*. In this sense the good is understood as the objective of human activities. They are the things to which we strive. Now, there are clearly many things that may be said to be things toward which we strive. They include health, wealth, and good reputation, to take three widely accepted examples. These are essentially the same (lower order) "pleasures" identified earlier by Plato. For Aristotle these goods are considered instrumental goods in pursuit of goods that are properly considered as ends in themselves. To understand the latter Aristotle asks us to consider what the proper function of man might be. It might seem odd to pose the question this way, but it is in keeping with Aristotle's overall method which consists in finding the final causes of things in general. A final cause of anything is understood in terms of its function or purpose. Man, for Aristotle, as for virtually all the ancient Greek thinkers, identifies the unique function of man in terms of his ability to reason. The ability to reason indeed is man's unique and outstanding virtue.

Aristotle identifies two sorts of human virtue corresponding to the two parts of the human soul. One applies to what he calls the appetitive part of the soul and the other that applies to the rational part of the soul. The latter are further subdivided into ethical (moral) and intellectual virtues. Moral virtues must be developed by training and education, though they begin with a disposition. Virtues can develop and/or deteriorate according to one's actions, and particularly one's choices. In taking the measure of a decision-maker's virtue, Aristotle relies on his infamous "doctrine of the mean." In this he means that with respect to any particular good or virtue there should never be either an excess or a deficiency. An oft-cited example concerns courage. An excess of courage would cause someone to act precipitously and to take ill-considered risks. A deficiency of courage would cause this same person to run from challenges that he should in fact undertake. The appropriate amount of this virtue is to be aimed for and defines the good. Similar moderation applies to external goods such as wealth. An excess amount of wealth will have a distorting effect on the character of the wealth-holder and cause that person to see wealth as a final end when, in fact, wealth should be thought of as a means to a higher end. A deficiency of wealth on the other hand will operate as a constraint on the individual's ability to develop his or her excellences.

Perhaps more than any other of the ancient Greek philosophers, Aristotle is given credit for developing economic ideas. In his *Politics* he describes that families were formed to satisfy the diverse needs of its members and that family members will specialize in particular productive activities to produce the goods and services that satisfy their various needs and desires. Long before Adam Smith Aristotle understood and wrote about the division of labor. The desire to form larger communities from combinations of families required the emergence of the state. Aristotle's conception of justice is developed from the tendency of human beings to combine into families, communities, and larger states in order to satisfy their varied needs.

A perennial question for ancient Greek philosophers is the status of pleasure as a good. Aristotle recognizes that human beings are pleasure-seeking, pain-avoiding creatures. This is an aspect of human nature that is shared with other animals. The pursuit of pleasure, then, is not peculiarly human and cannot for that reason represent the final good for man. Aristotle divides human needs into two broad categories: bodily needs and the needs of the soul. The first of these are once again instrumental to the fulfillment of the second, and they are necessarily limited. That is, man needs certain external goods to satisfy his bodily needs and in order to enable him to pursue the higher order needs of the soul. Consumption is not the final cause (purpose) of a well-lived life. Neither is utility maximization derived from consumption the proper object of an individual's, or household's, choice-making in contrast to the standard theory offered in economics textbooks. As a matter of fact, for Aristotle, the choices people make have profound ethical consequences, both revealing and contributing to the development of their characters. The happy man is the wise man. The wise man is the one who makes the right choices. Says Aristotle, "Now virtue of character is a state that decides; and decision is a deliberative desire. If, then, the decision is excellent, the reason must be true and the desire correct, so that what reason asserts is what desire pursues," (*Nicomachean Ethics*, (NE): 1139a).

This very brief review of some of the important ethical ideas of three of the most important philosophers of classical Greek antiquity is intended to provide a frame of reference by which we can appreciate both the influence they had on the Hellenistic period thinkers and how the Hellenistic schools extended and, in some ways, improved classical Greek ethics. In the next several sections we shall consider in greater detail the particular ideas of Hellenistic philosophy paying close attention to their ethical systems. We shall include some brief observations on the two comparatively minor schools of the Hellenistic period, the Cynics and Skeptics, and consider in more detail the more influential schools, the Epicureans and Stoics.

The Cynics

Cynicism often suggests an attitude to the modern mind that is at strong variance with its original ancient adherents' belief system. Even a close student of Cynicism takes a mildly deprecatory view of the group:

> To the student of ancient philosophy there is in Cynicism scarcely more than a rudimentary and debased version of the ethics of Socrates, which exaggerates his austerity to a fanatic asceticism, hardens his irony to sardonic laughter at the follies of mankind, and affords no parallel to his genuine love of knowledge. Well might Plato have said of the first and greatest Cynic, "That man is Socrates gone mad."
>
> (Dudley 1967: ix)

The founding of the Cynic school is usually credited to two major figures, Antisthenes (445–366 BC) and Diogenes of Sinope (412/403–324/321 BC). Of these two, Antisthenes is considered to be the first Cynic author/theoretician while Diogenes is considered the school's first important practitioner. Moreover, of the two, Diogenes is certainly considered the more interesting character.[5] He was the son of a banker in Sinope and was forced into exile for defacing the city's coins. "Defacing the currency" would thereafter become a guiding motto for Diogenes personally and for the larger movement which he led. It came to mean a relentless tendency to confront and overturn the conventional wisdom particularly as this wisdom pertained to ethical questions.

The identifying characteristic of Diogenes as a Cynic was his ascetic lifestyle. He was an itinerate philosopher for whom poverty was a conscious choice. He owned few possessions besides his cloak, his walking stick, and a small satchel, or wallet. He subsisted on what he could easily collect in his travels often at the side of the road. He slept in whatever public places he could find shelter. For these reasons he was referred to as "the dog," an epithet he would embrace. Diogenes admired the honesty and freedom dogs enjoyed and sought to imitate their lifestyle. Because the Cynics produced very little actual writing it has been argued that they hardly constituted a school at all. Indeed, they are not associated with any center of intellectual activity as were the schools associated with Plato (the Academy) or Aristotle (the Lyceum). Diogenes went so far as to ridicule speculative philosophy as practiced by Plato (Dobbin 2012: xxvii). He had little time or patience for metaphysics and considered what he had to offer as practical training for those who wished to pursue "the good life."

The good life for the Cynics is a life lived "according to nature," a familiar injunction for the ancient Greek philosophers. For the Cynics this recommendation had a substantially altered interpretation as compared to that given by other competing schools. While the Cynics urged a life of virtue, virtue itself was not wholly understood in terms of the exercise of reason. Rather, it consisted of the cultivation of certain important personal character traits along with the values that supported them. Primary among these personal character traits was that of self-sufficiency (*autarkeia*) in all its senses, physical, psychological, and with respect to social and political attachments. Such an attitude conforms to the minimalist consumption requirements of the Cynic life-style and also their tendency not to enter into marital or sexual relationships.[6] Social and political independence afforded them the freedom from patrimonial relationships with powerful men and, thereby, a license to speak truth to power. Such was not the typical position of many ancient Greek philosophers who often depended heavily on support from politically well-connected patrons. Dobbin (2012: xx) notes the following exchange between Plato and Diogenes (of Sinope) as reported by Diogenes Laertius:

> According to Diogenes Laertius, "Plato saw [Diogenes of Sinope] washing lettuces, came up to him and said to him under his breathe, 'Had you paid court to Dionysius, you wouldn't now be washing lettuces', and [Diogenes], answered, in a similarly confidential tone, 'If you washed lettuces, you wouldn't have to flatter Dionysius.'"

While the Cynics did not regard intense study as a road to develop the reasoning ability characteristic of the philosophic attitude found in competing schools, they did insist on the importance of training. This was true in both the mental and physical senses. A physically fit constitution is required to enable the Cynic practitioner to follow its rigorous life-style. Moreover, good physical condition is thought to be propitious to states of mind that are conducive to virtuous deeds, (Long 1996: 39). So demanding was the Cynic life-style that the Stoic Apollodorus described Cynicism as a shortcut to virtue. That is, according to this view, if one could maintain a Cynic life-style of minimal consumption and the pursuit of virtue, she would effectively approach the status of Stoic sage without a great deal of time and effort devoted to philosophic study that is characteristic of the Stoic ideal.

The Cynic rejection of conventional pleasures should not be understood as an arbitrary embrace of asceticism. Rather, avoidance of the false values associated with conventional pleasure-seeking or other "externals," such as wealth, power, or reputation, will distract people from a life lived according to nature. Not only will the pursuit of these externals deny people the leisure to pursue wisdom, gaining them will have an enervating, enfeebling effect. And as an empirical matter, it is noted by the Cynic philosopher, Teles, life in general has a larger share of pain than it does pleasure (Dobbin 2012: 128–129). The good life then would seem to be that which enables one to deal with pain, or avoid it altogether. From this perspective value systems that emphasize pleasure are false.

An additional and novel insight gained from the Cynics is their cosmopolitanism. Their itinerant life-style meant that they owed allegiance to no particular place. "I am a citizen of the world," proclaimed Diogenes. This attitude bespeaks not just a traveler's interest in the world at large, but rather a rejection of the conventional coercions and impositions of local authorities. At the same time there is a positive aspect to this cosmopolitan attitude as argued by Moles (1996). "I am a citizen of the world" signals the larger allegiance of the Cynic to humankind and to the earth itself. Cynic cosmopolitanism, in fact, expresses a commitment to non-human species. Cynic philosophers frequently took animal behavior as models of natural behavior. The Cynic commitment to humankind is not contradicted by neither their clear individuality nor by their strong emphasis on self-sufficiency. While they saw a dramatic chasm separating the wise from the masses of humanity, their mission was a proselytizing one in which they urged others to follow their example. Unlike either Plato or Aristotle, they did not view any person as standing outside candidacy for "wisdom" by virtue of gender, nationality, or class. Moreover, as Long (1996: 40–45) points out, what we know of the lives of the Cynics such as Diogenes and Crates is that they were entirely social personalities who sought out the company of their contemporaries in order to engage them in philosophical discourse. Crates even published satirical poetry that skewered the received wisdom and advanced Cynic ethical principles. Cynic self-sufficiency, then, should not be taken to imply social isolationism or indifference to the common good.

Epicurus

Epicurus lived from 341 to 271 BC and spent most of his life instructing his followers in Athens. These followers congregated in a community called "the Garden" and were less an academic group than a collection of like-minded individuals dedicated to a way of life based on the teachings of their leader. While our interest in Epicurean thought centers on its conception of the good life, an understanding of his cosmology and theory of science is helpful in providing a motivation for his *eudaimonia*. Epicurus was a thorough-going materialist, even "mechanist," who conceived of the universe in atomistic terms.[7] In *Letter to Herodotus*, Epicurus explains that the universe is composed of basic bodies, or atoms, and void.[8] These atoms have always existed and always will exist. They are indestructible and they are in continuous motion. The presence of void assures this dynamic quality of atoms. These basic bodies are also invisible. The visible reality that we perceive is the result of the combining of atoms into larger compounds as they collide. While atoms themselves are differentiated from one another only by size, weight, and shape, they otherwise do not manifest any other properties. Compounds, however, depending on how they are constituted, display all the properties of things that we can perceive with our senses.

Epicurus also explains sensory experience in material terms. Sight, for example, is explained by the tendency of objects to emit particles that collide with the eye and produce images. Smell is similarly explained in terms of particles impacted against the olfactory system. Epicurus is so thorough going a materialist that even his "metaphysics" is explained in materialist terms. The soul, claims Epicurus, is composed of very fine and very spherical atoms and, like all other essentially material things, it is finite. It dies when the body dies and its constituent elements, its basic bodies, return to be reconstituted as new compounds.

An important issue that follows from Epicurus's materialism concerns its potentially deterministic consequences. That is, if the universe is composed of atoms that simply collide and combine, and if the human mind and soul are themselves similarly constituted, how can we account for free will? Or is free will itself an illusion and prejudice that Epicurus wishes to overturn? The answer to the second question is that Epicurus wishes to preserve the concept of free will. He manages to do this by introducing into his system an important additional mechanism. This is the uncaused cause, or the "swerve." According to this account, while in general basic bodies move in a determined, (downward) straight-line fashion, occasionally some of them are liable to diverge from their pre-determined paths.[9] Absent this swerving tendency, atoms would fall without colliding into one another and it would be impossible for compounds to form. Since compounds are the stuff of our perception, it must be the case that atoms swerve. These facts according to Epicurean physics have important metaphysical and ethical implications which can now be outlined.

There is an important practical purpose to Epicurus's physics. It is to rid the world of religious superstition. In particular, he wished to free human beings from the belief that natural phenomena were the capricious expressions of divine intentions. Drought, hail, and storms did not represent the anger of the gods any more than adequate rainfall at the appropriate times and places represent their favor. Neither could the movement of the heavenly bodies (e.g., planets and stars) be understood in terms of the whims and preferences of the gods, contrary to the conventional wisdom of his day as per, for example, Plato (Long 1986: 42–43).

While Epicurus rejected the deism of his contemporaries and predecessors, this did not make him an atheist. Rather, he taught that god was a fully blessed and perfect being. As such He did not concern Himself with anything that was not similarly blessed and perfect, including humanity. For Epicurus and his followers the gods were not anthropomorphic meddlers. Instead, god provided a model to which wise people aspired. Wisdom in turn begins with a proper understanding of nature. Natural laws are knowable based on an atomistic understanding of the physical universe. This understanding is entirely a matter of a close observation of nature. Epicurean science is entirely empirical, sense-based, and rational. Epicurean rationalism is important for wisdom insofar as it dispels ignorance and fear. It also enables the wise to avoid the three motives – hatred, envy, and contempt – leading to injurious acts (Diogenes Laertius (DL) 1966). Besides a proper understanding of god, the wise person is instructed not to fear death. Death represents nothing more or less than the end of sentience. This implies that one ought not to fear an afterlife that does not exist, nor to yearn for immortality.[10]

Epicurus's conception of *eudaimonia* is typically expressed in terms of the pursuit of pleasure and the avoidance of pain. For this reason Epicurus is sometimes considered to be among the first utilitarians (Scarre 1994). The hedonism of Epicurus was of a highly qualified sort, however, and the Epicurean notion of pleasure was in his day, and continues to be, a source of controversy and confusion. Epicurus categorizes desires into those that are natural, necessary, and groundless, and advises the wise person to direct every preference and aversion toward securing health of body and tranquility of mind (DL: 653). This will enable him/her to be free of pain and fear whose absence is the essence of pleasure. Contrary to much misunderstanding, Epicurus did not recommend the life-style of the voluptuary or sensualist. Diogenes Laertius quotes Epicurus as follows:

> we do not choose every pleasure whatsoever, but oftentimes pass over many pleasures when a greater annoyance ensures from them. And oftentimes we consider pains superior to pleasures when submission to pains for a long time brings as a consequence a greater pleasure.
>
> (DL: 655)

Neither does Epicurus see pleasure in terms of consumption. In fact, the kind of peace of mind (*ataraxia*) that the Epicurean covets is as much a matter of self-control over the appetites as of consumption *per se*:

> Again, we regard independence of outward things as a great good, not so as in all cases to use little, but so as to be contented with little if we have not much, being honestly persuaded that they have the sweetest enjoyment of luxury who stand least in need of it, and that whatever is natural is easily procured and only the vain and worthless hard to win.
>
> (DL: 655)

Moreover, Epicurus understood that immediate pleasures were sometimes to be avoided especially when their enjoyment would entail subsequent pains, and that some immediate pains were to be chosen when they held out the promise of subsequent greater pleasure. The true Epicurean then would seem to understand that a certain healthy discipline is consistent with a life dedicated to the pursuit of pleasure.

Thus, the pursuit of pleasure, according to Epicurus required the exercise of virtue. That is, for Epicurus, virtue had important instrumental value that enabled the wise to realize the psychological freedom that is the essence of a eudaimonistic existence. In particular, Epicurus set great store by the virtue of prudence:

> Of all this the beginning and the greatest good is prudence. Wherefore prudence is a more precious thing even than philosophy; from it spring all the other virtues, for it teaches that we cannot lead a life of pleasure which is not also a life of prudence, honour, and justice; nor lead a life of prudence, honour and justice, which is also not a life of pleasure. For the virtues have grown into one with a pleasant life, and a pleasant life is inseparable from them.
>
> (DL: 657)

The greatest source of human happiness, according to Epicurus, is friendship:

> Of all the means which are procured by wisdom to ensure happiness throughout life, by far the most important is the acquisition of friends.
>
> (DL: 673)

The sources of this happiness are multiple. Friendship provides a source of security in times of need, but it is also a delight for its own sake. As far as the first of these is concerned the good of friendship is intimately connected with the virtue of justice. As the quotes above suggest the prudential selection of friends requires that we choose those who can be relied upon to share our outlook on the interconnectedness of honor, justice and pleasure. These same friends, in turn, can likewise rely on us. As far as the second is concerned, there is no presumption that the "delights" of friendship are always and everywhere immediate and easily realized. Pleasurable friendships presuppose certain virtues such as loyalty, patience, and beneficence. There is, in fact, an altruistic element in a satisfying friendship. Fortunately, according to the Epicurean account, the exercise of these virtues is itself a source of pleasure (Long and Sedley 1987: 138).

Among the virtues that Epicurus did not endorse are those associated with public life. For Epicurus the status and honor associated with a high public profile fell into the category of unnatural desires and were a profound source of unhappiness for those who pursued them. Better for the Epicurean wise man to withdraw to the community of like-minded pleasure seekers/pain avoiders and eschew the prizes of public life.

The Epicurean position has often been criticized as promoting an unacceptable degree of selfishness in its adherents and of being inconsistent with the promotion of a strong social basis upon which the Epicurean community itself depends. A.A. Long (2006) has risen to a defense of Epicurus in this regard. Long argues that Epicurus was aware that his community of pleasure seekers, (the Garden), depended for its subsistence on a larger stable and productive society. This larger stable society required a system of laws as well as procedures for their interpretation, enforcement, and amendment. For the Epicurean sub-community to stand outside these procedures, and yet benefit from their effectiveness, forces them to confront the charge of social parasitism. Long argues that the Epicureans may defend themselves from this charge in the following ways. First, he argues that the basic ethical theory of Epicurus promotes the general welfare insofar as people embrace its teachings on how to overcome their own internal obstacles to a life of pleasure. The Epicurean project is first and foremost an instructive one and as such has important social value (Long 2006: 187). Second, the Epicurean injunction that we live "honourably and justly" advances the cause of social welfare. Justice is seen as necessary so that people have a degree of security that is inseparable from a pleasurable life.[11] Long writes:

> The prudent Epicurean will want neighbors to share a commitment to justice; that is, to perceive the utility of the social contract that what I need for my own happiness can only be assured if I do nothing to frustrate your interest in the same goal for yourself. Epicurean justice is a commitment to the utility of not doing as one would not be done by.
>
> (Long 2006: 190)

Honorable living, moreover, argues Long, requires additional virtues beyond prudential justice, such as courage, beneficence, and nobility, that are also supportive of positive social relations. Such virtues are also strongly attached to friendship which Epicureans see as central to their program for a life of pleasure and avoidance of pain. The fact that these virtues have a strictly instrumental role in the pursuit of pleasure and avoidance of pain does nothing to diminish their social utility. Third, Long argues that the Epicurean explanation of social evolution, as expressed in the writings of his followers, provides an accounting steeped in the leader's ethics that combines utilitarianism with his notion of prudence. The educative function associated with Epicurean teachings enabled human society to emerge from the brutish life of primitives to the civilization of their own modernity. Epicurean ethical teachings, moreover, were regarded as necessary to prevent back-sliding to primitive life with its mental habits of superstition and irrationality. There is an important economic dimension to the Epicurean contribution to human social evolution since, absent civilization's progress, the ability to produce the basic goods and services necessary to sustain human life would be correspondingly limited, and there would be no starting point for a discussion of *eudaimonia*.

Long's defense is not an entirely convincing answer to the charge that Epicureanism avoids its full measure of social responsibility insofar as it promotes political quietism among its followers. While Epicureanism may contribute in some limited measure to the philosophical climate propitious to civilized life, it is clear that it avoids the heavy lifting associated with political leadership and policy formulation that advance the goals of social welfare. From an Epicurean perspective social welfare seems to amount to a simple additive formulation involving the individual utilities of persons. Absent is any consideration to the social benefits of public and quasi-public goods provision and their contribution to the realization of pleasure and the avoidance of pain. Epicurean ethics does not deny the utility of such goods; but it does not share in the responsibility for securing them. To do so would require direct involvement in the political process which the approach adjures.

The basis for Epicurus's advice to his followers to avoid public life is also questionable. His underlying assumption seems to have been that public life was no more than a forum in which individuals sought to satisfy their own personal ambitions for glory. Apparently, he could not conceive of the notion of a truly selfless public servant dedicated to advancing social welfare. The Stoics were not as imaginatively limited as we shall see in the next section. Before we consider the Stoics there is one remaining aspect of the Epicurean ethical outlook to explore. This one is related to the concept of the "swerve." Recall that the swerve is a tendency in Epicurean physics for a particle to spontaneously deviate from its otherwise determinant downward path. This phenomenon has ethical implications insofar as it raises the possibility of free will in our behavior and thereby imposes on us moral responsibility for our actions. That is, without the possibilities provided by the swerve, all our actions would be entirely determined by the undeviating movement of particles acting on our nervous and musculature systems. Spontaneity in our thoughts and movements would seem to require similar potential spontaneity in the basic bodies themselves.[12]

The Stoics

While the Epicurean system is centered on the thought of its originator, Epicurus, Stoic philosophy is associated with a number of ancient thinkers who can be identified with various stages in the system's development. The earliest Stoic philosopher was Zeno, whose life and thinking are described in detail by Diogenes Laertius. According to Diogenes's account of Zeno's thought, the virtuous life is one that is lived in accordance with nature. Self-interest also plays a primary motivating role in Stoic ethics, but Stoic thought rejects the belief that pleasure is the first object of self-interest (DL: 193). Rather, pleasure is taken to be a by-product of a well-lived life– a life lived in accordance with nature. So fundamental is nature to the Stoic system that it is identified with both absolute reason (*logos*) and with god.

The Stoics are similar to the Epicureans in holding to a materialist (corporeal) conception of the cosmos, though Long points out that it is better to characterize the Stoics as vitalists who regarded nature as a creative force (Long 1986: 154–155). The Stoic god (also corporeal), however, is a more active participant in the universe, though not to the point of taking a direct interest in the affairs of human beings. Matter (the inert fundamental principle) is seen as being acted on by god (the active fundamental principle) according to the latter's rational plan (*logos*). Universal development has a teleological, deterministic, and cyclical character. Human beings are said to participate in this development when they exercise their volitional "assent" to sense impressions.[13] Errors are avoided when reason is sufficiently disciplined. Significantly, knowledge of the physical cosmos is for the Stoics not an end in itself, but rather a means to *eudaimonia* – that is, a life in conformity with nature (White 2002: 128).

If the focus of Epicurean *eudaimonia* is pleasure, then for the Stoics it is virtue. Like the Epicureans the Stoics believe that the beginning of the search for the good life must begin with a rational apprehension of the world. A well-lived life is a life of reason and thus Stoic ethics is inseparable from its larger apprehension of the universe, its cosmology. In this the Stoics share another reference point with their Epicurean rivals. Both schools are essentially empiricist in their approach to knowledge. External reality leaves impressions on the human mind which is the beginning of knowledge (Long 1986: 124).

The Stoics draw an important distinction between virtues and goods. "All good is expedient, binding, profitable, useful, beautiful, beneficial, desirable, and just or right" (DL: 204–205). The good is instrumental in the development of virtue, a means to a desired end for one who aspires to wisdom and happiness. Evil refers to vices and vicious acts. Evil is the consequence of bad choices which are in turn the result of a lack of understanding or "right reason." Stoic philosophy then assigns an important function to education as an educated person can learn to act in accord with nature.

Some things are neither good nor evil and are referred to as "neutrals" or "indifferents." Though morally indifferent, some of these are preferred. They include things such as health and wealth. They are preferred in the sense that they do more benefit than injury, but they are neither necessary nor sufficient for happiness.[14] Neither does their absence necessarily result in misery. Preferred indifferents have value consisting in their contribution to harmonious living (DL: 211).

Elsewhere Diogenes describes the Stoic view of emotions as detrimental to the wise man's quest for virtue. Pleasure he describes as an irrational elation at the accruing of what seems to be choice-worthy. Desire or craving is an irrational appetency. Delight is the mind's propulsion to weakness. Good emotions by contrast are joy, caution, and wishing. The latter concept applies in the sense of well-wishing, or benevolence.

The Stoic wise man is also characterized by other personality traits such as modesty, indifference to praise or criticism, earnest for their own improvement, austere, and passionless. The latter characteristic is not to be equated with apathy. To the contrary, Stoic philosophers are adamant in their belief that the wise man has an obligation to be publically engaged in the effort to better his community and nation. The Stoic wise man is a good citizen who seeks public office not in the pursuit of power or personal aggrandizement, but to act as a servant to his community. Diogenes notes that Stoics will take part in politics in order to restrain vice and promote virtue, (DL: 225). Cicero argues that the Stoic wise man is engaged in the civic life of his community because reason compels him to be so engaged (Long 1996). While Epicurean quietism derives from a fear that political activity will devolve into a form of vanity and self-aggrandizement, the Stoics, and particularly Cicero, regard civic engagement as a normative extension of the essential rationality of human beings (Long 2007).

A particularly interesting feature of Stoic ethics concerns its views on the efficacy of human actions. From the Stoic perspective the moral worth of one's actions is judged according to one's intentions and not on the outcomes of one's actions. The Stoic wise man must resign himself to the fact that his best efforts may not pay the dividends he expects. This moral indifference to the outcomes of a Stoic's efforts is consistent with his overall worldview that asserts the unitary goodness of nature that does not focus exclusively on the particular fate of any individual. The Stoic must resign himself to this fact. The Stoic's well-being rests not on the realization of particular advantages, but in his disposition to whatever eventuates. This disposition is the one thing over which the he has control.

There was (and is) some concern on the parts of Stoic critics that the school's teachings implied a paralyzing determinism or fatalism. After all, given the strict materialism of its physics and the naturalism of its metaphysics, what place does it really provide for human agency and free choice? Put another way, if the universe is bound to unfold according to some divinely determined natural process, and we humans are an integral part of that order, what exactly is "up to us?" A possible answer to these questions is that human understanding of nature's unfolding is necessarily limited. In the face of that imperfect understanding we are urged by Stoic ethics to do two things: first, to understand universal nature better by a close study of it; and, second, to make choices that conform to nature as best we can. These are the things that are appropriate to our own nature as rational creatures. These are not easy tasks and are really only perfectly accomplished by "Sages." The pursuit of this understanding and the striving for appropriate understanding is the essence of virtue and, not coincidentally, a part of nature's unfolding. Thus, while Stoics see everything that happens as necessary parts of nature's plan, our own choices are also a part of that plan (Frede 2003).[15]

The Sceptics

A final philosophical movement identified with the Hellenistic period is called Scepticism. While our popular understanding of the term "Sceptic" refers to one who has doubt about some proposition, the literal translation from the ancient Greek is "searcher." Nonetheless, as we shall see, the movement identified with the Sceptics certainly strongly suggests doubt about our abilities to have real knowledge about the world and everything it contains. The figure most closely identified as the founder of the Sceptic movement is Pyrrho of Ellis (360–270 BCE). Diogenes Laertius tells us his philosophical outlook was influenced by his travels to India where he came under the ascetic influence of the Gymnosophists, or naked philosophers, though modern commentators have de-emphasized this influence (Hankinson 1995: 58–59).

The essence of Pyrrho's teaching is the denial of knowledge as a result of sense perception or as a result of pure thought. His argument is encapsulated in the following three assertions (Zeller 1870/2012): First, we can know nothing about the nature of things. Second, it follows that the appropriate attitude is to suspend judgment about them. Third, the payoff from this attitude is the peace-of-mind that follows from disengagement from dogma, or doctrine. Thus, as for the other schools of Hellenistic philosophy, the eudaimonistic objective for Pyrrho is a tranquil life, and by most accounts Pyrrho himself is said to have led an imperturbable life. Diogenes claims, for example that Pyrrho led a life consistent with his doctrine and "took no precaution facing all risks as they came leaving nothing to the arbitrament of the senses" (DL: IX 61–62). So, did Pyrrho depend on his friends to keep him from falling off precipices or down wells while ignoring the evidence of his senses? Perhaps not, because as a matter of both practical necessity and of doctrine he did place a lot of faith in his apprehension of the world *as it appeared* to him. That is, while a Sceptic denies that anyone could ever know the real nature of things, he could know how they appear to himself. On this basis he could make decisions and choices that result in a perfectly conventional life-style. The Sceptics argued, in fact, this is how people make decisions, on the basis of convention and custom, not real knowledge.

One might reasonably ask about the ethical adequacy of an approach that urges nothing more than intellectual disengagement as a means to psychological tranquility. It might be suspected that a view that urges a lack of cognitive commitment would be hard pressed to make any serious ethical commitments as well. In the chapters to follow, in fact, the teachings of the Sceptics will not figure as prominently as those of the other Hellenistic schools outlined in this chapter. There is, nonetheless I believe, an important contribution that Sceptic views make to the larger concerns of this book. It provides a bulwark against doctrinal purity, or dogmatism, in the contemporary sense of the word. The search for an improved normative/ethical basis for economic policy is not a search for the "one true faith." In this work I shall argue for both a critical eclecticism in the evaluation of the usefulness of the insights provided from Hellenistic philosophy as well as ethical pluralism as the basis of public policy. In the pursuit of these objectives the recommendation offered by the Sceptics that we suspend belief is often times well taken.

Why study the Hellenistic thinkers?

Aristotle in some sense represents the sort of value eclecticism I shall advocate inasmuch as he considered, for example, both virtue and external goods to be necessary ingredients to a well-lived life. Likewise, there occur in Plato's dialogs arguments that urge both virtue and pleasure are essential to *eudaimonia*. Why then should we focus on schools of thought that appear to take comparative extreme positions on the sources of human flourishing in comparison with Classical Greek philosophy? One answer to this question, which I hope this chapter has demonstrated, is that the Classical philosophers had a profound impact on the subsequent development of ancient ethics including and especially on the immediately subsequent Hellenistic schools of thought. Beyond this influence, however, there are good reasons to believe that the Hellenistic schools have contributed on their own an ethical legacy that is important to contemporary concerns and is one not found in the Classical tradition. Primary among these are its comparatively democratic and cosmopolitan aspects. Unlike the classical tradition the Hellenistic schools did not believe virtue is to be found in some classes and not in others. The Cynics were notorious for flouting the conventions of their day including those associated with socio-economic status. The simple pleasures of the Epicurean Garden of friends were open to all comers, including slaves. The Stoics believed that the sage could emerge from any walk of life, including the slave. Wisdom was the single perquisite, and this was a quality to which any human being; man or woman, slave or property holder, citizen or foreigner; could aspire. The extension of ethical consideration/"subject-hood" to those beyond the privileged classes marks an important moment in the history of western thought and might be said to begin with the Hellenistic thinkers.

A second ethical "breakthrough" provided by the Hellenistic thinkers that goes beyond the moral horizon of their Classical predecessors was their cosmopolitanism. By this I mean that the Hellenistic thinkers were far more inclined to think in terms of their moral obligations to the human race as a whole rather than merely their fellow citizens. This is undoubtedly partly a consequence of the fact that Hellenistic philosophy was developed during a period of emerging empire while Classical thought prevailed during a period when the chief form of social and political organization was the city-state. Alexander the Great's empire enlarged not only the geographical extension of Macedonian rule, but also the economic, cultural, and scientific worldviews of those who experienced it. Foreigners were no longer as likely to be dismissed as uncultured barbarians, and at the same time, one's allegiance to the local was correspondingly weakened. The period between the consolidation of Alexander's empire, its decline, and replacement by the Roman Empire was characterized by extremely unstable economic globalization and growing inequality combined with fractious intra-empire wars and conflict in which opportunism and political self-aggrandizement were largely unchecked. The Hellenistic philosophies to some extent represented a defensive reaction to the vulnerabilities and disenchantment that many felt in the face of these changing fortunes and the decline of familiar institutions (Erskine 1990: 34–37). This reaction took the form of the construction of ideal alternatives to the actually existing instability and conflict and in several cases it took the form of retreat from active political participation.

A moment's reflection should reveal that many of the insecurities and conflicts that plague the contemporary popular imagination in the United States and Europe bear a striking resemblance to those that afflicted the ancient Greek and Roman world during the Hellenistic period. Economic globalization, growing inequality of income and wealth, immigration and questions of citizenship, distrust of established political institutions and processes are all issues that produced social instability in the ancient world and they are each recognized as issues of contemporary concern, even if they have not yet provoked organized class resistance or rebellion. On the other hand, there has emerged in recent years an expanding literature that raises the same fundamental questions posed by the ancient Hellenistic philosophers regarding the search for happiness and questions, in ways similar to the challenges provided by the ancients, the received wisdom. It seems that on this basis alone a look back at the ideas of the Hellenistic thinkers on *eudaimonia* is justified. How these ideas might inform our modern public policy responses is the subject for later chapters. Before we get that far it may be useful to ask what influence the ancients have had on modern economists, if any. That is the task of Chapter 3.

Notes

1 See, for example, Sandel (2012), Frank (1999) and Skidelsky and Skidelsky (2012). In his discussion of Keynes's ethico-philosophical views, Skidelsky (2010) notes that economists (and others) have come to view the particulars surrounding the questions of what constitutes "the good life" as secondary ones subordinated to the primary goal of wealth accumulation. Interestingly, however, Skidelsky argues that for Keynes himself the expression "the good life" referred not to what makes life good for people, but to what it is that makes people good (p131).
2 The search for the answer to this question was not confined to the ancient Greeks, of course. Around the same period of the Hellenistic age India produced the Bhagavad Gita. A few hundred years earlier saw the beginnings of the development of Chinese Taoism and other schools of thought. There are some remarkable similarities in the goals of these disparate philosophies particularly in their goals of enlightenment and personal tranquility.
3 A philosopher would say that *eudaimonia* is a (human) teleological rather than an ontological concept. This means that it is a natural state toward which we develop rather than one that defines how we exist at some moment.
4 Socrates' superiority in this respect was purportedly established by the oracle at Delphi in response to the question, "Who is the wisest man in Greece?"
5 It is argued by Dudley (1967) among others that credit for the founding of Cynicism to Antisthenes was urged by the early Stoics who wished to establish the lineage of their own philosophy back to Socrates. The biographer Diogenes Laertius provides the key testimony in arguing that Antisthenes "learned his hardihood from Socrates, and inaugurated the Cynic way of life."
6 Diogenes of Sinope was notorious for his habit of public masturbation.

7 Epicurus's theory of existence, his *ontology*, is materialist. His theory of knowledge, or *epistemology*, would properly be characterized as empiricist. This follows from his belief that human knowledge starts from our perceptions of the world and the things in it. For more discussion of Epicurean epistemology, see Long (1986).
8 *Letter to Herodotus* and other Epicurean fragments can be found in Inwood and Gerson (1994).
9 This argument is found in *On the Nature of the Universe* by the poet Lucretius (Book 2, lines 216–224). Lucretius was a leading Epicurean spokesman.
10 These Epicurean positions will be explored and applied in Chapter 7.
11 The concept of Epicurean justice is explored in more detail in Chapter 8.
12 Yet, as Long (1986: 60) has pointed out, the swerve cannot provide a sufficient account for moral choices as they are random, physical events that can provide an impulse to act in a particular way. Only the trained Epicurean, however, can ultimately make a decision to act in a way that leads to a greater balance of pleasure over pain.
13 White (2002: 144–145) points out that certain versions of Stoic determinism was of the "soft" variety in order to allow for human volition and free choice. Human assent to an impression is "caused" by the antecedent event, the impression. But the assent itself is freely given by human choice.
14 Irwin (1986) provides a thorough review of the meaning of the Stoics "indifferents" and the role they play in their theory of *eudaimonia*.
15 The question of Stoic fatalism is taken up in more detail in Chapter 5.

References

Aristotle. 1999. *Nicomachean Ethics*, translated by T. Irwin, 2nd edition, Indianapolis: Hackett.

Diogenes Laertius. 1966. *Lives of the Eminent Philosophers, Volumes I, II*, translated by R. D. Hicks, Cambridge: Harvard University Press.

Dobbin, Robert. 2012. *The Cynic Philosophers from Diogenes to Julian*, New York: Penguin Classics.

Dudley, Donald R. 1967. *A History of Cynicism*, Hildesheim: Georg Olms Verlagsbuchhandlung.

Erskine, Andrew. 1990. *The Hellenistic Stoa*, Ithaca, NY: Cornell University Press.

Frank, Robert. 1999. *Luxury Fever: Weighing the Cost of Excess*, Princeton, NJ: Princeton University Press.

Frede, Dorothea. 2003. "Stoic determinism," in *The Cambridge Guide to the Stoics, 2nd edition*, B. Inwood (ed.), Cambridge: Cambridge University Press.

Hankinson, R. J. 1995. *The Sceptics*, London: Routledge.

Huby, Pamela M. 1967. *Greek Ethics*, London: Macmillan St Martin's Press:

Hulse, James W. 1995. *The Reputations of Socrates: The Afterlife of a Gadfly*, New York: Peter Lang.

Inwood, Brad and L. P. Gerson. 1994. *The Epicurus Reader*, with an introduction by D. S. Hutchinson, Indianapolis: Hackett Publishing Company, Inc.

Irwin, T. H. 1986. "Stoic and Aristotelian conceptions of happiness," in Malcolm Schofield and Gisela Striker (eds) *The Norms of Nature: Studies in Hellenistic Ethics*, Paris: Editions De La Maison des Sciences De L'Homme, pp205–244.

Long, A. 1986. *Hellenistic Philosophy: Stoics, Epicureans, Sceptics, 2nd Edition*, Berkeley, CA: University of California Press

Long, A. 1996. "The Socratic tradition: Diogenes, Crates, and Hellenistic ethics," in *The Cynics: The Cynic movement in Antiquity and its Legacy*, Branham and Goulet-Cazé (eds.), Berkeley, CA: University of California Press, pp28–46.

Long, A. 2006. *From Epicurus to Epictetus: Studies in Hellenistic and Roman Philosophy*, Oxford: Oxford University Press.

Long, A. A. 2007. "Stoic communitarianism and normative citizenship," *Social Philosophy & Policy*, 24, 2 (July): 241–261.

Long, A. A. and D. N. Sedley. 1987. *The Hellenistic Philosophers, vol. 1, Translations of the Principle Sources, with Philosophical Commentary*, Cambridge: Cambridge University Press.

Lucretius. 1994. *On the nature of the Universe*. Translated by R. E. Latham with an introduction and notes by John Godwin. London: Penguin Classics.

Moles, John L. 1996. "Cynic cosmopolitanism," in *The Cynics: The Cynic Movement in Antiquity and Its Legacy*, Branham and Goulet-Cazé (eds.), Berkeley, CA: University of California Press, pp105–120.

Rowe, Christopher. 1976. *An Introduction to Greek Ethics*, London: Hutchinson.

Sandel, Michael J. 2012. *What Money Can't Buy: The Moral Limits of Markets*, New York: Farrar, Strauss, and Giroux.

Scarre, Geoffrey. 1994. "Epicurus as a forerunner of utilitarianism," *Utilitas*, 6, 2 (November): 219–231.

Skidelsky, Robert. 2010. *Keynes, The Return of the Master*, New York: Public Affairs.

Skidelsky, Robert and Edward Skidelsky. 2012. *How Much is Enough: Money and the Good Life*, New York: Other Press.

White, Nicholas. 2002. *Individual and Conflict in Greek Ethics*, Oxford: Clarendon Press.

Zeller, Edward. 1870/2012. *The Stoics, Epicureans, and Sceptics*, London: Longmans, Green and Co., republished by Forgotten Books, Classic Reprint Series, www.for gottenbooks.org.

3 The impact of the ancients

It is common among historians of the Western intellectual tradition to note that the origins of that tradition reside in the ancient Hellenistic world. The ancient thinkers tended to develop whole systems that united explanations for their observations of physical phenomena with explanations of what could not be directly observed – that is, metaphysics. From both of these they drew ethical conclusions and, in some cases, they developed visions of the well-lived life and of the well-organized society. In certain areas of intellectual endeavor (e.g., science), ancient theories have been virtually entirely superseded by modern advances. The ancient philosophers had no conception of scientific method after all. In other areas the contributions of ancient Hellenistic thinkers continue to have a significant influence on modern thought. The literary and artistic contributions of the ancient Greeks, for example, continue to provide a source of inspiration to modern readers, museum patrons, and theater goers. Ancient Roman political and legal theories continue to inform modern political organization and jurisprudence. It is, however, the enduring influence of ancient ethical thought that most interests us here. In particular, we are interested in how ancient thought may have influenced early modern, or classical, economic outlooks. It is among the classical economists after all that moral philosophy had not yet become divorced from economics *per se*. That break would not become definitive for economics as a discipline until the latter part of the nineteenth century with the so-called "Marginalist Revolution." The intellectual preparation for this break began, however, two centuries earlier with the European Enlightenment. It will be useful by way of background, then, to trace the influence of Hellenistic ethical thinking to the Enlightenment political philosophers. To complete the picture, briefer forays on the impact of Hellenistic thought upon early Christian and Renaissance outlooks will also be provided. The overall intent is to show the relevance of Hellenistic ethical thought for what we might call the Western tradition. Of course, a thorough job of this would require a book in itself. In fact it will become clear from this review of the literature that many such volumes have, in fact, been written on just this theme. The more particular task of this chapter is to provide background to the more focused discussion to follow in subsequent chapters and in particular the next chapter that takes up important issues of method in economics.

The Hellenistic impact upon early Christianity

Historians of religion have noted that Christianity had its start as a relatively minor sect of Judaism. The question naturally occurs, then, as to how and why it emerged as one of the major religions of the world. An historical explanation is provided, in part, by the emergence of the Hellenistic empire that stretched eastward across the Mediterranean to link to Palestine. The fact of this empire was important to the emergence of Christianity for several reasons. First, it enabled the spread of ideas along its long east-west axis. Western philosophy became more religious as a consequence and Eastern religion became more philosophical. The spread of empire undermined the social and economic relations and structures that had characterized the Greek city-states (polis). After the death of Alexander in 323 BCE the empire was beset by dynastic and class struggle, civil wars, and revolts (Green 2008). Not surprisingly, these disturbances had important impacts on the established belief systems including a reconsideration of the established myth-based theology with its anthropomorphic gods. While in some instances there occurred a revival of traditional polytheism with official support for nationalist purposes, the average person sought a more personal religious experience for motives connected to succor and comfort (Randall Jr. 1970). These were provided by Eastern religions and were embraced throughout the empire not on nationalist grounds, but for their ability to provide "saviors." Randall Jr. (1970: 103) describes the religious fusion in the following terms:

> Paganism proved itself imperialistic: it welcomed and fused all these new Gods, with the sole exception of the jealous and exclusive deities of the Jews and the Christians. The only way to assimilate Christianity was to allow it to assimilate all the rest, which it eventually did: this was the path actually followed. The new cults were strong in the cosmopolitan cities, like Rome, Alexandria, and Antioch. Their growth began among the slaves, the soldiers, and the women, and then seeped upward to the upper classes.

A second important factor in connecting Western philosophy with Eastern religion was the dominance of the Greek language and culture. An important segment of the Jewish community had become Hellenized by the time of Paul, and the first Christian missionaries turned their attentions first to Hellenized Jews (Jaeger 1961). Jaeger notes that Paul's mission was conducted in the Greek language and early Christian literary forms (e.g., epistles) were patterned after Greek models. To generate tolerance for the new sect and to win converts the early Christian apologists needed to "market" its ethics in terms and symbols that would appeal to Greek sensibilities and established understandings. While Hellenistic philosophy was rooted in reason, Paul offered Christianity as a species of mystery cult offering redemption based on faith. It took the apostle John to make the appeal to reason. Writes Randall Jr. (1970: 157):

For John the Evangelist, salvation is to *know* God. The transformation of human nature effected by union with the Christ is an intellectual illumination, the change from dwelling in a "realm of darkness" to entering a "realm of light." Perhaps, if evidence from the Dead Sea scrolls may be believed, it is a continuation of the teachings of the Hellenized Hebraic sect of the Essenes. For John, Jesus is primarily a teacher, who came to *show* God to man … .

For John, the union with the Christ comes through faith, which he takes much more intellectually than Paul, as "belief." Hence John has to supplement such "faith" with "love," the mystical element and bond. In Paul, faith and love are fused together into one, which is his "faith." For Paul, faith is a mystical activity: for John, it is much more Greek: the spirit of receptivity toward the vision shown by the Christ.

Bultmann (1980) provides an interesting contrast between the Stoic and (Pauline) Christian perspectives on freedom and reason. The Stoic view is that reason (*logos*) does not operate as an irresistible and inevitable force in human begins. It represents rather a normative challenge that must be given assent to. And yet the failure to provide such assent is the result of (correctable) error alone. Given time and appropriate instruction, human beings are capable of exercising *logos*. And this is precisely what consists in their freedom. It is an inner freedom entirely under their control and impervious from external considerations. From Paul's perspective, by contrast, man is fallen from the start and is incapable of redemption without divine assistance. What freedom human beings possess is a gift of grace (Bultmann 1980: 145).

Paul's redeemer religion is of a type referred to as Gnosticism. More generally, the Gnostic vision was dualistic separating reality into spirit and matter with those seeking redemption emphasizing asceticism. Randall Jr. explains that the extreme dualism of the Gnostics provoked a reaction among many Christians and against the theology of Paul in the second century AD. Leading this reaction were the Alexandrian theologians, philosophers in the Hellenistic tradition, who sought to create a synthesis of Christian ethics interpretable in terms of Greek *logos* (Randall Jr. 1970: 162). Randall Jr. (1970: 173) provides an illustrative example:

Justin Martyr is typical of these ex-Stoic apologists. He sounds to our ears very much like the much later eighteenth-century Deists. He emphasizes what they took to be the three tenets of their rational religion: there is an omnipotent God; He has commanded a law of righteousness; and He will reward and punish men in a future life. Man is a free being, but he is stupid and forgetful: he needs to be reminded of these truths, which he could reach by his natural reason. Christ, a second God, came, not to bring men magic grace, not to give them essentially new teaching, but to remind men that God means what he has said. Christ merely reaffirmed the true philosophy of Heraclitus, Socrates, and Plato. These Greek philosophers were all really Christians, because they were right, and the Logos was inspiring them.

The problem from this "syncretistic" perspective is not that man has fallen from grace as a result of original sin, but has lost his way as a result of ignorance.[1] The solution, in turn, does not reside in redemption via magic, but a decision to act in one's true best interest beginning with an appropriate exercise of reason. The evil versus ignorance debate, of course, is one that continues to bedevil policy discussions to this day. It shows up, for example, in contending positions on criminal justice that emphasize punishment or rehabilitation.

Early Christian philosophy developed in the third century in Alexandria in the hands of theologians who sought to incorporate and reconcile the beliefs of classical Greek philosophy with the Gnostic elements of the redeemer religion. Prominent among these were Clement and Origen who based their synthesis on the most religious of the Greeks, Plato. Of the two, Jaeger (1961: 60) has this to say:

> They try to see Christianity in the light of the supreme concept of what the Greeks had contributed to the higher life of the human race. They do not deny the value of that tradition, but they claim that their faith fulfills this paideutic mission of mankind to a higher degree than had been achieved before. Considering the importance of this overarching idea of padidea for the evolution of a unified culture in the Greek intellectual world, this step in the discussion between Christianity and the Hellenistic tradition marks the beginning of a decisive development in the aspiration of the Christians toward the goal of a Christian civilization.

Of Clement, Jaeger notes that he understood Plato's philosophy as derived from the Hebrew tradition either directly from Moses, or at the least divinely inspired (1961: 61).[2] Of Clement's more systematic pupil, Origen, Jaeger cites his belief that god's creation could not have been perfect if He had denied man the freedom to choose the good for its own sake, a typically Platonic and Stoic point of ethics. Christianity then represents an extension of the Platonic paideia (i.e., education of man) (65). For Origen, moreover, Christ's role in this Christian philosophy was that of transmitter of god's pedagogy to humankind. Jaeger (1961: 67) writes:

> Christ is for Origen the educator who transfers these sublime ideas to reality. But for him the salvation that comes through Christ is not a single historical event. Unique in its importance as it is, it had been preceded by many steps of a similar nature, beginning with Creation itself, which made man into an image of God; and after the fall of Adam there was a long line of the prophets of Israel and the great philosophers of Greece and the wise lawgivers through whom God had "spoken."

The meaning of the Renaissance

The word *Renaissance* means "rebirth." Applied to history it typically refers to that period between the thirteenth and sixteenth centuries bounded by the Middle, or Dark, Ages and a subsequent era beginning in the seventeenth century called the Enlightenment. The earlier era suggests an epoch without intellectual progress, a period of scientific and cultural stagnation.[3] This is a popular misconception but it is undeniable that the frequent wars and invasions had an inhibiting effect on population growth and economic development. It was also a period during which allegiance to religious faith trumped discovery. Literacy was low and limited to the ruling and religious elites. Intellectual concerns were focused on matters of religious doctrine and classical scholasticism. By the latter term I have in mind the attempt to reconcile Classical philosophy (e.g., Aristotelianism, neo-Platonism) with Christian teaching.

From the perspective of philosophy the term Renaissance refers to the recovery, or re-discovery, of a particular *attitude* toward knowledge that had not dominated since classical antiquity. Randall Jr. (1976: 111) describes this change in the following terms:

> Nevertheless, though the old forms and old beliefs persisted relatively unchanged, that period which we loosely call the Renaissance was marked by the increasing prevalence of attitudes and interests that had hitherto played a minor role in the life of Western Europe. These growing interests burst the bonds of the narrow if intricately carved medieval world and left men toying with the fragments. It was for the next age to seek the broad foundations upon which those fragments could be builded (sic) into a new structure.

This same author makes clear the ancient intellectual tradition that provided the source of these "broad foundations":

> Eagerly they turned to the literature of Greece and Rome, which revealed to them men who had similar interests, and eventually led them on to investigate the actual world in which they were living. The complex hierarchy of medieval society, with its fixed group control, proved increasingly inadequate to satisfy the new needs and demands of human nature, and to organize men's diversified and changing activities. The forces centered in the individual members broke down the nicely adjusted binding ties, and in every field of human endeavor, in religion, in science, in art, in economic life, in political control, more and more emphasis was laid on the growth and expression of the potentialities of the individual elements and less and less on the organization of these elements into wholes, toward which the individual members felt a diminishing sense of responsibility (112).

The term applied to the new interests and forces Randall Jr. describes in this passage is *humanism*. Its emphasis is on secular rather than scholastic concerns, and there is a preference for the near and now as opposed to the hereafter typical of the Middle Ages. There is also a renewed emphasis on empiricism and reason as opposed to revealed truth. The recovery and dissemination of ancient thought fueled these new enthusiasms. While the humanist scholars of the Renaissance were inspired by the ancient philosophers for their emphasis on reason, they were also keen on showing their consistency with, or at least not their blatant contradiction of, Christianity. Aristotelianism and Neo-Platonism were the dominant ancient sects from which the humanists drew, though many scholars saw much to admire in Stoicism and Epicureanism despite the comparative paucity of available texts for the latter two schools.

The father of Italian humanism is said to be Francesco Petrarch (1304–1374). Petrarch's *Remedies for Good and Bad Fortune* is said to have enabled the transmission of Stoic ideas, including the notion that virtue is the only good and that pain, for example, is not an evil (Kraye 2001). As evidence he offers the suffering of Christ and holds him up as a Stoic model. A particularly intense debate among Renaissance thinkers concerns the Stoic injunction against grief combined with their doctrine that death is not an evil. The disputants in this case were Francesco Zabarella (1360–1417) and Coluccio Salutati (1331–1406). Zabarella urged on Salutati the conventional Stoic wisdom that death is not an evil since only vices are evil. Inasmuch as death is universal and inevitable, it cannot be considered evil. Grief in the face of death then is inappropriate from a Stoic perspective. Salutati was predisposed to the Stoic outlook until the untimely death of his beloved son. He responds to Zabarella by observing that while death may not be a moral evil, it is an evil nonetheless since it is the privation of a good, namely life (Witt 1997). Salutati here implicitly rejects the Stoic doctrine that virtue is the only good. He further presses this line of argument to observe that virtue, far from constituting the sole or ultimate good, is actually instrumental to the realization of higher order goods such as "beatitude" or blessedness in the case of individuals, and peace and security in the case of nations. As far as the figure of Jesus as a model of Stoic equanimity in the face of pain and death is concerned, Salutati cites Christ's passion as evidence that death is an evil.

As noted earlier, Renaissance admirers of Stoic ethics were very concerned to show its consistency with Christian teachings. The Flemish humanist Justus Lipsius (1547–1606) is the most prominent such "apologist" of the Renaissance period (Young 1997). In his *A Guide to Stoic Philosophy in Three Books* he relies heavily on the Stoic authority of Seneca and Cicero to argue that the Stoic sage is an ideal type who does not exist in nature. Such a figure, however, is useful in providing us with a model to emulate. He further defends the Stoic argument that virtue is sufficient for happiness and that externals such as health, wealth, reputation, etc. may be conducive to evil as well as good and, on that basis, must be rejected. In the course of this argument he urges his listener to follow nature which he equates with god. He cites both the

Hebrew author of the Psalms as well as the early Christian fathers Clement and Ambrose as authorities for the view that the Stoic sage finds his counterpart in the Christian-Judaic tradition. A similar roster of authorities is recruited to give support to Lipsius's contention that the Stoics were correct in maintaining that the virtuous could find happiness even while suffering bodily torment, arguing that good may emerge precisely in the face of adversity.

Not surprisingly, many of these pro-Stoic positions were challenged. In some cases the argument was made on behalf of the primacy of Christian doctrine that Stoic doctrine was actually derived from more ancient Biblical sources. Francisco de Quevedo (1580–1645), for example, contrary to any plausible notion of historical chronology, argued that the Stoic model of the imperturbable sage is based on the study by Epictetus of the Old Testament Book of Job (Deitz and Wiehe-Deitz 1997). In other cases, critics argued that on some important points of both theology and ethics, Stoicism fell well short of the high level set by The Scriptures. de Quevedo and others, for example, criticized Seneca for recommending suicide as an option for those for whom the burdens of life had become unbearable while praising Epictetus for recommending the opposite counsel.[4] Several humanist thinkers were highly skeptical of the "pain is not an evil" claim of the Stoics. Cosma Raimondi argued that the Stoics erred in not considering that man is composed of both mind and body, and that when the body suffers the mind cannot help but be affected (Kraye 2001/2002: 28). Martin Del Rio (1551–1608) criticized the school for advancing the belief that the sage's happiness is perfectly under her control requiring her to only to "follow nature." To the Renaissance humanists this belief seemed to obviate any need for divine salvation and was on that basis unacceptable.

Epicureanism received a similarly mixed reception by the Renaissance thinkers. In fact, it is probably more accurate to say that Epicureanism received a more hostile reception than its competitor school.[5] The main difficulty it faced was that its metaphysics stood in clear contradiction to the Christian belief system, though it might be also said that the primacy of the pleasure principle in Epicurean ethics presented it with an uphill struggle for the hearts and minds of humanists. This is not to say that Epicurus did not have his defenders, among them Raimondi who, as we have just noted, rejected the mind-body dualism of the Stoics. In *A Letter to Ambrogio Tignosi in Defence of Epicurus*, Raimondi endorses as obvious the Epicurean position that pleasure is the supreme good and rejects the Stoic view that virtue is necessary and sufficient for happiness (Davies 1997). Moreover, he makes a very modern sounding argument that links the condition of the body to the condition of the mind – an argument that amounts to a "naturalistic" account of pleasure. In what eventually became a standard defense of the Epicurean pleasure principle, Raimondi makes clear what the Master really had in mind by the term "pleasure," insisting that he expounded on the pleasures of the mind in preference to those of the body.

Francisco de Quevedo also comes to the defense of Epicurus, just as he had for the Stoics, motivated once again by a desire to demonstrate the essential consistency of ancient thought with the precepts of Christianity. In this instance de Quevedo credits Seneca for debunking the popular view of Epicurus as a depraved glutton and suggests that Epicurus's opponents had an axe to grind on the basis of his rejection of dialectics as an analytical method (Deitz and Wiehe-Deitz 1997: 217). Epicurus also scores points for having rejected suicide (according to Seneca!) and for showing Stoic fortitude on the day of his own death. Epicurus's faults according to de Quevedo were those of a pagan for which he could not be held blameworthy.

Other Renaissance scholars, however, were less forgiving. Kraye (2001) notes that entrenched prejudices against Epicurus were difficult to overcome even after new evidence had been provided by recently available translations of the works of Diogenes Laertius and the poet Lucretius. There was a particularly strong reaction against the Epicurean belief in the materiality and mortality of the soul. Renaissance humanism would only go so far in its toleration of such heretical views. Kraye (2001: 106) writes:

> The broadminded case for toleration that the French political thinker Jean Bodin (1530–96) put in the mouths of the interlocutors in his *Colloquium of the Seven about Secrets of the Sublime*, a clandestine work that circulated in manuscript until the nineteenth century, specifically excluded the Epicureans on the ground that it was "much better to have a false religion than no religion." Epicurus, in "trying to uproot the fear of the divinity," had committed the "unpardonable sin" of removing the sanction of rewards and punishments in the afterlife, without which civilization would descend into anarchy.

Just as was the case for the Stoics and Epicurean schools, there were available few primary sources representing ancient skeptical thought and the school probably had even less influence than the others on ethical thinking during the Medieval period. St. Augustine's *Contra Academicos* strong rejection of skepticism is considered by Schmitt (1983) to be the last word on academic skepticism before its recovery during the Renaissance. Skepticism becomes more influential during the fifteenth and sixteenth centuries with the recovery of works by Cicero, Diogenes Laertius, and Sextus Empiricus, with the last of these being the most widely read and influential. These works were initially studied in the centers of Italian learning (e.g., Rome, Venice, and Florence) and later spread to northern Europe in the sixteenth century.

As Schmitt makes clear, academic skepticism ought not to be confused with religious skepticism. The former amounts to a denial that we can have certain knowledge of the world through natural (e.g., via our sense experience) means (1983: 229). As such the doctrines of the school can be used as a weapon against secular dogma and in defense of religion. This was precisely the strategy employed by Gianfrancesco Pico (1469–1533) who made use of Sextus to critique Aristotle in the name of Christianity (1983: 236) That is, by undermining confidence in empirically based knowledge, he sought to elevate belief derived from Scripture. The skeptical attitude is a two-edged sword, however. Schmitt notes that early Byzantine scholars regarded skepticism as a threat to the Church (1983: 235) and the school would become an important source of intellectual inspiration in the hands of religious skeptics in the seventeenth century, the century most closely associated with the Enlightenment.

The Enlightenment and the neo-Epicurean, neo-Stoicism debate

If the Hellenistic schools were comparatively marginal in their influence during the Renaissance, they came into their own during the subsequent period in Western intellectual development, referred to as "The Enlightenment." The Enlightenment, just as for the Renaissance, was not a single, regionally concentrated historical phenomenon. The term has application to England, France, Germany, and Northern Europe. It also applies to Russia and other non-Western, non-European areas. For our purposes, given the focus of this book on the relationship between ethics and economics, it shall be particularly advantageous to focus on the Scottish Enlightenment, some of whose outstanding figures were Frances Hutcheson, David Hume, and Adam Smith. The last of these is, of course, of especial interest as the so-called "father" of economics.

Peter Gay (1966) argues that Enlightenment philosophers (*philosophes*) were particularly inspired by the ancient Greeks and Romans inasmuch as they regarded them as kindred spirits concerned to liberate mankind from the dogma of received religious belief that they regarded as grounded in superstition. They saw themselves as occupying a similar position relative to the Medieval Schoolmen as the classical and Hellenistic philosophers did in relation to the Homeric era Greeks who sought explanations in terms of their capricious and anthropomorphic gods and goddesses. They were aided by the greater availability of Latin translations of the ancient Greek texts, as well as by the fact that these had become standard in their educational curriculums. Gay (1966: 44) notes:

> While a program of study is not normally a reliable intellectual pedigree, the philosophes' classical education had special, lifelong meaning for them: it offered them an alternative to Christianity. There were critical moments in their lives, in adolescence and later, when they appealed to the ancients not merely for entertainment but for models, not merely for decoration but for substance, and not for bland substance – such as the staples of Horatian satire: complaints about crowded city life, laments on the brevity of existence, or the menace of bores and bluestockings – but for a philosophical option. Books forced on reluctant schoolboys are rarely more than hateful exercises, laboriously mastered and quickly forgotten, but all over Europe and America, for the philosophes alike, the ancients were signposts to secularism.

Whereas Renaissance humanism sought to find ways of reconciling ancient ethical thought with Christian teachings, Enlightenment thinkers used these sources to advance ethics on a secular basis as well as for a scientific understanding of the universe. Gay further notes that Enlightenment Neo-Stoicism operated as a cure for the sixteenth-century civil wars. He profiles the Dutch humanist and statesman Dirck Coornhert who translated Cicero and Seneca and promoted public service and intellectual brotherhood as an antidote to sectarian religious conflict (1966: 299). He also describes the influence of Lipsius's Stoic-inspired work on Enlightenment thinkers Gibbon, Montesquieu, Diderot, Voltaire, and others, observing the following:

> The official ideology of Christian civilization had united ethics and politics and subjected both to theology. In Lipsius's writings these bonds were weakened: his *De Constantia,* with his sympathetic exposition of Stoic ethics as the doctrine of the good life according to nature, was both cause and symptom of the separation of ethics from theology; his *Politicorum,* with its treatment of the state as a rational construct guided by realistic considerations of power, was both cause and symptom of the separation of ethics from politics. The Christian tinges of this Stoicism were evidence of the tenacious hold of religion over men's minds, but his eighteenth-century readers treated Lipsius as the Church Fathers had treated Cicero: they kept what they found congenial and threw the rest away.
>
> (Gay 1966: 302–303)

Epicureanism's strong imprint on Enlightenment thought came largely thanks to the mediating influence of Pierre Gassendi (1592–1655). Gassendi's project to rehabilitate Epicurus's reputation as an atheist and voluptuary, however undeserved, was a formidable one. He managed this once again by a selective embrace of the Epicurean system, an approach that ignored those doctrines most unacceptable to Christian sensibilities such as the corporality and mortality of the soul (Olster 2003: 32). Gassendi accommodated Epicurean atomism by crediting god as the creator of the atoms while exempting Him from any of the laws to which atoms are otherwise subject.[6] He also reinterpreted Epicurean ethics by recognizing that Epicurus argued for a hierarchy of pleasures. Gassendi then asserts the highest of all pleasures to be the beatific vision of god while maintaining that He instilled in human beings a natural propensity to seek pleasure, a natural aversion to pain, and free will (Olster 2003: 40). The prudent exercise of the latter will providentially lead man to choosing the most sublime of pleasures. Gassendi's reinterpretation then is consistent with Epicurus's own argument that virtue bears an instrumental relationship to pleasure.

Gassendi also employed Epicurean principles to map out a political philosophy that is highly suggestive of a social contract theory of the state. According to this theory, in order to secure tranquility (*ataraxia*), people establish contracts to protect their property and persons. These contracts imply rights which are defended by a system of laws. Civil society then is perceived as a natural outcome of human pleasure-seeking, pain-avoidance inclinations. The Epicurean/Lucretian philosophy in turn had a pronounced impact on the Enlightenment social contract theorist, Thomas Hobbes. Hobbes rejected the philosophies of Plato and Aristotle in preference to the materialism of Epicurus. He further endorsed the Lucretian account of the origins of the state (Wilson 2008: 188).

We now turn our attention to the Scottish Enlightenment. The Scottish Enlightenment is worthy of particular attention for several reasons. The first is that late seventeenth-century Scotland was resource poor with a stagnant population. It was also highly dependent economically and politically on England. It sought to overcome its disadvantages by placing a high value on education in order to develop its manufactures as well as to expand its trade opportunities both within and outside of Britain (Emerson 2003). It therefore engaged in an intense national debate regarding economic development and international trade. The fact that economic matters were so central a part of Scottish national concern makes its intellectual history a particularly interesting one for our study. Relatedly, the Scottish Enlightenment included two personages, David Hume and Adam Smith, who are major figures in the history of economic thought. While the Scottish thinkers were cosmopolitan in outlook, their status as a part of Britain meant, of course, a special relationship with England. In some important sense then the Scottish Enlightenment bears an intimate relationship and similar intellectual development with its southern and more powerful neighbor state. Our story of Scottish Enlightenment moral theory begins with a late seventeenth-century British moralist.

Anthony Ashley-Cooper (1670–1713), the 3rd Earl of Shaftesbury and commonly referred to simply as Shaftesbury, posed the following question: "Why is there so much immorality in a nation which professes such a moral religion as Christianity?" Two opposed responses offered themselves as possible answers: the Negative Answer (NA) and the Positive Answer (PA) (Gill 2006). NA starts from the assumption that man is fallen and thus he acts sinfully and selfishly. Thomas Hobbes is assigned a large portion of the credit (or blame) for propagating this outlook and for building a theory of the state around it. Shaftesbury, however, stood strongly opposed to this vision of human nature and advocated for the PA. The PA argues that human beings are endowed with virtuous impulses that lead them to act in virtuous ways. They are then entirely capable of being motivated by unselfish desires. An important aspect that the NA and PA share is that they are each self-fulfilling phenomena. That is, for example, if people embrace the NA as an accurate characterization of human behavior, they are more likely to act in selfish ways.[7] Contrariwise, selfless, virtuous acts will engender in people a love of such behavior leading to more such other-directed behavior.[8]

Shaftesbury also criticized John Locke for his denial of the innate sociability of human beings. Locke held that morality consists of the entirely arbitrary word of the sovereign, or of god, and that human compliance to that word is motivated by the fear of punishment and/or the desire for heavenly reward. The importance of Shaftesbury for the development of the Enlightenment outlook on morals resides in the fact that he is the first to maintain that virtue requires no particular religious obligation and that even an atheist is capable of virtue (Gill 2006: 85). For Shaftesbury human beings are possessed of other-directed affections as a matter of their nature regardless of their religious convictions. Shaftesbury then is an important figure in the movement to secularize moral theory.

Francis Hutcheson (1694–1746) also contended with the NA as a part of his upbringing in his Scottish Presbyterian household. His teacher was John Simpson who held to a PA view, and Hutcheson embraced Simpson's "heresies" (Gill 2006: 136). Hutcheson was also attracted by Shaftesbury's version of the PA and like the British moralist held to a "virtue-as-benevolence" outlook (Gill 2006: 141). This view came under attack by Bernard Mandeville in his infamous book *The Fable of the Bees* published in 1714. In this work Mandeville argues that people are always and everywhere motivated by self-interest, and what we are in the habit of as describing as virtue is nothing more than self-interest disguised. That is to say, any action that might be described as selflessly or socially motivated is, in reality, an act designed to answer a selfish need to act selflessly or socially.[9] Thus, according to Mandeville, the very notion of virtue is an illusion. Hutcheson rejected this outlook in very strong terms and, as Gill describes, utterly demolishes it.

Hutcheson's first move in this demolition is to argue that human beings are capable of making disinterested judgements of value. Aesthetic judgements are a case in point. Granting the possibility of disinterested judgements of this sort, we can then also imagine that people are capable of making similarly disinterested moral judgements. "Disinterested" in this context means, of course, not serving one's own narrowly understood interest, rather than indicating a general indifference to the moral issue at hand. Now, egoists can spin seemingly coherent accounts of how other concern meets some need of the supposedly selfless individual. Hutcheson maintains, however, that these accounts are hardly plausible. The care and concern that one exhibits toward a friend or family member, for example, might be motivated by a "selfish" concern with avoiding the distress that we might feel should they encounter difficulties. In this sense the egoist could always semantically turn each and every act into a selfish one. The assertion of egoism, however, would only be true then as a matter of unsatisfying tautology. This sort of explanation, moreover, is exceedingly insufficient inasmuch as it offers no account of the *disposition* to be other concerned in the first place (Gill 2006: 146–149). And this disposition is precisely that which requires an accounting. It is this selfless, or social, disposition that Hutcheson and Shaftesbury term virtue.

Another argument mounted by Mandeville claims that politicians manipulate the public into an admiration of those who serve the public welfare for their own (the politicians') selfish ends. This amounts to additional evidence against the belief that virtue, in this case public virtue, is what it is claimed to be. Hutcheson counter-argues that Mandeville's position does not hold up since it relies on the existence of an antecedent disposition in the public for public virtue. That is, if people were not predisposed to public virtue in the first place, they would not be vulnerable to this alleged manipulation. If Mandeville recognizes this predisposition then the case for psychological egoism falls apart (Gill 2006: 150).

While Gill traces the roots of Hutcheson's moral theory to both Cambridge Neo-Platonism and Neo-Stoicism, a recent article by Christian Maurer (2010) locates Hutcheson more firmly under Stoic influence. Moreover, his argument suggests that Hutcheson makes a contribution to moral theory that addresses a key difficulty often identified in the Stoic outlook. Maurer notes that Hutcheson, following the Stoics, makes a distinction between (calm) affections and (violent) passions (2010: 35). The distinction arises inasmuch as the Stoics believed that emotions have a cognitive element. Affections arise from a rational apprehension of good, or evil, whereas as passions arise from violently confused sensations when confronted with provocative circumstances that compel us to apprehend a good or an evil (Stoic), a pleasure or a pain (Hutcheson). In Maurer's interpretation of Hutcheson's distinction he notes the following (2010: 38):

> In contrast to affections, passions have a problematic tendency to reflect on the consequences and the appropriateness of one's actions. They cannot be simply controlled by correcting one's opinions, whereas affections allow for such indirect control. Without self-cultivation, the violent passions risk opposing the calm affections, tend to override them and might cause actions that are in conflict with private or public interest.

Maurer sees an interesting asymmetry in the ancient Stoic (as represented by Cicero) treatment of this distinction as compared to Hutcheson's parallel understanding. Cicero does not recognize the legitimacy of a calm emotion in the face of a present evil for the Stoic sage. The reason is that, for the sage the only good is virtue and the only evil is vice, each of these being entirely internal states of the sage. That is, as we may recall from our earlier discussion of Stoic virtue, for the sage the good in no way depends upon anything external to herself. But Hutcheson wishes to count benevolence as an attitude worthy of virtue. Benevolence is defined as concern for the welfare of others with no account taken for self-interest.[10] Clearly, Hutcheson's conception of virtue conflicts with that of the "lower rate of Philosophers of the Stoick Sect" (Maurer 2010: 44) since benevolence, being relational and other directed renders the sage's happiness vulnerable to the welfare of others (i.e., an external good). Moreover, Hutcheson finds psychologically and morally implausible the notion of virtue as a "private sublimely selfish discipline."[11]

Hellenistic philosophy and early modern economics

Early modern economics, called classical economics, was strongly influenced by ancient Western philosophy. This is hardly surprising given that classical economics was part and parcel of the British/Scottish Enlightenment and, as we have seen in the previous section, acquaintance with ancient Greek and Roman philosophy was a part of the standard intellectual toolbox of educated Enlightenment thinkers. In this section I wish to draw attention to the impact of ancient philosophy upon the theories of three classical economists who are often also considered to have made important contributions to moral philosophy. These are Adam Smith, John Stuart Mill, and Karl Marx.

Adam Smith

The influence of Hellenistic thought on classical economics is perhaps particularly notable given the especially strong influence of the Scottish moralists and the fact that two important classical economists, Adam Smith and David Hume, were themselves Scots.[12] Here we focus on Smith, considered to be the "father" of modern economics based on the seminal impact of *The Wealth of Nations*, (WN), published in 1776. We are, however, more interested here in the development of his ethical thought, and, for that reason, attention will be concentrated on his earlier major work, *The Theory of Moral Sentiments*, (TMS), whose first edition was published in 1759. TMS went through four more additions between 1759 and 1781 with a sixth published in 1790 shortly before his death. The sixth edition is particularly relevant for our present concerns inasmuch as it added an entirely new Part VI entitled "Of the Character of Virtue." It has become the scholarly consensus that Stoic philosophy had a strong influence, perhaps the dominant influence, on Smith's ethical thinking.[13] This influence is no more obvious than in Part VI of TMS.

The first thing to note in comparing Smith's ethical theory with that of the ancient Greek and Roman philosophers is an important point of difference in their respective foundational assumptions. This difference resides in the fact that while ethics for the ancients is grounded in reason (*logos*), for Smith it is grounded in feeling, or sentiment.[14] That is, the starting point for the ancients is a metaphysical belief in reason as an immanent force in the universe, while for Smith it is an empirical observation of human nature. In particular, Smith observed that the great ethical motivator for people was the approval of their fellow human beings. More than the approval of their peers is necessary, however. If approval is not felt to be deserved, it won't have value. Thus, people seek to be *praise-worthy* as well.

The question immediately arises as to whom, or to what, falls the responsibility of setting the standard for "praiseworthy"? Smith's answer is to propose a sort of abstract judge which he calls the Impartial Spectator. The Impartial Spectator has several roles to play in Smith's ethical system. One of these is to set the rules by which people interact and to define the appropriateness of those interactions. The Impartial Spectator then acts to bring reason into Smith's ethics. As Vivenza (2001) points out, however, in Smith's ethics reason follows sentiment. Ethical assessment begins with an initial perception when an action evokes a feeling of approval or disapproval. A second job of the

Impartial Spectator is to assess the appropriateness of the *degree* of feeling (i.e., passion) that an action provokes. If this degree is appropriate, neither insufficient nor excessive under the circumstances, it is said to meet the standard of propriety. The standard against which propriety is established is not that of the Stoic sage. It is that of the ordinary man and is one which it is expected that anyone would be able to meet (Waszek 1984: 596).

How then do the ancient philosophers inform Smith's ethical outlook? Vivenza has noted a similarity between Smith's conception of propriety of passion and Aristotle's "golden mean" (46–47). Propriety consists of a certain emotional mediocrity. They are also similar insofar as they both regard propriety's threshold point as differing across the passions. That is, for example, an "excess" of one passion (e.g., affection) is less objectionable than of others (e.g., anger) (48). Vivenza also notes a parallel between Smith's Impartial Spectator and Aristotle's "man of practical wisdom" (*phronimos*). In each case these abstractions act to introduce an element of control into the determination of appropriate moral behavior and assessment the absence of which would imply an unacceptable degree of relativism.

While Aristotelian (and Platonic) elements can be identified in Smith's ethics, the greater influence, as noted, is typically attributed to the Stoics. Raphael and Macfie (1976: 5) assert, for example, "Stoic philosophy is the primary influence on Smith's ethical thought."[15] An especially salient point of contact between the Stoics and Smith concerns the roles of nature and Providence in their ethical outlooks. For the Stoics, nature is that universal and beneficent force in which humankind participates. Divinely directed, it operates in the general interest even when the immediate results of its workings do not appear to serve particular human interests. Smith similarly refers to nature as a machine, or system, of whose workings individuals participate towards beneficent ends of which they are dimly aware outside of the operation of their instincts:

> Mankind are endowed with a desire of those ends, and an aversion to the contrary; with a love of life, and a dread of dissolution; with a desire of the continuance of the species, and with an aversion to the thoughts of its intire extinction. But though we are in this manner endowed with a very strong desire of those ends, it has not been intrusted to the slow and uncertain determinations of our reason, to find out the proper means of bringing them about. Nature has directed us to the greater part of these by original and immediate instincts. Hunger, thirst, the passion which unites the two sexes, the love of pleasure, and the dread of pain, prompt us to apply those means for their own sakes, and without any consideration of their tendency to those beneficent ends which the great Director of nature intended to produce by them.
>
> (TMS II.i.10)

As the above passage makes clear, Smith shares in Stoic providentialism, but with a twist. Rather than claim that people conform to the dictates of nature via the exercise of reason, he argues that this occurs due to something more primordial: instincts and passions. It is typical of Smith to appropriate and adapt ancient thought to his own purposes.[16]

Smith's discussion of the virtue of self-command illustrates very well his tendency to offer a qualified endorsement of Stoic virtue. The love of propriety instills in us a respect for the self-command required to serve as a check on the passions. Absent such self-restraint, the exercise of the other virtues would become problematic. The inability to exercise control over fear and anger, for example, would imperil our ability to practice the virtue of justice. Similarly, absent control over our love of ease and pleasure, we would not be able to practice the virtues of temperance and moderation.

For Smith the exercise of the virtue of self-command is admirable not only for the results it produces in terms of the other virtues, but it is also productive of the intrinsically attractive virtue of magnanimity:[17]

> The command of each of those two sets of passions, independent of the beauty which it derives from its utility; from its enabling us upon all occasions to act to the dictates of prudence, of justice, and of proper benevolence; has a beauty of its own, and seems to deserve for its own sake a certain degree of esteem and admiration. In the one case, the strength and greatness of the exertion excites some degree of that esteem and admiration. In the other, the uniformity, the equality and unremitting steadiness of that exertion.
>
> (TMS VI.iii.4)

Smith's appreciation of the intrinsic value of self-command (i.e., "a beauty of its own") recalls the Stoic insistence that the sage pursues virtue for its own sake.

It can be argued that the Stoic impact shows up in Smith's economics as well. Prudence, for example, is an economic as well as ethical virtue. The ability and willingness to defer immediate gratification in the interest of a greater future benefit, is, of course, a defining feature of the commercial/ capitalist personality.[18] Prudence, however, is precisely the sort of virtue that presupposes the anterior virtue of self-command.

While Smith was an admirer of the Stoic emphasis on the virtues he was not, as noted, uncritical of several of their key propositions. He decidedly (and predictably for a sentimentalist) rejected Stoic apathy which he understood in terms of the sage's advice to minimize, if not extirpate entirely, the exercise of the passions. Smith considered such advice to be an unnatural imposition on human psychology. From Smith's ethical perspective, grounded as it is in "sympathy," properly regulated passions are the building blocks of social relations and an ethical approach that attempts to ignore or deny this fact would ignore important facts about human nature and its essential sociality (Montes 2008: 36).[19] Smith also takes a strong stand against the Stoic position that suicide is not an unmitigated evil. After having reviewed Stoic arguments on this matter, and considered the ancient historical record as to the actual practice of suicide, Smith concludes:

> Nature, in her sound and healthful state, prompts us to avoid distress upon all occasions; upon many occasions to defend ourselves from it, though at the hazard, or even the certainty of perishing in that defence. But, when we have neither been able to defend ourselves from it, nor have perished in that defence, no natural principle, no regard to the approbation of the supposed impartial spectator, to the judgement of the man within the breast, seems to call upon us to escape from it by destroying ourselves. It is only the consciousness of our own weakness, of our own incapacity to support the calamity with proper manhood and firmness, which can drive us to this resolution.
>
> (TMS VII.ii.I.34)

We'll close the discussion of Smith with a focus on a concept that both links Smith to Stoicism and that links TMS to WN. This is the concept of self-interest. In the latter of these two links resides the concept of self-interest relevant to the so-called "Adam Smith problem."[20] The issue here is how we might reconcile the seemingly contradictory ethical presuppositions of Smith's work as they reveal themselves in his two most important works. In *The Theory of Moral Sentiments*, Smith is at pains to show the variety and subtlety of moral motivations at work in society and to devise a corresponding account of ethical evaluation. By contrast, in *The Wealth of Nations*, he appears to reduce ethical motivation to that identified with the psychological egoism so familiar to modern students of mainstream economics. So the underlying question posed by the Adam Smith problem is, how do we understand what Smith meant by self-interest?

Given the strong Stoic influence on Smith an appropriate place to start is to ask what the Stoics understood by self-interest. Here the salient Greek concept is *oikeiosis*, or familiarization. The Stoics gave a development account of *oikeiosis* that began with the claim that every living thing had a natural concern with its own preservation and well-being (i.e., self-love, self-interest). Thus, in the earliest stages of life all living organisms seek to gratify their needs by being attracted by whatever will provide them with succor and being repelled by those things they regard as threats. This is true of all living organisms; but what is distinctive about the human species is its rationality, and rationality according to the Stoics has a developmental aspect to it.[21] Thus, as reason develops, *oikeiosis* ensures that the reach of those things understood to be in the individual's sphere of concern (i.e., self-interest) is extended. The lines of extension are described by the Stoic Hierocles in roughly the following terms: from the individual to one's parents, to one's extended family, to village/community, to city, to nation, to the world in ever-expanding circles of concern. From this vision is derived the Stoic reputation for cosmopolitanism (Forman-Barzilai 2010) and impartiality (Annas 1993). The process of *oikeiosis* results, at least from the perspective of the Stoic sage, in the transformation of an understanding of "self-interest" from narrowly conceived expression of egoism to one encompassing the virtue of universal benevolence.

Now Smith appropriates this Stoic conception of familiarization up to a point. For Smith the Stoic doctrine of *oikeiosis* is useful as a sociological account of the reach and limits of sympathy. Smith's account begins at TMS VI.ii.1.1 where he presents his own version of the Stoic concentric circles metaphor. Here he explains that sympathy is extended outward from the individual in weakening degrees of affection in the manner described by Hierocles. Human affection is derived from physical closeness and habitual interaction, says Smith. The more remote our relationships and less habitual our interactions, the weaker are our affections. Moreover, says Smith, not only are our sympathies, but our abilities to make our benevolence affective, are strictly determined by nature to reach their limits at the national border. At TMS VI.ii.2.6 we find:

> The most extensive public benevolence which can commonly be executed with any considerable effect, is that of the statesmen, who project and form alliances among neighboring or not too distant nations, for the peace and tranquility of the states within the circle of their negotiations. The statesmen, however, who plan and execute such treaties, have seldom any thing in view, but the interest of their respective countries.

The Stoic admonishment that the sage extends *oikeiosis* to include all of nature and all of humanity is met with Smith's disapproval on the basis of its psychological implausibility for the common man and is, therefore, rejected as morally objectionable, (Forman-Barzilai 2010: 125–127). What human beings are incapable of, they should not be expected to attempt, argues Smith. What falls outside of human capabilities is left to god:

> The administration of the great system of the universe, however, the care of all rational and sensible beings, is the business of God and not of man. To man is allotted a much humbler department, but one much more suitable to the weakness of his powers, and to the narrowness of his comprehension; the care of his own happiness, of that of his family, his friends, his country: that he is occupied in contemplating the more sublime, can never be an excuse for his neglecting the more humble department; and he must not expose himself to the charge which Avidius Cassius is said to have brought, perhaps unjustly, against Marcus Antoninus;[22] that while he employed himself in philosophical speculations, and contemplated the prosperity of the universe, he neglected that of the Roman Empire. The most sublime speculation of the contemplative philosopher can scarce compensate the neglect of the smallest active duty.
> (TMS VI.ii.3.6)

John Stuart Mill

In his autobiography, John Stuart Mill claims that he cannot recall when he started learning Greek, but he estimates that it began at age three at the instruction of his father, James Mill, (Mill 1970). Latin was begun at age eight. John Mill notes his instruction was not merely intended to inculcate linguistic and literary skills, but also for the lessons that the ancient writers had to teach. Among his early moral influences, John Mill cites the influence of his father whose own moral influences included ancient Greek philosophers:

> My father's moral convictions, wholly dissevered from religion, were very much of the character of those of the Greek philosophers; and were delivered with the force and decision which characterized all that came from him. Even at the very early age at which I read with him the Memorabilia of Xenophon, I imbibed from that work and from his comments a deep respect for the character of Socrates; who stood in my mind as a model of ideal excellence … . At a somewhat later period the lofty moral standard exhibited in the writings of Plato operated upon me with great force. My father's moral inculcations were at all times mainly those of the "Socratici viri"; justice, temperance (to which he gave a very extended application), veracity, perseverance, readiness to encounter pain and especially labour; regard for the public good; estimation of persons according to their merits, and of things according to their intrinsic usefulness; a life of exertion in contradiction to one of self-indulgence and sloth (47).

Further, John describes his father's outlook on life as being largely in accordance with ancient philosophy.

> In his views of life he partook of the character of the Stoic, the Epicurean, and the Cynic, not in the modern but the ancient sense of the word. In his personal qualities the Stoic predominated. His standard of morals was Epicurean, inasmuch as it was utilitarian, taking as the exclusive test of right and wrong, the tendency of actions to produce pleasure or pain. But he had (and this was the Cynic element) scarcely any belief in pleasure; at least in his later years, of which alone, on this point, I can speak confidently (47–48).

Both John and James are closely associated with the utilitarian philosophy and of its founder, Jeremy Bentham. Bentham, in fact was a close friend of James Mill and had a hand in John's education. John Mill's utilitarianism, despite his up-bringing in the tradition, is at substantial odds with that of Bentham. According to Mill, Bentham improperly attaches an exclusive weight on the utilitarian pleasure-pain calculus as the basis for his moral philosophy. This error in turn is grounded in Bentham's inadequate understanding of human nature. He thus criticizes his teacher in the following terms:

Man is never recognized by him as a being capable of pursuing spiritual perfection as an end; of desiring, for its own sake, the conformity of his own character to this standard of excellence, without hope of good or fear of evil from other source than his own inward consciousness. Even in the more limited form of Consciousness, this great fact in human nature escapes him. Nothing is more curious than the absence of recognition in any of his writings of the existence of conscience, as a thing distinct from philanthropy, from affection for God or man, and from self-interest in this world or in the next.

(Mill 1969a: 95)

Much as Smith had earlier criticized the Epicureans for their utilitarian reductionism, so does Mill criticize Bentham. Mill's criticism is not that Bentham's emphasis was wholly wrong-headed, but rather far too exclusive:

The unusual strength of his early feelings of virtue was, as we have seen, the original cause of all his speculations; and a noble sense of morality, and especially of justice, guides and pervades them all. But having been early accustomed to keep before his mind's eye the happiness of mankind (or rather of the whole world), as the only thing desirable in itself, or which rendered anything else desirable, he confounded all disinterested feelings which he found in himself, with the desire of general happiness: much as some religious writers, who loved virtue for its own sake as much perhaps as men could do, habitually confounded their love of virtue with their fear of hell.

(Mill 1969a: 96)

Bentham's excessively narrow understanding of human motivation leads him, says Mill, to an inappropriately consequentialist theory of ethics. For Mill, intents and motivations also matter as reflecting character and should also be taken into account in our moral assessments of human behavior. A more well-rounded ethical theory, moreover, is important not just for philosophy's sake, but for the good of policy. A negative focus of legislative philosophy that merely proscribes certain behaviors in the interest of the general welfare is insufficient for Mill. He seeks rather an approach that encourages virtue, not one that merely produces happiness (Mill, 1969b).

The virtue content of Mill's ethics can be traced to the inspiration of the Stoics. He explicitly cites Stoic inspiration in his acknowledgement of the highest moral excellence of those who are willing to sacrifice for the benefit of others and, as paradoxical as it may seem, the willingness to make such sacrifices is itself the best guarantee of happiness in an imperfect world (Mill 1971: 24). He is equally explicit in what he regards as the insufficiency of the Epicurean utilitarian system even given its superiority to a sensation-based hedonistic calculus. An adequate moral system must include, he writes, many Stoic, as well as Christian, elements (1971: p18).

J. S. Mill notes the Hellenistic roots of utilitarianism and corrects the mis-apprehension of those who criticize the Epicureans on the grounds that they appeal to the least noble hedonistic impulses in people. Mill reminds these critics that Epicurus always made a distinction between higher and lower sources of pleasure. He takes modern utilitarian writers to task for not properly appreciating these higher pleasures. He makes both points as follows:

> But there is no known Epicurean theory of life which does not assign to the pleasures of the intellect, of the feelings and imagination, and of the moral sentiments a much higher value as pleasures than to those of mere sensation. It must be admitted, however, that utilitarian writers in general have placed the superiority of mental over bodily pleasures chiefly in the greater permanency, safety, uncostliness, etc., of the former – that is, in their circumstantial advantages than in their intrinsic nature. And on all these points utilitarians have fully proved their case; but they might have taken the other and, as it may be called, higher ground with entire consistency.
>
> (Mill 1971: 18–19)

Among Mill scholars the question is debated as to whether Mill's revision of Bentham's utilitarianism raises more problems than it solves. By allowing for qualitative differences in pleasures, how can the utilitarian method, which depends on a quantitative standard of measurement and comparison, be applied? The utilitarian rule, after all, is to make the choice that maximizes total utility. Or, does admitting the relevance of virtue considerations, as Mill seems to do, militate against his professed allegiance to utilitarianism? In sum, is Mill really a utilitarian, or isn't he? In recent years a number of scholars have advanced interpretations of Mill's revisionism that recall the influence of his early classical education. Geraint Williams (1996) argues that Mill had a concept of happiness that differed from Bentham's utility and, in fact, was much closer to the Greek concept of *eudaimonia*. The critical difference in these two conceptions is that while the first is purely a subjective matter based on the individual's experience, the second is grounded in some objective standard that provides a framework within which pleasure is experienced. Higher-ordered pleasures are those realized within that standard. The key for Mill's project of integrating virtue with utility was his recognition that in the eudaimonistic conception of happiness, virtue was not merely a means to happiness, as per the Epicureans, but also constitutive of it. This followed from the belief that virtuous activities are characteristic of human nature (Williams 1996: 11). Taking this view of human nature enables Mill to embrace the distinction between higher and lower order goods without abandoning his essentially utilitarian commitment.

A similar line of argument is pursued by Don Habibi (1998) who locates Mill's higher/lower pleasures distinction in terms of the potential for human growth in his value system.[23] Here an important related distinction is made by Mill as it relates to the idea of happiness. There exists the notion of happiness emphasized by Bentham as a state of mind (i.e., the experience of pain or pleasure). But there also exists for Mill a higher state of pleasure related to the development of higher-order human faculties (e.g., intellectual, creative, moral, spiritual). It is interesting in this respect to compare Mill's higher/lower pleasures to those found in the Epicurean system. Mill is similar to Epicurus in his recommendation in favor of the exercise of prudence in the selection of pleasures. Not all pleasures are equally preferable, or preferred in the short run, inasmuch as some are more likely to lead to greater pleasure in the long run. As far as that is concerned, both Mill and Epicurus would recommend pains, frustrations, and disappointments that result in greater long term pleasures.

A second commonality shared by the Epicurean and Millsean outlooks is their respect for expert opinion. For Epicurus these experts are those who choose to join the Master in the Garden and who devote themselves to a life of study of his principles. For Mill experts are those who are acquainted with both lower and higher pleasures, and are thus positioned to identify the higher pleasures from the lower, and to make recommendations to others regarding the superiority of the latter. It is also significant that for neither Epicurus nor Mill were these societies of the elect closed ones by virtue of one's station as determined at birth. Each, for example, was open to women.

In one important respect Mill's ethical theory differed from that of Epicurus. This deference concerns their respective ultimate conception of pleasure. For Epicurus, recall, the highest pleasure was *ataraxia*, or tranquility, or freedom from disturbance. For Mill, on the other hand, the ultimate pleasure was something that we might describe as involving a more active principle – namely, human development. We might also note a decided difference separating the two in terms of the implications of their views for social and political action. While for Epicurus it is hard to avoid the conclusion that his ethics recommends political quietism, this is certainly not the case for Mill. Like his nineteenth-century mentors, James Mill and Bentham, John Mill was a social and political reformer who hoped to fashion institutions that would aid and abet the development of the potential of all citizens.

It would be misleading to leave the reader with the impression that among the ancient Greeks Epicurus was the sole, or even the dominant, influence on Mill's thought. Both Nussbaum (2004) and Saunders (2010), for example, point to Aristotle as having left the stronger imprint on Mill's ethical theory. Loizides (2013) meanwhile draws attention to the importance of Plato in John Mill's overall intellectual development by way of James Mill and Samuel Coleridge. Nussbaum defends Mill from charges of incoherency in his views of happiness by arguing that Mill, like Aristotle, understood happiness to consist in a combination of heterogeneous elements, including, critically, a sense of dignity which compels people to choose higher-order pleasures (64–65). Saunders likewise comes to Mill's defense by invoking (via Rawls 1999) the so-called Aristotelian Principle which states: "other things being equal, human beings enjoy the exercise of their realized capacities (their innate or trained abilities), and this enjoyment increases the more the capacity is realized, or the greater the complexity," (Rawls 1999: 374). This is an outlook shared by Mill and one that he connects to a sense of dignity (Saunders 2010: 60).[24] Loizides argues that John Mill's own intellectual development, as well as his views on how truth could be reached, owed much to James Mill's enthusiasm for, and his son's training in, Plato's dialectics. It was this training that enabled J.S. Mill to move beyond the "narrow creed" of Bentham and pursue an enlarged view of utilitarianism that respected individual development, diversity of outlook, and intellectual progress. Moreover, John Mill's embrace of the Romantics (i.e., Coleridgeans) convinced him that truth contain emotional and aesthetic aspects.

Karl Marx

Karl Marx is similar to both Adam Smith and J. S. Mill, and many other Enlightenment thinkers, insofar as he was educated in, and retained a strong affinity for, the ancient classics. He is said to have had 89 volumes authored by ancient Greek and Roman writers, many of them in their original languages in which he had working knowledge (DeGloyer 1992: 115).[25] Unlike the other two political economists we have surveyed here, however, we would not classify Marx as doing dual duty as a moral philosopher. In fact, there are those who would argue that Marx's social, political, and economic analyses of capitalism are determinedly *amoral*. Indeed, the language used by Marx himself reveals him to be dismissive, and even contemptuous, of the moralizing attitude of others. But does Marx's attitude toward bourgeois morality, or his choice not to articulate a moral theory, render him or his work amoral? The answer to this question provided by recent scholars is decisively, "no," on both counts.[26] Moreover, the balance of this scholarship suggests that Marx's implicit moral outlook has important elements in common with what I have described as *eudaimonia*, and the eudaimonistic understanding of the good. This should not come as a surprise given what has just been described as Marx's education in, and affinity for, the ancient Greek tradition. I shall return to Marx's moral understanding in due course. For the moment I wish to focus on the more general influence of the ancient Greeks on his thought.

   Of the ancient Greek philosophers who had an influence on Marx's thinking, two stand out – Epicurus and Aristotle. Of these two figures, it is more difficult to determine which had the dominant influence on Marx; but the answer to this question may hinge on the stage of his intellectual development considered. Thus, Marx's doctoral dissertation involved a comparison of the atomism of Democritus and Epicurus.[27] Marx takes a strong stand in favor of the Epicurean atomistic view of the universe on the grounds that Democritus's interpretation is too mechanical and amounts to a purely deterministic view of reality, including of human behavior. Epicurus avoids the determinism of Democritus by positing the existence of a phenomenon called by Marx

(1975a) "declination" and by others, "the swerve." Recall in Chapter 2 that the swerve is that element in Epicurean physics that explains how it is that atoms, that otherwise fall in a straight-line path through the void, are able to collide and combine to form the substance that we sensuously apprehend as material reality. Marx notes that while both ancient and modern critics took Epicurus to task for his seemingly *ad hoc* explanation, he rises to his defense and argues that Epicurus, in comparison to Democritus, is the superior proponent of the atomistic outlook and the outstanding figure of the Greek Enlightenment.[28] The details of Marx's defense are conducted in the spirit of Hegelian idealistic philosophy, and there exists a lively scholarly debate as to whether or not Marx could be considered a philosophic idealist or materialist at the time of his dissertation (Burns 2000). Marx was included in the group known as "the Young Hegelians" and was a close student of Hegel's philosophy. Soon he would reject the idealism of Hegel and adopt a materialist understanding of historical change.

Materialism is a defining characteristic of Marx's analytical method throughout his life's work and it is no surprise that he was drawn at a very early age to the writings of Democritus and Epicurus. His preference for the Epicurean rather than the "Democritean" version of materialism has a lot to do with Marx's ethical worldview which attaches great importance to human freedom. In fact, in steering a course between Hegelian idealism and mechanical materialism, Marx, along with other "Young Hegelians" such as Ludwig Feuerbach, developed a form of humanism that he regarded as consistent with materialism and yet allowed for free will:

> Indeed, Marx is quite happy to describe his own views at this time as being materialist. For example, in the *Paris Manuscripts* he explicitly describes the humanism of Feuerbach as a form of materialism. He refers there to Feuerbach's "great achievement" as being "the establishment of *true materialism* and of real science". And in his contribution to *The Holy Family* (1844) he refers to the fact that speculative idealism, as it is to be found in the philosophy of Hegel, "will be defeated for ever by *materialism* which has now been perfected by the work of speculation itself and coincides with humanism". It is clear that Marx sees no logical inconsistency between a commitment to materialism, on the one hand, and a commitment to humanism, of the sort advocated by Feuerbach, on the other.
>
> (Burns 2000: 31–32)

Marx's embrace of Epicurean atomism is important for the development of what would become his analytical method, dialectical materialism. It may also pre-sage his revolutionary fervor hinted at in his dissertation where he notes the following:

> *Lucretius* therefore is correct when he maintains that the declination breaks the *fait foedera* (the bonds of fate), and, since he applies this

immediately to consciousness, it can be said of the atom that the declination is that something in its breast that can fight back and resist.

(Marx 1975a: 49)

While Epicurus held the dominant sway over the thinking of the younger, humanist Marx, for the more mature political economist, the ideas of Aristotle are brought into high relief. Thus, Marx begins his *magnum opus, Capital*, with an examination of the fundamental unit of exchange, the commodity, and immediately makes reference to "the first to analyse so many forms, whether of thought, society, or nature, and amongst them also the form of value. I mean Aristotle" (Marx 1975b: 59). Like Marx in volume 1 of *Capital*, Aristotle in book V of his ethics is concerned to determine the rate of exchange of commodities. To manage this they understand that they must establish what it is that commodities of different sorts in use (i.e., use values) have in common that enables them to be exchanged (i.e., to have exchange value). Aristotle maintained that the invention of money was motivated by the need for a mechanism by which exchange value could be measured and exchanges effectuated. From the *Nicomachean Ethics* we read:

> This is why all items for exchange must be comparable in some way. Currency came along to do exactly this, and in a way it becomes an intermediate, since it measures everything, and so measures excess and deficiency – [for instance,] how many shoes are equal to a house. Hence, as builder is to shoemaker, so must the number of shoes be to a house; for if this does not happen, there will be no exchange and no community. But proportionate equality will not be reached unless they are equal in some way. Everything, then, must be measured by some one measure as we said before.
>   In reality, this measure is need, which holds everything together; for if people needed nothing, or needed things to different extent, there would be either no exchange or not the same exchange. And currency has become a sort of pledge of need, by convention; in fact it has its name (*nomisma*) because it is not by nature, but by the current law (*nomos*), and it is in our power to alter it and to make it useless.
>
> (V.5.10–11)

Marx gives Aristotle credit for recognizing that exchange requires a means for expressing and measuring commodities as commensurable quantities, but argued that he failed to see the value relationship in its deepest, most mean-ingful incarnation (i.e., as the result of human labor). Marx argues that Aristotle in this sense was limited by the world in which he lived. Marx writes:

> There was, however, an important fact which prevented Aristotle from seeing that, to attribute values to commodities, is merely a mode of expressing all labour as equal human labor and consequently as labour of

equal quality. Greek society was founded upon slavery, and had, therefore, for its natural basis the inequality of men and of their labor powers. The secret of the expression of value, namely, that all kinds of labour are equal and equivalent, because, and so far as they are human labour in general, cannot be deciphered, until the notion of human equality has already acquired the fixity of a popular prejudice. This, however, is possible only in a society in which the great mass of the produce of labour takes the form of commodities, in which, consequently, the dominant relation between man and man is that of the owner of commodities. The brilliancy of Aristotle's genius is shown by this alone, that he discovered, in the expression of the value of commodities, a relation of equality. The peculiar conditions of the society in which he lived, alone prevented him from discovering what, "in truth," was at the bottom of this equality.

(Marx 1975b: 59–60)

Comparing these two passages we can appreciate that, at least from Marx's perspective, Aristotle misidentified the fundamental source of exchange value "in reality" as residing "in need" when "in truth" it resided in the fact that it represents a given quantity of abstract labor power. One way to consider the difference between Marx's notion of value determination and that of Aristotle, is to note that for Marx value is determined in the sphere of the social conditions of production, while for Aristotle it is determined by relative demand(s) for commodities.[29] This is a critical distinction since for Marx the social conditions of production are central to his theory of how a mode of production operates as well as of his moral evaluation of it.

McCarthy (1990) urges us to consider the parallels between Aristotle's notion of practical knowledge, *phronesis*, and Marx's concept of praxis. The use of the adjective "practical" carries the warning that it does not connote instrumentality, prediction, or explanation. Such meanings would be appropriate to a modern "positivist" interpretation, but not to an Aristotelean or Marxian (or Hegelian) usage. Practical knowledge for Aristotle is that which guides human behavior toward "the good." Implicit here then is some conception of "the good." McCarthy notes that this conception involves "human freedom and rationality – the telos of man" (1990: 106). Marx's idea of praxis combines this practical knowledge with political action directed, again, to the goal of human liberation:

Like Aristotle, Marx believes that ethics is a form of political and economic knowledge. For Aristotle the criterion of truth is that which leads to the good and to happiness, while for Marx it is that which leads to liberation and humanization of consciousness. In both cases, truth is determined not through the classical correspondence of consciousness and reality, but instead lies in the process of acting itself.

(McCarthy 1990: 111)

Brenkert (1983: 104), like McCarthy, also highlights the focus of Marx's ethical position in terms of human freedom. He describes Marx's ethics in fact as a variant of virtue ethics wherein freedom is the cardinal virtue:

> It (freedom) is not simply a power or an ability to do certain things, nor is it a principle of action or set of rights. Rather, Marx's treatment of freedom is best understood as the characteristic of a kind of life, a way of being, which we morally ought to realize. He urges us, at this historical juncture, to "Be free!" This requires one's self-development or self-objectification to an extent determined by one's own desires within the constraint that this development enables one to rationally and essentially direct one's activities with and relations to other people, social institutions, and natural forces.[30]

Marx's life work can be understood as an attempt to explain how historically specific forces and relations of production act to limit, or deny, people precisely the kind of self-objectification necessary for self-determination, as well as the requirements that must be met for positive freedom to be realized. Critical in Marx's understanding is the idea that self-determination is a social and not an individual matter. This is true in a double sense: the first being that the task of transforming productive forces and relations necessary to enable the kind of self-objectification characteristic of freedom cannot be the task of any individual. It is rather a class-based undertaking. The second sense in which the tasks of self-objectification/self-determination are social rather than individual resides in the fact that human beings are inherently social beings and self-determination requires *real* community. Marx's real community is a normative concept that recognizes the essentiality of human relationships to our self-objectification project(s). Production, for example, is production *with* and *for* other people. Marx's notion of self-determination also requires that the individual recognize the other as an essential part of her own essence; that is, human beings share a *species being*. The contrast between Marx's real community and that of the illusory community of bourgeois society are manifest. The latter simply connotes a community in which the class antagonisms that separate people are mediated and resolved by a state, typically in favor of the interests of members of the dominant class. Marx's real community by contrast requires the harmonization or unity of people which in turn requires the elimination of class-based antagonisms. Only as such will they see themselves as integrated in a larger social and rational order (Brenkert 1983: 119).

McCarthy notes that Marx is supported by Aristotle in his view of the essential sociality of human beings and contrasts this to the individualism of other eighteenth-century theorists. He also contrasts the meanings of Aristotle and Marx in the following way: Whereas for Aristotle human social development is a part of the individual's *telos*, his/her individual potential; for Marx this development includes the capacity of a class to overcome its cultural and ideological delusions and to create the institutions that enable its liberation (McCarthy 1990: 113).

There is little or nothing to be found in Marx's writing, or in the secondary literature of which I am aware, that suggests that the Stoics had a strong influence on his outlook. Nevertheless, there are perhaps at least a couple of points of tangency between the Stoic ethical outlook and that of Marx, each of which is suggested by Brenkert's argument that Marx's ethical perspective is, at bottom, a kind of virtue ethics. The first point is that Marx's cardinal virtue of freedom is an end in itself. Thus, as for the Stoics, Marx's virtue is not regarded as instrumental to some other end; rather, it is that good for which human development strives. Marxian *eudaimonia* is conceived as a state of being, or consciousness, just as it is for the Stoics. The second point relates the Stoic concept of *oikeiosis* to the Marxian concept of alienation. These two concepts are in fact antonyms: *oikeiosis* refers to "familiarization to" while alienation means "estrangement from." Recall from our earlier examination of the concept, Stoic *oikeiosis* concerns the rational disposition of the sage to extend her concern to ever widening circles of humanity such that, in the limit, the entirety of the species is included. Marxian alienation describes the obverse condition faced by human beings when they are unable to recognize their essential human and social relationships insofar as they labor under a consciousness distorted by an economic system predicated on commodity production and exchange and geared to the private accumulation of capital. *Oikeiosis* could then be interpreted from a Marxian perspective as the condition of a revolutionary self-consciousness that enables humankind to rid itself of class-based antagonisms and create the real community envisioned by Marx under communism. While there are important differences separating the Stoic understanding of *oikeiosis* and the parallel and corresponding Marxian notion (i.e., *species being*), they have in common that each is the result of an evolved and universal rationality.

In the late nineteenth century the divorce between economics and moral philosophy had become final. The emergent neoclassical school acknowledged no debt to ancient moral philosophy and instead preferred to point out Aristotle's errors (Theocarakis 2006). The positivist split between fact and value, and of science from ethics, begun by the time of David Hume's *A Treatise of Human Nature* (1740), by the early twentieth century had become conventional wisdom. As well, by the late nineteenth century, the focus of economics as a discipline had switched from a concern with the dynamic (and political) questions of economic growth, development, and income distribution to a concern for the static equilibrium conditions for resource allocation. Questions of commodity value had shifted from an objectivist (labor, or cost of production-based) to a subjectivist (neo-utilitarian) perspective, while questions of ethical values had been sidelined altogether. Economics had become "scientific." Within the new dominant paradigm the very concept of human rationality took on a new and narrow understanding. It is to this last question that we turn in the next chapter.

Notes

1 Randall Jr. points out that the Christian synthesis had its roots not only in Judaism (Hellenized or otherwise). It includes elements of Persian dualism, Syrian mystery cults, Stoic ethics, and Platonist thought (1970: 142).
2 Hatch (1970: 126–127) also notes that some Christian apologists, including Justin Martyr, believed that the best of the Hellenistic philosophical doctrines were inspired by the Divine Word made incarnate in Jesus Christ while others had appropriated their teachings from the Scriptures.
3 The Middle Ages are said to stretch from the fifth to the fifteenth centuries and are typically disaggregated into the Early, High, and Late periods. By the Late Middle Ages there was a perceptible increase in the pace of scientific advance, technological change, and state formation. This was accompanied by an acceleration of long-distance trade and exploration. The period is often referred to as the Age of Discovery.
4 Petrarch made a similar criticism of Seneca (Kraye 2001: 100).
5 Dante, for example, relegated Epicurus and his followers to the sixth circle of hell (Kraye 2001: 103).
6 Olster (2003) notes that the only law to which god is subject in Gassendi's reinter-pretation of the Epicurean system is the law of non-contradiction.
7 There is empirical evidence that economics students, trained in the methods of neoclassical theory at whose center rests the image of *homo economicus*, will behave in the manner described by that model far more often than students in other academic disciplines. See, for example, the empirical papers by Frank and Schulze (1998) and Frank et al (1993).
8 As we have seen, virtue as an end in itself is part of the mind-set of the Stoic sage. Gill (2006: 78–79) cites Cambridge Platonism, and specifically the sermons of Benjamin Whichcote, as the dominant influence on Shaftesbury's outlook in this regard.
9 This attitude is known as "psychological egoism" and will be addressed again in the following chapter.
10 Beneficence, by contrast, is defined as other-directed actions motivated by the self-approbation they may generate. Such actions are without moral value by Hutcheson's accounting, (Maurer 2010: 41).
11 Hutcheson is joined in this opinion by contemporary philosopher Martha Nussbaum (1986).
12 Skinner (2003) also mentions Hutcheson and Sir James Steuart as important figures in early Scottish political economy which as a whole was marked by a focus on socio-economic context and a method that owed much to Isaac Newton.
13 A partial list of the literature includes Raphael and Macfie (1976), Waszek (1984), Heise (1995), Vivenza (2001), Force (2003), Montes (2008), and Forman-Barzilai (2010).
14 Smith is considered to belong to a group of British moral philosophers that includes Hume, and a moral philosophical tradition called "sentimentalism."
15 The high regard for the Stoics is asserted by Smith himself at TMS VII.ii.I.29, "The spirit and manhood of their doctrines make a wonderful contrast with the despondent, plaintive, and whining tone of some modern systems," and again at TMS VII.ii.I.47, "That the Stoical philosophy had very great influence upon the character and conduct of its followers, cannot be doubted; and that though it might sometimes incite them to unnecessary violence, its general tendency was to animate them to actions of the most heroic magnanimity and most extensive benevolence."
16 In this regard Montes (2008) refers to Smith as "eclectic" while Vivenza (2001) characterizes his approach as "alchemical." Forman-Barzilai (2010) writes of the "hybridity" of Smith's thought.

17 Hanley (2009) provides an interesting discussion of magnanimity as a moment in the dialectical development of virtue in Smith's ethics.
18 This approach to prudence as a virtue is obviously an instrumental one and ascribes to Smith an Epicurean motivation. Hanley (2009: 39–40) notes the Epicurean sentiment in Smith's description of commercial society and its inherent threat to happiness understood in terms of tranquillity. Hanley notes that while for Smith tranquillity is a prerequisite for happiness, it is not sufficient (39, n38).
19 As Maurer (2010: 38) points out, some Stoics as represented by Cicero had a more subtle appreciation of the emotions and made a distinction between "affections" and "passions." The exercise of reason enabled the sage to give or withhold assent and thereby maintain control over the perceptions evoked by the emotions and their potential deleterious consequences. All of this seems entirely in keeping with Smith's attachment to propriety.
20 For a recent review of the Adam Smith problem and a wealth of relevant scholarly citations see Forman-Barzilai (2010: 29–55).
21 Ancient and modern conceptions of rationality are explored and compared in the following chapter.
22 Smith is referring here to Roman emperor and Stoic philosopher Marcus Aurelius.
23 The opportunity to promote such growth was an objective that Mill shared with Bentham, notes Habibi. Bentham's philosophy, after all, had a legislative agenda whose objective was the refashioning of institutions in such a way that recruited the pleasure–pain calculus that motivated individuals to act in ways to serve social welfare (90–92).
24 Saunders (2010: 64) also draws our attention to an argument made by Mill that defends his use of the "competent judge" in matters of determining which of the pleasures are higher and/or lower. Here Mill argues that such an appeal to authority is not avoided by Bentham's quantitative concept of utility since some such judge must render a ruling on which of two pleasures (or pains) is more or less intense.
25 Marx studied for several years at the University of Berlin, center of the German neo-humanist movement that replaced the Greek New Testament with Greek classics writings in the last 25 years of the eighteenth century. By the time of Marx's study, Berlin had become the undisputed center of classical scholarship (Degolyer 1992: 117).
26 See, for example, Brenkert (1983), Peffer (1990), West (1991), McCarthy (1992), Blackledge (2012).
27 Foster et al (2008: 84–85) have recently noted that Marx's interest in Epicurus is revealed as early as his Gymnasium (high school) days in Trier when he wrote an essay comparing the Epicurean and Christian views. In this instance Epicurus comes off second best to Christ – an outcome that is reversed several years later when Marx reaches university age.
28 "Epicurus is therefore the greatest representative of Greek Enlightenment, and he deserves the praise of Lucretius" (Marx 1975a: 73).
29 This interpretation of Aristotle runs the risk of anachronism since he did not in fact have any conception of market demand as it is understand by modern economics. For discussion of this see, for example, Pack (2010) and DeGolyer (1992). Marx understood that demand (use value) was essential to the concept of an exchangeable commodity. Exchange value of commodities, however, the source of surplus value and capital accumulation, were determined by the quantity of socially necessary value time embodied in their production.
30 "Self-objectification" is Marx's variant of a Hegelian notion that expresses the human need to express their personalities in concrete form, typically for Marx, via the labor process. It has different implications for freedom (i.e. self- determination) depending on the historical moment, mode of production, etc.

References

Annas, Julia. 1993. *The Morality of Happiness*, New York: Oxford University Press.

Aristotle. 1999. *Nicomachean Ethics*, translated by Terence Irwin, 2nd edition, Indianapolis, IN: Hackett.

Blackledge, Paul. 2012. *Marxism and Ethics: Freedom, Desire, and Revolution*, Albany, NY: SUNY Press.

Brenkert, George G. 1983. *Marx's Ethics of Freedom*, London: Routledge & Kegan Paul.

Bultmann, Rudolf. 1980. *Primitive Christianity in its Contemporary Setting*, Reginald H. Fuller (trans.), Philadelphia, PA: Fortress Press.

Burns, Tony. 2000. "Materialism in ancient Greek philosophy and in the writings of the young Marx," *Historical Materialism*, 7, 1: 3–39.

Davies, Martin. 1997. "Cosma Raimondi," *Cambridge Translations of Renaissance Texts, Volume I: Moral Philosophy*, Jill Kraye (ed.), Cambridge: Cambridge University Press.

DeGolyer, Michael. 1992. "The Greek accent of the Marxian matrix," in *Marx and Aristotle: Nineteenth-century German Social Theory and Classical Antiquity*, George E. McCarthy (ed.), Savage, MD: Rowman & Littlefield.

Deitz, Luc and Adelheid Wiehe-Deitz. 1997. "Francisco de Quevedo," *Cambridge Translations of Renaissance Texts, Volume I: Moral Philosophy*, Jill Kraye (ed.), Cambridge: Cambridge University Press.

Emerson, Roger. 2003. "The context of the Scottish Enlightenment," in *The Cambridge Companion to the Scottish Enlightenment*," Alexander Broadie (ed.), Cambridge: Cambridge University Press.

Force, Pierre. 2003. *Self-Interest before Adam Smith: A Genealogy of Economic Science*, Cambridge: Cambridge University Press.

Forman-Barzilai, Fonna. 2010. *Adam Smith and the Circles of Sympathy: Cosmopolitanism and Moral Theory*, Cambridge: Cambridge University Press.

Foster, John Bellamy, Brett Clark, and Richard York. 2008. *Critique of Intelligent Design: Materialism versus Creationism from antiquity to the Present*, New York: Monthly Review Press.

Frank, Björn and Gunther G. Schulze. 1998. "How Tempting is Corruption? – More Bad News about Economists," *Social Science Research Network Working Paper Number 164* (April). Available at SSRN: http://ssrn.com/abstract=100968.

Frank, Robert H., Thomas Gilovich, and Dennis T. Regan. 1993. "Does studying economics inhibit cooperation?", *The Journal of Economic Perspectives*, 7, 2 (Spring): 159–171.

Gay, Peter. 1966. *The Enlightenment: An Interpretation, vol.1 The Rise of Modern Paganism*, New York: Alfred A. Knopf.

Gill, Michael B. 2006. *The British Moralists on Human Nature and the Birth of Secular Ethics*, Cambridge: Cambridge University Press.

Green, Peter. 2008. *The Hellenistic Age: A Short History*, New York: Modern Library, Random House Inc.

Habibi, Don. 1998. "J. S. Mill's revisionist utilitarianism," *British Journal for the History of Philosophy*, 6, 1: 89–114.

Hanley, Ryan Patrick. 2009. *Adam Smith and the Character of Virtue*, Cambridge: Cambridge University Press.

Hatch, Edwin. 1970. *Influence of Greek Ideas on Christianity*, Gloucester, MA: Peter Smith.

Heise, Paul A. 1995. "Stoicism in the EPS: the foundation of Adam Smith's moral philosophy," in *The Classical Tradition in Economic Thought: Perspectives on the History of Economic Thought, Vol. XI*, Ingrid Rima (ed.), London: Edward Elgar Publishers.

Jaeger, Werner. 1961. *Early Christianity and Greek Paidea*, Cambridge, MA: The Belknap Press of Harvard University Press.

Kraye, Jill. 2001/2002. "Stoicism in the Renaissance from Petrarch to Lipsius," *Grotiana* (New Series), 22/23, 1: 21–46.

Loizides, Antis. 2013. "Taking their cue from Plato: James and John Stuart Mill," *History of European Ideas*, 30, 1: 121–140.

Marx, Karl. 1975a. *Karl Marx, Frederick Engels Collected Works, Volume 1*, New York: International Publishers.

Marx, Karl. 1975b. *Das Kapital, Volume 1*, New York: International Publishers.

Maurer, Christian. 2010. "Hutcheson's relation to Stoicism in the light of his moral psychology," *The Journal of Scottish Philosophy*, 8, 1 (March): 33–49.

McCarthy, George E. 1990. *Marx and the Ancients*, Savage, MD: Rowman & Littlefield.

McCarthy, George E. (ed.) 1992. *Marx and Aristotle: Nineteenth-century German Social Theory and Classical Antiquity*, Savage, MD: Rowman & Littlefield.

Mill, John Stuart. 1969a. "Bentham," in *Essays on Ethics, Religion and Society*, in *Collected Works of John Stuart Mill, Volume X*. J.M. Robson (ed.) Toronto: University of Toronto Press.

Mill, John Stuart. 1969b. "Remarks on Bentham's Philosophy," in *Essays on Ethics, Religion and Society*, in *Collected Works of John Stuart Mill, Volume X*. J.M. Robson (ed.) Toronto: University of Toronto Press.

Mill, John Stuart. 1970. *Autobiography*, London: Longman, Green, Reader, and Dyer (an authorized facsimile produced in 1970 by University Microfilms, Ann Arbor, MI).

Mill, John Stuart. 1971. *Utilitarianism with Critical Essays*. Samuel Gorovitz (ed.), Indianapolis, IN: Babbs-Merrill Company, Inc.

Montes, Leonidas. 2008. "Adam Smith as an eclectic Stoic," *The Adam Smith Review*, 4: 30–51.

Nussbaum, Martha. 1986. *The Fragility of Goodness: Luck and Ethics in Greek Tragedy and Philosophy*, Cambridge: Cambridge University Press.

Nussbaum, Martha. 2004. "Mill between Aristotle & Bentham," *Dedalus*, 133, 2 (Spring): 60–68.

Olster, Margaret J. 2003. "Early modern uses of Hellenistic philosophy: Gassendi's Epicurean project", in *Hellenistic and Early Modern Philosophy*, Jon Miller and Brad Inwood (eds.), Cambridge: Cambridge University Press.

Pack, Spencer. 2010. *Aristotle, Adam Smith and Karl Marx: On Some Fundamental Issues in 21st Century Political Economy*, Northampton, MA: Edward Elgar.

Peffer, Rodney G. 1990. *Marxism, Morality and Social Justice*, Princeton, NJ: Princeton University Press.

RandallJr., John Herman. 1976 (1926). *The Making of the Modern Mind: A Survey of the Intellectual Background of the Present Age, Fifth Anniversary Edition with a forward by Jacques Barzun*, New York: Columbia University Press.

RandallJr., John Herman. 1970. *Hellenistic Ways of Deliverance and the Making of the Christian Synthesis*, New York: Columbia University Press.

Raphael, D. D. and A. L. Macfie. 1976. "Introduction," *The Theory of Moral Sentiments*, Oxford: Clarendon Press.

Rawls, John. 1999. *A Theory of Justice*, Cambridge, MA: Cambridge University Press.

Saunders, Ben. 2010. "J. S. Mill's conception of utility," *Utilitas*, 22, 1 (March): 52–69.

Schmitt, C.B. 1983. "The rediscovery of ancient skepticism in modern times," in *The Skeptical Tradition*, Myles Burnyeat (ed.), Berkeley, CA: University of California Press.

Skinner, Andrew S. 2003. "Economic Theory," in *The Cambridge Companion to the Scottish Enlightenment*, Alexander Broadie (ed.), Cambridge: Cambridge University Press.

Smith, Adam. 1976. *The Theory of Moral Sentiments*, Oxford: Clarendon Press.

Theocarakis, Nicholas J. 2006. "Nicomachean Ethics in political economy: the trajectory of the problem of value," *History of Economic Ideas*, 14, 1: 9–53.

Vivenza, Gloria. 2001. *Adam Smith and the Classics: The Classical Heritage in Adam Smith's Thought*, Oxford: Oxford University Press.

Waszek, Nobert. 1984. "Two concepts of morality: A distinction of Adam Smith's ethics and its Stoic Origin," *Journal of the History of Ideas*, 95, 4 (October–December): 591–606.

West, Cornel. 1991. *The Ethical Dimensions of Marx's Thought*, New York: Monthly Review Press.

Williams, Geraint. 1996. "The Greek origins of J. S. Mill's happiness," *Utilitas*, 8, 1 (March): 5–14.

Wilson, Catherine. 2008. *Epicureanism at the Origins of Modernity*, Oxford: Clarendon Press.

Witt, Ronald G. 1997. "Coluccio Salutati," *Cambridge Translations of Renaissance Texts, Volume I: Moral Philosophy*, Jill Kraye (ed.), Cambridge: Cambridge University Press.

Young, Robert V. 1997. "Justus Lipsius," *Cambridge Translations of Renaissance Texts, Volume I: Moral Philosophy*, Jill Kraye (ed.), Cambridge: Cambridge University Press.

4 Conceptions of rationality: thin, thick, and ancient

An operating hypothesis of this book is that the normative/ethical presupposi-tions of the conventional economics wisdom, typically expressed in terms of the neoclassical economic model, are inadequate to serve a class of public policy problems that require we go beyond the model's standard assumptions and methods. This hypothesis is hardly novel having a substantial and growing intellectual lineage in the development of modern economic thought. The standard economic model shares with ancient Greek philosophy one extremely important underlying assumption which I would like to examine in some detail in this chapter. This assumption concerns the defining characteristic of the human animal, namely, rationality. The apparent similarity of the modern economic and ancient philosophical outlooks, however, is largely superficial. The most obvious difference between the two is often said to consist in the fact that while for the ancient Greeks the term "rational" had unmistakable ethical implications, for modern economics it does not. That is, for modern economics "rationality" has been understood as positively describing human choice-making unburdened with any particular normative-ethical baggage. And yet, it is interesting to note, this modern "scientific" theory grew out of a nineteenth-century ethical tradition, utilitarianism, whose shadow it has never been able entirely to escape.

The argument that the ethical/normative presuppositions of modern economics are too "thin" to enable the discipline to provide a basis for many important public policy issues presupposes, of course, that modern economics is in fact grounded in some sort of normative/ethical worldview. The particular ethical presuppositions of the discipline emerge in part from what it takes as the defining features of rationality and rational economic behavior. Modern eco-nomics is keen to fashion itself as a science and, as such, is equally keen to stand apart from normative/evaluative prescriptions. It is also a discipline that fashions itself as being of particular usefulness for purposes of policy formulation and implementation. It is a statement of faith among "positivist" thinkers, among whom we would include most social scientists, that one cannot derive an "ought" from an "is." The meaning of this is that objective analysis of reality necessarily stands apart from our value judgments. To handle the twin tasks of positive analysis of economic behavior while providing a basis for inherently normative policy recommendations, modern economics has consigned the latter normative issues to a sub-discipline referred to as welfare economics. Here such concepts as consumer and producer surplus, optimality, and efficiency are pressed into service to provide policy-makers guidance. This is done, however, without a reformulation of the basic understanding of human behavior that lies at the center of its standard model. I shall argue in this chapter that this basic understanding is a highly restrictive one that underestimates the range of actual human motivations that operate to influence choice-making. Thus, in part, my position is that the standard economics theory is "thin" both in its assessment of human behavior as well as "thin" in the ethical presuppositions that ought to be taken into account in the formulation of the policies that both derive from and seek to shape that behavior.

In this chapter I pursue four objectives. The first is to describe the approach that I characterize as revealed choice utilitarianism (RCU). I shall describe the origins of the approach as well as show how it emerged as the theory of decision-making that has dominated not only modern economic theory, but also to spread its influence across the social sciences. Second, I wish to give an account of the thinness of the theory. This involves a critical review of RCU as well as a review of the attempts to modify, or "thicken," it. "Thicken" here refers to attempts that have been made to address the limitations of the approach identified by critics as well as extensions of the method that allow for its relevance across a wider range of observed behaviors. Third, I shall provide a more detailed accounting of the understanding of "reason" and "rationality" as it is understood by the ancient thinkers. Fourth, and finally, I shall detail some ways that contemporary philosophers have up-dated the ancient virtue ethics and suggest briefly how their insights might point the way forward for policy discussion.

The rise of neoclassical economics

The uneasy relationship between mainstream economics and questions of value, moral and otherwise, has a history as long as the discipline itself. Adam Smith, widely acknowledged as the "father of modern economics," made his living as professor of moral philosophy at the University of Glasgow. For Smith the idea that economics was an extension of moral philosophy was a natural one. While he assumed that economic behavior was largely explained by the individual's search for advantage, he recognized that human behavior more generally was motivated by a variety of additional motivations, including the esteem of one's neighbors. The RCU view of value, however, has its roots in the utilitarianism that began with Jeremy Bentham around the same time as Smith in the late eighteenth century. In contrast to Smith, Bentham held a highly reductionist view of human motivation. If people were motivated by a desire for the esteem of their fellows, it was because this esteem served them as a source of utility (pleasure) while their disapprobation was a source of disutility (pain).

The view of human behavior as essentially egotistical and utility-seeking dominated conventional economic theory throughout the eighteenth century up through and including the so-called "Marginalist Revolution" that began around 1870. The Marginalist Revolution was important in the history of economic thought for a variety of reasons, but perhaps most importantly because it represents the moment when economics begins the attempt to become purely and purposefully scientific. In order to do this, the revolutionists thought, it was necessary to remove from the discipline any element of value judgment. Stanley Jevons, the British economist, thus claims that it is not possible as an empirical matter to make comparisons of utility between individuals. In contrast to Bentham, who did believe that such comparisons could be made, he rejected on this basis redistributive taxation proposals that sought to increase the sum of welfare by increasing the incomes of the poor whose marginal utility of income was higher than that of the rich. The Austrian Carl Menger also insisted on the purely scientific character of economics and added that as a scientific matter the discipline could only be studied from the perspective of the individual economic agent (e.g., consumer or firm owner). Scientific economics in other words has nothing to say regarding *social* welfare considered apart from the aggregate welfare of the individuals that constitute society (Hunt, 1979: 251). Thus he advanced the cause of methodological individualism that is part and parcel of modern mainstream economics. Finally, Léon Walras developed a system of equations that demonstrated the simultaneous determination of all prices in the economy, commonly known as general equilibrium. This highly mathematized construction itself represents an important moment in the development of economics as a scientific discipline at least insofar as quantification is seen as prerequisite to the rigor associated with science.

Revealed choice theory

But, for all its seeming scientific advance, economics was still wedded to a version of the utilitarianism of its predecessors. While the assumption that utility could be measured in some absolute, cardinal sense was replaced by a weaker assumption that consumers need only be able to rank their preferences in an ordinal sense, the fact remained that the theory of individual choice was still firmly tied to some psychological postulate of utility. And as utility, being not only unmeasurable but also unobservable in any direct way, made life uncomfortable for those who insisted on economics as an empirically-based science, some means was sought to develop a theory of rational choice that removed utility from the picture outright. The way forward was provided by a bit of early twentieth-century scientific method called *logical positivism*. The essence of logical positivism is that the truth value of a theory resides in its predictive capacity, and not in the realism of its assumptions. Applied to a theory of consumer choice then, what matters is, does the theory predict how consumers will respond to a price change for a good? It matters not at all *why* they respond in the way they do. It only matters for the validity of the theory at hand whether they respond in the manner predicted by the theory. The great advantage of this approach is that it renders the economic decision-maker's motivation quite moot. This decision-maker could be motivated by a desire to maximize utility, or by altruism, or by some other psychological prior. It really doesn't matter for the theory, called revealed choice theory in economics, since its one and only concern is, does the observed behavior of the decision-maker accord with the prediction of the theory? A second significant advantage of this approach is that the theory itself can be motivated by a very small number of assumptions. That is, the approach is "parsimonious."[1] The particular assumptions, called axioms, of revealed choice theory are the following:[2]

1   Reflexivity: any bundle of goods is as good as itself. Or, for a bundle, x, $x \geq x$.
2   Completeness: for any two bundles x and y, either $x \geq y$ or $y \geq x$.
3   Transitivity: for any three bundles x, y and z, if $x \geq y$ and $y \geq z$, then $x \geq z$.
4   Continuity: it is possible to make marginal substitutions between items in a bundle x such that one is indifferent between the resultant bundle and the first bundle. Thus, no particular item in a bundle is essential such that additions of another good do not provide adequate compensation for its removal.

The first three of the above axioms is sufficient to provide a "preference ordering." The additional axiom (4) allows this preference ordering to be represented by a set of indifference curves familiar to beginning students of microeconomics with the alleged important difference that there is no need to invoke any notion of utility, ordinal or otherwise, to motivate economic decisions. The decision-maker acts "as if" he were driven by a utility function to choose in a manner that maximizes utility.

Yet a third advantage of the revealed preference approach is its generality. While the customary economic application of the approach concerns the issue of consumer choice, there is nothing in the axioms that limits the choices to consumption "bundles." The word "bundle" could be substituted for by "choice" and the system could apply equally well to any choice-making context. Thus the method is capable of providing an account of such diverse decision-making as family size and the amount of time spent brushing one's teeth.

Finally rational choice theory has been adapted to take into account situations involving risk and uncertainty. In such cases choices are said to be made over "prospects" rather than bundles where the former is defined as a weighted sum of outcomes. The weights in this case are given by the probabilities of particular outcomes. Additional axioms follow (Hargreaves Heap et al 1992: 13), but the result is that decision-makers are still found to be able to act *as if* they maximized "expected utility" and once again, the approach is said to have broad application to both economic and less obvious economic contexts including cases involving strategic interactions among "players" (e.g., game theory). So influential has the revealed preference approach been in the social sciences that it is no longer considered to be the singular province of economics and has emerged as an equally influential, if not dominant, method in political science, international relations theory, and psychology. At the same time, however, it has also been subject to a great deal of critical review and revision.

Criticisms and limitations of revealed preference theory

The above-described method has spawned a virtual sub-industry dedicated to its elaboration in response to its clear limitations. These limitations are a consequence of two of its considered strengths, its parsimony and its potential for general application. The criticisms fall into two categories: (1) arguments that the theory does not in fact accurately predict behavior, at least not in many important contexts and cases; (2) the theory is not normatively neutral. Let's consider these criticisms in turn.

That revealed choice (or preference) theory is not predictively accurate would seem to be a particularly damning criticism to make of a theory that owes its genesis to a philosophical outlook (logical positivism) predicated precisely on the power of its predictive accuracy. As Kahneman (2011: 270) has pointed out the rational agent model is not, nor was ever intended to be, a theory of human psychology. It is rather a specific kind of logic that was pressed into serviced by economists to serve as the behavioral foundation of their discipline.

The specific claims made against the theory are not all a matter of the adequacy of its axioms. Part of the difficulty is what it retains from the utilitarian tradition from which it evolved. Despite the claim that the approach is independent of any particular psychological category such as utility, it is still tied to its close cousin, preference. Moreover, the economics version of revealed choice theory invariably retains the familiar auxiliary assumption that decision-makers are essentially selfish. In the attempt to then explain apparently altruistic choices it is proposed that such decision-makers either derive utility from altruism, or that they seek to avoid the disutility of confronting the distress of others. In either case it is argued that apparently altruistic choices are in fact selfish ones. This line of argument is a patently tautological (and therefore trivial) one inasmuch as its conclusion is built-into its assumptions.[3] By this line of reasoning, any particular choice, even one that appears to be motivated by concern for others, may be read as motivated by the selfish pursuit of utility. The failure to provide some account of why some choice or other provides utility, or is preferred, amounts to a theoretical evasion (Sen 1990). It also fails to provide a testable hypothesis of the revealed preference approach itself.

There are other shortcomings of RCU. One is that is it provides no accounting of, nor even allows for, changes in preferences, beyond noting that such changes may occur. This is an important lacuna in contexts where the decision-making has an inter-temporal aspect to it. As far as that is concerned, inter-temporal decision-making may involve information demands that RCU cannot meet. In the uncomplicated situation the decision-maker is assumed to have a well-defined preference ordering which presupposes that she possesses all the relevant information necessary to rank her preferences. This requirement becomes far more problematical when time enters as a significant contextual issue. It may be an order of magnitude more difficult to know what conditions will obtain in the future that might have a bearing on contemporaneous decisions, or how one's preference function might change over the time horizon under consideration.

Thick rationality

There have been a number of attempts to address these short-comings of the neoclassical approach. One category of such alternatives is called "bounded rationality." This approach relaxes the assumptions that decision-makers possess perfect information and that they make decisions that are maximizing or optimizing. In its place it assumes that they make decisions based on the available information and engage in "satisficing" behavior. Operationally, bounded rationality is said to work by employing rules of thumb that substitute for the precise equilibrium conditions associated with optimizing behavior. Thus, for example, firms might choose to attach a mark-up over costs to determine their sales prices rather than to attempt to calculate profit maximizing prices. Workers or consumers might anticipate future prices on the basis of last period prices (adaptive expectations) rather than on the basis of anticipated impacts of monetary policy and other structural features of the economy (rational expectations). As this approach seeks to describe how economic agents actually go about decision-making, it is often alternatively identified as *procedural rationality* (PR).

Some have questioned if bounded, or procedural, rationality really amounts to a "thickened" account of rationality. Hargraves Heap (1992) declares the version of PR advanced by Herbert Simon to be an "ersatz" form of the instrumental rationality (IR) associated with the neoclassical model. That is to say, PR hardly amounts to a thicker conception of rationality if it leaves untouched our understanding of "the rational" strictly in terms of means in relation to ends. But this is not the only way in which broad rationality might be conceived. Hargraves Heap notes that the rules of thumb associated with PR provide the building blocks of a society's culture (1992: 18). Practical rules of thumb develop in a social context that addresses itself to a variety of relational issues besides means and ends ones, and the concept of bounded rationality may be grounded in *homo sociologicus* as much as in *homo economicus*.

Jon Elster (1983) draws a distinction between the thin rationality related to the standard means and ends model employed in social science and what he terms "broad rationality." The latter concept seeks to examine the substantive rationality of ends and desires themselves. This raises, of course, the question as to how we assess the substantive rationality of our ends. Elster's answer to this question begins by noting that broadly rational desires are a result of the way they are shaped. He writes, "All desires and beliefs have a (sufficient) causal origin, but some of them have the *wrong sort* of causal history and hence are irrational (emphasis added)" (16). Elster is concerned to interrogate the conventional theory of choice at both the individual as well as at the collective levels. He notes two important assumptions regarding traditional social choice theory. First, the only alternative to the aggregation of preferences is the censoring of preferences. Second, the censoring of preferences is always objectionable. Elster challenges these assumptions by observing that the central concern of politics is (and should be) unanimous and rational consensus, not an optimal compromise among irreducibly opposed interests. Like Hargraves Heap, Elster argues for the essential sociality of desires and yet, for broad rationality, also wishes to emphasis the importance of autonomy. Autonomy he admits is difficult to define, but he draws a parallel to the ability possessed by some people to exercise judgement. He writes, "Just as there are persons well known for their judgement, there are persons that apparently are in control over the processes whereby their desires are formed, or at least not in the grip of processes with which they do not identify themselves" (21). Significantly, the ability to form desires autonomously is linked by Elster to such character-forming philosophies such as those associated with the Stoics, Buddhism, and Spinoza.

Martin Hollis (1992) also takes up the concept of autonomy in an attempt to flesh out the meaning of rationality. He begins by recalling the familiar distinction between negative and positive freedom. *Homo Economicus* of RCU fame is said to possess negative freedom inasmuch as he is free to choose the utility-maximizing bundle of commodities given his independently derived preference function. The model of consumer sovereignty, however, makes some strong supporting assumptions regarding the availability and quality of information. Hollis asks the pertinent question, what are we to make of this conception of the autonomous decision-maker in a world of incomplete, imperfect, or selectively provided information (e.g., advertising)? Neither is any account given of the resource demands that accompany (and may constrain) the exercise of (negative) freedom according to this model.

The question arises as to what the requirements are for the exercise of positive freedom that we might associate with authentic autonomy. Moreover, Hollis asks, how is our understanding of rationality modified under such authentic autonomy? The answer to the first of these questions suggests considerable demands on the information requirement. Consider again, for example, the challenges posed by time and the variability of preferences over time. Consider as well the impact of choices made at one moment in time on the future preferences of the choice-maker (79). Such considerations lead Hollis to stipulate that authentic autonomy presupposes a *reflectively rational* decision-maker which in turn requires the development of character. Citing

Mill and Kant, Hollis also raises the possibility that the autonomous life that embodies positive freedom may be one that involves moral purpose (80–87).

Economist Albert Hirschman (1984) believes that economics has paid insufficient attention to the questions of non-instrumental motivations and actions. He makes a distinction between "wanton" and reflective preference change. By wanton preference Hirschman refers to one that is given or unexamined. This is the type of preference that is the domain of RCU. These are contrasted to "metapreferences," a type of higher order preference.[4] Changes in preferences are evidence for the existence of metapreferences, as is the fact that people sometimes make choices that are "against their better judgement"–"their better judgement" reflecting their metapreference. Metapreferences may also change, and when they do they signal a change in values. These sorts of changes are decidedly non-wanton and typically involve serious internal conflict, i.e. they require the exercise of reflective rationality (14–15).

One could argue, notes Hirschman, that the proper field for the RCU method is precisely wanton preference change. But economics has not seemed content to limit itself to say explaining, for example, under what circumstances people will prefer apples to oranges. Rather the discipline has evinced a tendency to spread its influence and explanatory apparatus to all manner of decision-making and to characterize all values in commercial terms. Moreover, this same apparatus, as noted earlier, has become highly influential in other social science disciplines. The result is that even such non-instrumental motivations (e.g., love, altruism, virtue) have been given an instrumental cast. Not only does the reductionist tendency of the RCU approach do damage to the analytical coherency of the social sciences, it may also imperil the functioning of the social and economic system it seeks to describe. Writes Hirschman (1984: 25):

> once a social system, such as capitalism, convinces everyone that it can dispense with morality and public spirit, the universal pursuit of self-interest being all that is needed for satisfactory performance, the system will undermine its own viability, which is in fact premised on civic behavior and on the respect of certain moral norms to a far greater extent than capitalism's official ideology avows.

The above review of efforts to provide a thicker, more satisfying account of rational choice-making is only partial. Additional testimony is available.[5] It is sufficient, however, to accomplish two objectives. The first is to demonstrate the inability of the standard model (RCU) to provide an adequate description of the range of motivations that drive human decision-making without undue semantic violence (i.e., attributing all choices to utility by defining all choices in terms of utility). Second, it makes a chimera of the strong separation of fact and value that has been the default assumption in science since Hume. Recent writers have argued the connection between "is" and "ought" operates through the mechanism of neurobiology. Harris (2010), for example, has noted that the concept of human well-being, as difficult as that concept may be to define with precision, is nonetheless identifiable and describable in neurological and psychological terms. Moreover, it would appear to amount to philosophical pettifogging to doubt that human well-being is part and parcel of "the good" for human beings. Applied to the domain of social science, particularly where there exists an imperative for policy recommendations, the imagined breach between fact and value is particularly untenable. The entire premise of social scientific understanding in such cases is the desire to enable people to live better lives. This is precisely the vision that motivated ancient philosophy to which we now return.

The role of reason in ancient Hellenistic thought

While it is indeed true that modern social science and ancient philosophy share a common interest in the concepts of reason and rationality, these notions do far more work in the latter systems than they do in the former. For most schools of modern social science rationality has been reduced to providing an algorithm for choosing between and among commensurable options defined in terms of utility or some other common denominator; for the ancient philosophers it is defined in terms of apprehending the universe and one's place in it. Recall from Chapter 2 the ancient Greek concept of *logos*. This term translates as reason, but reason understood as universal force, sometimes identified with god, or the gods. Human rationality was thought to partake of this universal *logos* which was thought to constitute the defining characteristic of our species. So, reason for the ancients is no mere tool in the hands of human beings to achieve particular ends or states as it is for so-called consequentialist outlooks such as RCU.[6] Rather the ancient conception of reason/rationality has both ethical as well as developmental content and implications. *Ethical*, inasmuch as reason is considered essential to virtuous activity, and *developmental* inasmuch as the capacity to reason well is not an intrinsic, or automatic, attribute of human behavior.

Not all the ancient philosophers thought in exactly the same way about what and how people reasoned. Aristotle and Plato, for example, believed that the human soul was comprised of both rational and irrational elements, while the Stoics believed that irrationality stemmed from a lack of knowledge. What most of these thinkers had in common, however, is the belief that the exercise of reason is connected to virtue. The concept of practical reasoning (*phronēsis*) refers to the *disposition* of the virtuous decision-maker, action-taker to do the right thing, in the right way, at the right time, and for the right reason(s) (Annas 1993: 73). It suggests a disposition to deliberation rather than to act on impulse. The centrality of virtue in "practical" reasoning may seem puzzling. After all, the idea of practical choices or actions might seem to involve all sorts of things that have no particular moral dimension to them, such as which breakfast cereal I might choose on any given morning. For the ancients, however, all seemingly isolated, episodic choices fit into a more general "all things considered" context and with a view to an overarching end (i.e., to the well-lived life). Neither did the ancients believe that there was anything necessarily automatic about this deliberatively virtuous disposition. *Phronēsis* is a state that the virtuous actor develops over a lifetime via study and practice. Beginning or aspiring, virtuous decision-makers may rely on rules to help guide them, while the fully mature and virtuous decision- maker internalizes the virtues and has no need for rules. Virtue becomes part of the disposition of the latter, but, again, there is no guarantee of this development. It does not develop without time, effort invested in understanding the principles that underlie virtue, and the experience in the exercise of virtue(s).

Stoic rationality

The developmental view of rationality is perhaps clearest in the Stoics who differed from their classical era predecessors in modifying the notion of a multipartite division of the soul, or psyche. Rather than divide the soul into rational, irrational and appetitive components, the Stoics conceived of reason as the "governing principle" of the soul (Long 1986: 171). This governing principle is set in motion by an impulse that follows upon some perception. Impulses are rational responses inasmuch as they give rise to actions. Moreover, impulses are necessarily evaluative inasmuch as the action(s) they inspire are predicated on some good to be attained, or bad to be avoided, by the decision-maker. If they are excessive they are considered "passions." The Stoic denigration of passions then follows not from their essential irrationality, but from the failure of a properly regulated rationality. "Right reason" is, by contrast, reason properly regulated and whose evaluation is concerned strictly with the pursuit of virtue. This is not to suggest that other values never enter into the choice-making of Stoic sages. As discussed in Chapter 2, external values such as health, wealth, and reputation have *selection* value for the sage but are not considered good as such. This selection value has been variously interpreted by commentators as instrumental value or "planning value" (Brennan 2003) insofar as they support the pursuit of virtue.

Conventionally understood economics is concerned with the production and distribution of what from the Stoic sage's perspective are considered "indifferent values." Brennan (2003: 281) poses an interesting question for the sage:

> We may stipulate that all of the Sage's actions are virtuous actions, but it also seems that every virtuous action consists in a virtuous way of responding to indifferents. In any situation, the Sage will have an infallible grasp of which indifferents require attention, what their respective planning values are, and which actions are likely to result in the production of which further indifferents with which further values. But how does that knowledge function in the Sage's deliberations?

Citing the Stoic authority of Cicero (*De Officiis*), Brennan suggests that something like the model of bounded rationality could operate wherein the sage would select indifferents in a way that does not conflict with virtue. That might be consistent with maximizing some function of indifferents subject to the requirements of virtue. But it might also be consistent with some other virtue prioritizing approach as well. Brennan (2003: 283) asks some additional questions:

> Is the Sage's consideration of planning value a maximizing one or not? Does he attempt to maximize or otherwise distribute planning value only for himself or for other agents as well? Perhaps the algorithmic model is wholly inappropriate, and they were intuitionists of some form? These are central questions in moral psychology; our current inability to answer them points to important avenues for research on the Stoics.[7]

Epicurean rationality

Epicurean rationality contains elements that appeal to modern sensibilities. First, it is derived from a materialist/empiricist rather than metaphysical attitude to knowledge. All "reasonable" assertions about the world must stand the test of the senses. Sense perception itself is taken to be a reliable guide to existing reality. The primacy of sensory impressions in establishing knowledge follows from Epicurus's physics which has as its base the movement of atoms through the void. The collision of atoms moving through the void and coming into contact with those in the human brain are the cause of perceptions. We note in Epicurus's account then an incipient form of neuro-biology. Second, at the center of Epicurean moral reasoning is pleasure.[8] The pursuit of pleasure and the avoidance of pain provide us with all we need to motivate our moral choices. This would seem to have a great deal in common with modern consequentialist ethical theories and in particular the utilitarianism associated with modern welfare economics. And yet, as it does for nearly all of the ancient schools, virtue emerges as an important element in the Epicurean account of pleasure. Moreover, virtue is regarded by Epicurus as instrumental to pleasure. That is, while pleasure is the sole source of human happiness, virtue is a requirement for the realization of Epicurean pleasure. On the face of it then, the structure of Epicurean ethical rationalism shares with RCU the latter's means-ends formulation. Of course, the "special sauce" for RCU is information rather than virtue.

An understanding of Epicurean pleasure helps us to understand why virtue is central to the good life. We can start by noting that Epicurean pleasure has nothing to do with episodic ecstasy as it might with more conventional notions of pleasure. Rather for Epicurus pleasure is better understood as a tranquil, or untroubled state of mind. Zeller (2012: 449) describes Epicurus's understanding of pleasure as follows:

> In calling pleasures the highest object in life, says Epicurus, we do not mean the pleasures of profligacy, nor, indeed, sensual enjoyments at all,

but the freedom of the body from pain, and of the soul from disturbance. Neither feasts nor banquets, neither the lawful or unlawful indulgence of the passions, nor the joys of the table, make a happy life, but a sober mind discriminating between the motive for action and for inaction, and dispelling the greatest bane of our peace, prejudices.

Epicurus made a distinction between static and kinetic pleasure. Kinetic pleasure is ephemeral, temporary. You eat a good meal and you realize kinetic pleasure which soon passes until your next good meal; similarly, for all such sensual pleasures. Static pleasure, *ataraxia*, is a final state and, as Annas (1993: 85) argues, subject to the constraints and qualifications that all such end states are bound. *Ataraxia* (tranquility), in fact, is the measure of *eudaimonia* according to the Epicurean outlook. It is therefore better understood as an aspirational goal of life rather than a distinctive, one-off experience of life. While the RCU approach to choosing might have some application to kinetic pleasure, it fails entirely in providing insight into static pleasure thus conceived. It is hard to imagine how one would increase or decrease such a state, let alone maximize it. Neither would various satisficing strategies seem to apply to Epicurean static pleasure. If rules of thumb are sought, they would seem to require those that would codify Epicurean principles.

As for the Stoics and their classical epoch predecessors, Epicurean reason and rationality is not a simple endowment of human beings. It is an intellectual and ethical aspiration available to those who have access to the proper instruction as well as the commitment to follow. Achieving *ataraxia* is not assumed to be automatic or guaranteed. In fact, it is unlikely to be realized in the absence of a commitment to philosophy, or a life of reason. Epicurus urged his followers to retreat to the Garden where they would have the leisure to study as well as to enjoy the company of like-minded disciples. For Epicurus, in fact, friendship was the highest and most reliable source of pleasure.

Comparing ancient and modern conceptions of rationality

Do the efforts to improve on the short-comings of the standard model of rationality in social science provide us with an adequate normative basis from which to conduct public policy? I wish to suggest that thickening approaches that seek only to improve on the limited "means-ends" purposes of thin rationality do not go far enough in allowing us to address some pressing policy issues. Bounded rationality seeks to elaborate on the *means* portion of the decision algorithm by replacing the full information, maximizing assumptions with rules of thumb and satisficing assumptions. But they do not call into question the ultimate *ends* of thin rationality. Other efforts to elaborate on the standard model, however, do in fact attempt to broaden our assumptions regarding the ultimate objectives of rational behavior. Several writers (e.g., Elster, Hollis) regard *autonomy* as an end state that motivates "reflective rationality," a position that both requires and engenders personality characteristics that thin rationality pays no attention to. Likewise, Hirschman invokes the notion of reflective rationality as a means of identifying the distinction between wanton and meta-preferences suggesting that an understanding of the latter require an examination of the decision-makers' values. It should be clear that in their attempts to flesh out the thin account of rationality provided by the standard model, these writers extend their normative concerns from the types of final objectives to include the characters of choice makers. In this they take a step in the direction of ancient thought and wisdom.

It emerges from what we have seen in this chapter that the ancient conception of rationality differs from the modern conception. The key difference separating ancient understandings from modern is the centrality of virtue as an element in the choice-making process. This suggests in turn a level of normativity for the ancients that is absent from modern theories of rationality such as RCU. For the ancients, good choices are made by good people whereas for the modern theory people choose between goods. There is an overriding objective of choice-making in each case. For the moderns this is some measurable level of welfare. For the ancients it is something larger (i.e., a good flow of life).

There is a perhaps an understandable tendency for those of us who are not professional philosophers to think that ancient thought is largely irrelevant to modern times. This is a consequence of a belief that when intellectual progress is made the old thinking becomes superseded and replaced by more up-dated and correct thinking. If this view is applied to ethical theory, it is correct only to a degree. The ancient schools of ethical thought retain their contemporary relevance via their influence on modern schools in direct and indirect ways. Where the former is concerned, for example, we can point to writers who unreservedly refer to themselves as Platonists, Aristotelians, Epicureans, and Stoics.[9] As we might expect, these neo-ancient tendencies in contemporary ethical thought do not embrace *in toto* all that the ancient masters propounded, but they retain enough of the old wisdom to be recognizably identified with their ancient schools. An advantage to considering these neo-ancient approaches is that having chronologically emerged following the establishment of the standard model, they are in a position to confront the claims and limitations of that same model from the vantage point of their received, (albeit modified) ancient-inspired doctrines. What is particularly remarkable about these neo-ancient theories is their common attempt to provide a rational basis for ethical theory. That is, they attempt to derive "ought" from "is", a move that was considered unacceptable to the founders of the standard model.

Neo-ancient ethical outlooks

Rosalind Hursthouse (1999) takes a neo-Aristotelian view of the "is–ought" link which emphasizes a "naturalistic" basis for virtue ethics. By a "naturalistic basis" is meant that ethical principles, and the behavior that we would identify as ethical, is derived from an objective understanding of human nature. The challenge here is to come up with an account of virtues based on a description of human nature that does not merely describe particular human dispositions and behaviors as virtues. The circularity (and illegitimacy) of such an argument is apparent. Hursthouse argues in fact that the ethical naturalism she justifies operates from "within an ethical perspective."[10] Given an ethical perspective, however, ethical evaluations must take into account the empirical facts that confront the decision-maker including those that relate to her flourishing as a member of a social species. Hursthouse argues that "the good" for a social animal is that which ensures (1) its survival as an individual; (2) the continuance of its species; (3) its characteristic freedom from pain and characteristic enjoyments; and (4) the characteristic functioning of its social group. The modifier "characteristic" is used here pointedly. Members of a species may be defective if, for example, it does not feel appropriate pain at appropriate times. Pain, as we know, often operates in the interest of our survival. Certain pleasures may be detrimental to it.

"The good" as it is used here is said to be *attributive*. That is, it is an adjective attached to nouns so that our understanding of the good depends on the particular noun it modifies. But, she argues, the same attributive function applies to our use of the good in a context of ethics.[11] Like other social animals, humans act; but unlike other animals, social or otherwise, they are rational. They act from reasons. So, we need to ask, what can we say is *characteristic* about human pains, pleasures and functionings, and how does the answer to this question relate to our truly identifying feature as a species, our reason? Hursthouse (1999: 222–223) explains:

> Our characteristic way of going on, which distinguishes us from all other species of animals, is a rational way. A "rational way" is any way that we can be rightly see as good, as something we have reason to do. … But to maintain, as I am recklessly doing, that our "characteristic way of going on" is to do what we can rightly see we have a reason to do, is to give up with a vengeance any idea that most human beings do what it is "characteristic" of human beings to do. The notion is avowedly normative, and is clearly going to yield judgements to the effect that many human beings are *not* going on "in the way characteristic of the species" and are thereby defective human beings.

Hursthouse anticipates the objection that the normativity implied in this concept of "characteristic" runs against its claims to naturalism. She responds, however, that the context within which this notion of characteristic must operate are the other four ends of the social animal enumerated above. She explains:

> I cannot just proceed from some premises about what is reasonable or rational to do to some conclusion that it is rational to act in such-and-such a way, and hence that a good human being is one who acts that way. I have to consider whether the corresponding character trait (if

such a thing could be imagined) would foster or be inimical to those four ends.

(1999: 224)

It is interesting to also consider the views of a neo-stoic, Lawrence Becker (1998) who describes stoic ethics as a species of eudaimonism. Becker writes in the first person plural voice to convey the impression that stoicism is a contemporary school of philosophy while referring to such figures as Zeno, Chrysippus, and Cleanthes as "our ancient brethren." He argues that the metaphysical elements in Hellenistic era Stoicism owed to the limited reach of its science and expresses confidence that, given the strong emphasis they placed on "following nature," they would have adapted their doctrines to incorporate scientific discovery.[12] Becker (1998: 6) writes:

> It is interesting to try to imagine what might have happened if stoicism had had a continuous twenty-three-hundred-year history; if stoics had had to confront Bacon and Descartes, Newton and Locke, Hobbes and Bentham, Hume and Kant, Darwin and Marx, and the vicissitudes of ethics in the twentieth century. It is reasonable to suppose that stoics would have found a way to reject teleological physics and biology when scientific consensus did; that they would have found ways to hold their own against the attacks on naturalism launched in the modern era.

While contemporary stoicism, Becker argues, does not adopt wholesale the metaphysics of its ancient Greek forebears, it retains from the ancient view a holistic evaluative outlook as the focus of its eudaimonism. Becker (1998: 21) contrasts the new stoicism with other alternative evaluative traditions in the following terms:

> The whole-life frame of reference, together with a plausible account of the variety of ways in which life can be a good one, keeps stoicism sharply distinct from Epicurean doctrines, or their modern "welfarist" off-shoots.[13] How well my life is going from the inside, so to speak, in terms of the quality of my experience, is only one of the things that enters into a stoic evaluation of it.

Just as for the neo-Aristotelean Hursthouse, for the neo-stoic Becker there is a kind of naturalism involved in defining "the good" for human beings and the pursuit of the good life as a process of discovery of the appropriate facts. Hence the exercise of practical reason is essential in this pursuit. Moreover, Becker asserts that virtue is, for the rational agent, the perfection of agency. Becker shares with the standard economic model the notion that the agent is a self-interested optimizer. Becker's stoic agent, however, is not interested in maximizing utility or any other affective state of mind. Instead she seeks to optimize the number of her successful multiple endeavors. The pursuit of these endeavors requires the exercise of practical reason and a corresponding set of norms, particularly as some of them may conflict with one another. Practical reason will be required to resolve these conflicts. The whole-life frame of reference referred to above implies that the set of endeavors pursued by the agent include occurrent as well as prospective ones placing considering demands on practical reason and the development of agency. The stoic agent is then a highly reflective one.

Becker relies heavily on modern developmental psychology to explain how agents construct and improve their agency. Agents start out with certain received, primal elements including their physical bodies, instinctual impulses, reactive endowments, informational processing abilities, and agent energy. These endowments undergo development via routine into dispositions whose character are a function of salient events. The agent's affective experiences are also developmentally important as are the attachments she forms to her own body, other people, objects, states of mind, etc. Add to these structures the basic capabilities for representation and logical processing (including language acquisition) together with "basic tenors of personality" and the stage is set for the agent to begin the deliberate construction of agency.

The task of agency construction (and perfection) involves the exercise and development of "practical reason." This development also involves a foundational stage wherein the agent identifies patterns that can be expressed propositionally. These propositions are subject to re-evaluation and revision as the agent seeks congruence between actions undertaken and desired results as well as the integration of multiple endeavors. The process is described by Becker (1998: 94) as follows:

> deliberation and choice become reflexive, determinative conditions of revisions of their own routines. The effort to get the practical reasoning right is in part the attempt to generalize, regularize, and make practical inferences about the reasoning process itself. Success in this reflexive effort to improve the congruence between practical conclusions and outcomes motivates the wider, and more deeply dispositional, incorporation of practical reasoning routines into the determinative conditions of action in our various endeavors. Thus, unhindered primal agents construct and recursively reconstruct themselves into agents who deliberate and choose in an increasingly determinative way in an increasing number of their endeavors.

There are a number of notable features of this neo-stoic understanding of agency and of its centrally important instrument, practical reason, that distinguishes it from thin or even thick accounts of rationality considered earlier. First and foremost, rationality so considered by Becker's neo-stoicism is far more than a "means-end" algorithm. It is a development objective. The rational agent is not simply endowed with practical reason. He is endowed with some of the elements necessary for its development, but its actual development requires other necessary acquired elements. Second, and relatedly, the acquisition of these additional necessary traits, once again, is not automatic. They are rather deliberately constructed and are therefore a matter of choice. It should also be clear that their construction requires effort. Third, it follows that perfected agency is not a state that is going to be realized by everyone. In fact, in true Stoic form, Becker assures us that the greater likelihood is that perfected agency is unlikely to be realized by anyone. Perfected agency, or sagehood, then is an aspirational ideal. Unlike the ancient Stoics, however, Becker's neo-stoicism allows for the possibility that some agents can approximate this ideal and it makes sense to consider various degrees of agency health.

Collective rationality and social justice

Since a key focus of this book is on public policy it is appropriate that we consider the contrast between thin, thick, ancient, and (now) neo-ancient notions of rationality as they apply to the collective, or social, body. Correspondingly, we should also consider how these notions relate to the question of social justice, which is a prime objective of government and policy.

As Sugden (1992) notes, utilitarianism makes no distinction between "the good" and "the just" since both ends are served when utility is maximized. The collective utility function to be maximized is taken to be simply the sum of the individual utility functions of the constituent members of society. The maximizing agent is the rational utility-maximizing government. As previously noted, according to the older Benthamite tradition, social utility maximization could well involve a redistribution of society's resources in the case where the marginal utility of low income groups is higher than that for higher income groups. This, of course, presupposes that utility is measurable in a cardinal sense, a claim that was rejected by theorists in the second half of the nineteenth century.

John Rawls in *A Theory of Justice* (1971) argues that utilitarianism is "psychologically unstable" inasmuch as it may require the more productive to make permanent uncompensated sacrifices in order to improve the welfare of the less productive, such a request being psychologically untenable. Rawls also advocates for inequality where it can be shown to promote the absolute position of the least advantaged members of society. This might be true when inequality provides incentives to the more productive members to raise the living standards of the less productive.[14] Rawls also criticizes utilitarianism for its failure to attach any normative force to individual liberty. An even more fundamental principle of justice according to Rawls is that each individual has a basic claim to equal rights and liberties. Rights and liberties are parts of what he more generally refers to as *primary social goods*. Primary goods are defined to be those that any rational agent may be presumed to want in order to formulate and pursue a rational plan of life.

It would seem that much hangs on what is understood by "rights and liberties" as well as "any rational agent" in this context. Rights and liberties can be defined in strictly negative terms to indicate the limits imposed on an agent's actions that prevent her from impinging on the rights and liberties of another. To illustrate, seventeenth-century British philosopher John Locke defined the right to property accumulation to the extent that it left "enough and as good for others."[15] But rights and liberties can also be defined positively to refer to the claims an agent may have that make her agency effective. Thus, gainful employment, for example, may be considered a primary social good insofar as without such the agent lacks the material basis to pursue her agency. The notion of "rationality" employed in contract theories like Rawls's are also open to multiple interpretations (Hausman and McPherson 1996). Mutual advantage versions of contract theory, such as those identified with Hobbes and Hume, are premised on the self-interested agent understanding of rationality. A social contract is the result of bargaining that enables agents to pursue their self-interests more harmoniously than in the absence of an agreement. Justice as impartiality relies on terms that "no person could reasonably reject," (i.e., consensus). The Rawlesian contract, to take a third understanding of rationality, is premised on reciprocity. Here the assumptions motivating agreement to the rules of justice are such that one might at times act against one's best interest under the belief that others are, when necessary, dispose to do likewise.

Ancient notions of justice differ in an important way from modern conceptions insofar as it (justice) is understood as a virtue attached to individuals rather than as an attribute of institutions that binds their behavior. And yet the mediating notions of reciprocity and impartiality that we identify with modern theories of justice figure importantly in ancient accounts of "non-politicized" justice as well. The Stoic concept of social *oikeiosis*, or familiarization, extended beyond those most near and dear to us to include, in its rational limit, the rest of humanity, has led scholars to consider the Stoic school to be the progenitors of "natural law" and "natural rights." Thus, Long (2007) argues that a natural rights theory of justice is present in several principles given by Cicero.[16] These are:

1 It is contrary to nature for one person to gain advantage at the cost of another's disadvantage (3.21).
2 Natural law permits persons to give preference to themselves in securing material resources provided they do not do so at other people's expenses (3.22).
3 Natural law urges persons to be social benefactors rather than solitary pleasures lovers (3.25).
4 Natural law prescribes that one human being should want to consider the interests of another, whoever the person may be, for the very reason that he or she is a human being (3.27).

From a resource allocation, that is economic, perspective, these principles raise some interesting questions. The fact of resource scarcity, for example, suggests any number of possible scenarios involving zero-sum allocation outcomes that would appear to be incompatible with the requirement implied by principle (1). One need not subscribe to a philosophy of market fundamentalism to believe that principle (2) may be unworkable in many situations involving fixed resources. Nor does it hold out much promise in any program of redistribution whatever might be the shape of the intended social welfare function. That is, for example, according to (3), redistributive public finance proposals might well be interpreted as contrary to Stoic conceptions of natural law.

On the other hand, the prescriptions advanced by principles (3) and (4) would appear to hold out much greater promise for a communitarian policy outlook. Each runs contrary to the individualist ethos standard in neoclassical economics which assumes that unconstrained self-maximizing behavior of individuals is social welfare maximizing. Principle (3) itself implies the non-commensurability of values suggesting the superiority of social values to those of individual hedonism. While this outlook is embraced by Epicureanism, it has no place in neoclassical economic value theory. Implicit then in the Stoic natural law approach motivated by social *oikeiosis* is an outlook that proposes a hierarchy of material goods that responds to a fully mature rationality. The "solitary pleasures" identified by Cicero hold the place of "preferred indifferent" in the Stoic ordering and are subordinated to virtue as the guiding motivation for the well-lived life. The question of our individual commitment to the Stoic ordering is raised again by Long (2007) in the following terms:

> Stoicism challenges us to consider that rationality and mutual reverence are not only values of a categorically higher order but are also integral to our sheer survival as a civilized race. Is it the case that these higher-order values are at risk precisely because our cultures have placed so great a premium on the supposed necessity of non-essential material goods?

Concerns for social justice also motivate what has in recent decades been referred to as the capabilities approach (CA) pioneered by welfare economist Amartya Sen (1985, 2009) and developed along neo-Aristotelian lines by Martha Nussbaum (1988, 2011). Sen was the first to articulate the now widely adopted and explored CA while Nussbaum has drawn attention to its Aristotelian content. The CA is understood as a conceptualization of human well-being that focuses on the quality of life in terms of "functionings" (i.e., beings and doings) and capabilities. Not coincidentally it is also a way to assess the goodness of the state insofar as it enables citizens the freedom to realize functionings and capabilities. Sen describes functionings in the following terms:

> The relevant functionings can vary from such elementary things as being adequately nourished, being in good health, avoiding escapable morbidity

and premature mortality, etc., to more complex achievements such as being happy, having self-respect, taking a part in the life of the community, and so on. The claim is that functionings are constitutive of a person's being, and an evaluation of well-being has to take the form of an assessment of these constitutive elements.

(Sen 1992: 39)

Capabilities are the combinations of functionings that a person can achieve that enable the person the freedom to choose how to live in one manner or another. Capabilities are, says Sen, "well-being freedom" and subject to influence (or neglect) by public policy. A "good" social state is one that has a positive role to play in the promotion of capabilities among its citizens. Sen also places heavy emphasis on what he calls "agency freedom" as an important functioning. This he defines as a person's freedom to bring about the achievements she values and attempts to produce. Such freedom may extend well beyond concerns for the person's own, immediate well-being narrowly understood to include the well-being of others including one's country or community or some other larger concern (Sen 1992: 56–57). Sen further notes that while well-being freedom and agency freedom are distinct functionings they are also clearly inter-dependent. One's ability to achieve agency goals are affected by one's well-being strictly understood, and one's successful (or frustrated) agency may have consequences for one's well-being.

While broadly in agreement with Sen's capability outlook, Nussbaum sees her own capability approach in a different light. More than Sen, Nussbaum wishes to more clearly specify the content of capabilities rather than treat the approach merely as a way to attach value to freedom(s). Towards this end she specifies what she considers to be ten "central capabilities", (Nussbaum 2011: 33–34).[17] Nussbaum is keen to point out that these capabilities apply to the individual even as individuals have desires and projects that extend beyond their own particular interests. She also emphasizes the essential non-commensurability of these capabilities in the sense that we cannot talk about substitutability among and between them as one might in an RCU-type approach to welfare.

Nussbaum's insistence on the non-commensurability of the central capabilities is clear evidence of her Aristotelian priors. The plurality and concreteness of these capabilities is additional evidence. The fact that they relate to human activity and have value only in relation to human activity is still additional evidence of Aristotle's relevance. Particularly salient, claims Nussbaum (1988: 160), is Aristotle's emphasis on what she describes as *internal capabilities* (I-capabilities) developed in *Nicomachean Ethics*. I-capabilities are the traits of intellect, body, and character that enable people to choose and act well under the appropriate circumstances. These are developed by education and, Nussbaum notes, Aristotle's repeated concern that the state promote the public good via the provision of public education. More generally, public policy plays an important role in providing the circumstantial context, called by Nussbaum external capabilities, within which I-capabilities can develop in the young and flourish in the already mature.

Aristotelian naturalism is given a strong endorsement by Nussbaum's criticism of the limits of Sen's own CA outlook. She argues that he needs to be more radical in his criticism of utilitarian welfare theory, while providing an objective account of human functioning along with a procedure for evaluating objectively how particular functionings contribute to human welfare, (Nussbaum 2011: 176). Like her neo-Aristotelian co-religionist, Hursthouse, Nussbaum draws on Aristotle's concept of "characteristic human functioning" as the starting place for an account of the human good to argue that the critical "linking" functioning connecting all other functionings consists in the exercise of practical reasoning. Applying this to her own understanding of the CA she notes:

> A reflective scrutiny of our most basic values, of our judgements about which functionings are so important to us that we take them to be definitive of who we are, informs us that there is a common core of all the functions we come up with. Reason is what all the functionings have in common; and this is, as well, the architectonic function that holds them altogether (182).

This practical reasoning functioning operates in a society of human flourishing both at a micro as well as at a macro level. At the micro level it enables individuals to identify and pursue the I-capabilities and functionings for the well-lived life along with the externals that support such a life. It also enables them to identify and avoid those externals superfluous, or counter-productive, to a eudaimonistic existence. It operates at the macro level of public policy both to sustain the individual in her pursuit of the well-lived life, as well as to foment practical reason itself. Nussbaum writes:

> The central task of the city will, then, be to give its people (all the ones who *can* lead such lives, in the sense of B-capability) the conditions of fully human living; living in which the essential functionings according to reason will be available. This means, don't just give out food and allow people to "graze": make it possible for people to choose to regulate their nutrition by their own reason. Don't just take care of their perceptual needs in a mechanical way, producing a seeing eye, a hearing ear, etc. Instead, make it possible for people to use their bodies and their senses in a truly human way. And don't make all this available in a minimal way: make it possible to do these things well (183).

Finally, Nussbaum also notes that Aristotelianism also suffers from two important short-comings. These are related to Aristotle's belief that the state's role in promoting *eudaimonia* applies only to its citizens. Aristotle's citizens are a fairly restricted class. It excludes, for example, women who are thought to lack the perquisites of character for citizenship. It further excludes people who work for a living, including slaves, since these groups lack the necessary leisure to exercise the rights and duties of citizens. And finally, Aristotle's advocacy of the development of capabilities and functionings reaches its limit where the city-state ends. None of these restrictions would, of course, have any relevance to a modern theory of justice that recognizes the universality of human rights. Not surprisingly, in her most recent writing on the philosophical sources supporting the CA, Nussbaum cites the importance of Stoicism. In citing the relevance of the Stoics for the CA she notes:

> The Stoics taught that every single human being, just by virtue of being human, has dignity and is worthy of reverence. Our ability to perceive ethical distinctions and to make ethical judgements was held to be the "god within," and as such is worthy of boundless reverence. Ethical capacity is found in all human beings, male and female, slave and free, high-born and low-born, rich and poor.
>
> (Nussbaum 2011: 129)

> More than most, the Stoics put their views into practice: they campaigned for the equal education of women, and their ranks included one former slave (Epictetus), one foreigner from the far reaches of the empire (Seneca, born in Spain), and various women (whose writings, unfortunately, do not survive), not to mention the "new man" Cicero, whose nonaristocratic origins are a constant theme in his writings. Because their thinking was not bounded by the walls of the city-state, they developed elaborate doctrines of duties to humanity, including proper conduct during wartime.[18]
>
> (Nussbaum 2011: 129)

In up-coming chapters we shall examine the relevance of Hellenistic ethics in the context of public policy formulation. Whether or not the ancient ethical accounts can offer a coherent theory of social justice as it applies to institutions, there would seem to be much that they contribute to a view of the good life conceived in eudaimonistic terms. The relevant question then might be posed as follows: can (and should) policy choices promote a eudaimonistic conception of the good? As the forthcoming chapters make clear, my own belief is that properly conceived public policy is capable of promoting *eudaimonia*, just as it is capable of promoting social and individual utility as these latter terms are more narrowly understood. The question of *should* policy seek to promote *eudaimonistic* ends is concerned with the more fundamental questions as to the proper role of policy, and of the state, in a liberal democracy. The basic tenets of liberalism do not endorse an "official" view of the good in substantive terms. Rather, these tenets seek to provide free individuals with the freedom to construct and pursue their own conception of the good on free and equal terms. Can policy in a liberal democracy then legitimately pursue the promotion of *eudaimonia* understood as "right reason", or "virtue", or "following nature" as the ancients conceived it? I would argue that the answer is "yes" as long as these goals are identical with Becker's "new stoic" vision of "the perfection of agency." As Becker himself makes clear, there is nothing in this objective that is incompatible with the agent's own freedom to determine the content of her whole life's endeavors. The coordination, integration, and pursuit of such whole life endeavors in an optimal way, as Becker notes, are no mean feat. Becker argues that the perfection of agency entails the development of virtue. While I find his reasoning compelling, I would add that the perfection of agency may be aided by appropriate public policies. Perhaps the most obvious instance in which public policy provides for the development of the kind of agency Becker identifies with the "new stoicism" is with respect to educational opportunity. This connection is explored in Chapter 8. More generally, however, we might usefully equate Becker's stoic goal of ideal agency with policy recommendations via the capabilities approach identified with Sen and Nussbaum.

Notes

1 Economics models are thought to be subject to Occam's razor which suggests that one model is preferred to another if (1) it explains (predicts) the phenomenon in question at least as well as another and (2) it makes fewer assumptions. It is not entirely clear why the principle of parsimony adds value to a model except that it might aid in developing other models that make additional accurate predictions regarding additional observations not included in the primary model.
2 The list of axioms reviewed here is taken from Hargreaves Heap et al (1992) who take them to describe a theory of "instrumental rationality."
3 Recall Hutcheson's "demolition" of Mandeville's argument discussed in the previous chapter.
4 The distinction between preferences and metapreferennces calls to mind the possibility discussed in Hargreaves Heap et al (1992: 330–331) of so-called *lexicographic* preference orderings. This is the notion that our choices may be ranked in different orders by different criteria. To resolve potential conflicts in the orderings requires some rule by which we determine which of the criteria are dominant. In Hirschman's discussion metapreferences dominate wanton preferences via the operation of values.
5 See, for example, Schmidtz (1995), Etizioni (1998), and Myrdal (1984).
6 Annas (1993) makes this point in noting that for the ancients the final end of a rational agent relates to how she *acts*, rather than how she is (37).
7 Some possible answers to these questions are provided by the neo-stoic Lawrence Becker, whose views are explored in more detail later in this chapter.
8 Epicurus was not the first ancient Greek thinkers who endorsed a form of ethical hedonism. It occupies a prominent place in Plato's dialog *Protagoras*. I thank Spencer Pack for calling this to my attention.
9 Oftentimes these identifiers are preceded by the "neo" prefix as in neo-Platonist, neo-Stoic, etc.
10 As Hursthouse (1999: 193) notes, we might agree that human beings are by nature social beings. The ethical perspectives, however, of boy scouts, for example, will probably differ considerably from that of gangsters notwithstanding the fact that both are social organizations.

11 Hursthouse credits Foot (1995) with this line of development in ethical naturalism.
12 Becker considers the expression "following nature" to have unfortunate metaphysical associations and chooses to re-interpret it to mean "following the facts" of the world we live in as well as of our own powers as we deliberate as to how we should act (43).
13 Note Becker's partisan support for stoicism against potentially competing schools such as neo-Epicurean ones.
14 This is known as the "Difference Principle."
15 This is known as the "Sufficiency Principle."
16 References are to Cicero's *De Officiis/On Duties*.
17 These are enumerated by Nussbaum as follows: life; bodily health; bodily integrity; senses, imagination, and thought; emotions; practical reason; affiliation; other species; play; and control over one's environment.
18 Nussbaum also recognizes the limits of Stoic doctrine as it applies to CA. In particular, she takes exception to the Stoic view of "invulnerability" as psychologically implausible and as promoting an incompatible quietism. As we've seen, the Stoic denial of the relevance of "externals" was not embraced by all Stoic thinkers, at least not without important qualifications.

References

Annas, Julia. 1993. *The Morality of Happiness*, New York: Oxford University Press.

Becker, Lawrence C. 1998. *A New Stoicism*, Princeton, NJ: Princeton University Press.

Brennan, Tad. 2003. "Stoic moral psychology," in *The Cambridge Companion Guide to The Stoics*," Brad Inwood (ed.), Cambridge: Cambridge University Press.

Elster, Jon. 1983. *Sour Grapes: Studies in the Subversion of Rationality*, Cambridge: Cambridge University Press.

Etizioni, Amitai. 1998. *The Moral Dimension: Toward a New Economics*, New York: The Free Press.

Foot, Philippa. 1995. "Does moral subjectivism rest on a mistake?," *Oxford Journal of Legal Studies*, 15: 1–14.

Hargreaves Heap, Shaun, Martin Hollis, Bruce Lyons, Robert Sugden, and Albert Weale. 1992. *The Theory of Choice: A Critical Guide*, Cambridge, MA: Blackwell.

Harris, Sam. 2010. *The Moral Landscape: How Science Can Determine Human Values*, New York: The Free Press.

Hausman, Daniel M. and Michael S. McPherson. 1996. *Economic Analysis and Moral Philosophy*, Cambridge: Cambridge University Press.

Hirschman, Albert O. 1984. "Against parsimony: Three easy ways of complicating some categories of economic discourse," *Bulletin of the American Academy of Arts and Sciences*, 37, 8 (May): 11–28.

Hollis, Martin. 1992. "Autonomy," in *The Theory of Choice: A Critical Guide*, Hargreaves Heap et al (eds.) Cambridge, MA: Blackwell.

Hunt, E.K. 1979. *History of Economic Thought: A Critical Perspective*, Belmont, CA: Wadsworth Publishing.

Hursthouse, Rosalind. 1999. *On Virtue Ethics*, New York: Oxford University Press.

Kahneman, Daniel. 2011. *Thinking, Fast and Slow*, New York: Farrar, Strauss and Giroux.

Long, A. A. 1986 (1974). *Hellenistic Philosophy: Stoics, Epicureans, and Sceptics*, Berkeley, CA: University of California Press.

Long, A. 2007. "Stoic communitarianism and normative citizenship," *Social Philosophy & Policy*, 24, 2 (July): 241–261.

Myrdal, Gunnar. 1984. "Implicit values in economics," in *The Philosophy of Economics*, Daniel Hausman (ed.), Cambridge: Cambridge University Press, pp250–259.

Nussbaum, Martha C. 1988. "Nature, functioning and capability: Aristotle on political distribution," *Oxford Studies in Ancient Philosophy*, 6: 145–184.

Nussbaum, Martha C. 2011. *Creating Capabilities: The Human Development Approach*, Cambridge: The Belknap Press of Harvard University Press.

Rawls, John. 1971. *A Theory of Justice.* Cambridge: Harvard University Press.

Schmidtz, David. 1995. *Rational Choice and Moral Agency*, Princeton, NJ: Princeton University Press.

Sen, Amartya K. 1985. *Commodities and Capabilities*, Amsterdam: North-Holland.

Sen, Amartya K. 1990. "Rational fools: A critique of the behavioral foundations of economic theory," in *Beyond Self-Interest* by Jane J. Mansbridge (ed.), Chicago, IL: University of Chicago Press, pp25–43.

Sen, Amartya K. 1992. *Inequality Re-examined*, Cambridge, MA: Harvard University Press.

Sen, Amartya K. 2009. *The Idea of Justice*, London: Allen Lane.

Sugden, Robert. 1992. "Social Justice," in *The Theory of Choice: A Critical Guide*, Hargreaves Heap et al (eds.) Cambridge, MA: Blackwell.

Zeller, Edward. 2012 (1870). *The Stoics, Epicureans, and Sceptics*, Classic Reprint Series. London: Forgotten Books.

Part II
Ethics and public policy

5 The problem of pathological consumption

From a standard economic perspective the ultimate purpose of production is consumption. Production of capital and intermediate goods, for example, are justified by their subsequent use in the further production of consumption goods and services. This basic relationship, moreover, is not altered when we consider the private–public goods distinction. Economists typically speak of the collective and individual consumption of such goods as public health services, national security, and government-provided amenities such as parks and recreational goods and services. The resources dedicated to environmental quality are also said to provide society with the opportunity to *consume* a stream of environmental services. Thus, in some fundamental sense it is accurate to view consumption as the motor force of economics.

The standard model as we saw in the previous chapter maintains that people will allocate their incomes over the variety of consumption goods and services, and over time periods, in such a manner as to maximize their individual and collective consumer utilities. As far as this model is concerned, utility maximization is tantamount to not only to the good life, but to the best that life has to offer. I argued in the previous chapter, however, that the standard model, which I referred to as revealed choice utilitarianism (RCU), while perhaps adequate for some apples versus oranges-type consumer allocation decisions, offers only a thin account of human decision-making, and may be inadequate for certain important decisions we make as individuals and as a society. It was argued there that the underlying account of rationality, an account consisting of a short list of decision-making rules, or axioms, was not sufficient to explain, for example, why people under certain circumstances might make decisions that run contrary to their own self-interest. Moreover, it was argued that the normative outlook, or welfare theory, that follows from the RCU model fails to provide adequate policy guidance for some important issues requiring a more expansive view of the human good. In this and the following three chapters we shall take up several of these particular policy issues. The first of these issues to be considered in the present chapter is, in fact, concerned with a kind of consumption. It is not, however, consumption of the apples and oranges kind. It may, in fact, be considered pathological consumption. By pathological consumption I mean consumption that does not contribute to human flourishing, but rather renders it harder to realize.

Before we begin an examination of pathological consumption it will be useful to offer a few observations on the relation between ethical outlook and policy in general. It was pointed out in Chapter 1 that ethical theories can be categorized as consequentialist, deontological, and virtue-based. All of our formal and informal rules and codes of ethical behavior can fit into one or more of these categories, but most of our economic policies undoubtedly fit into the consequentialist description.[1] This is so since utilitarianism is a type of consequentialist ethics. It can also be said that policy, in general, is necessarily consequentialist since policies, after all, are concerned with producing particular outcomes which is the whole point of consequentialism. So the question naturally arises as to how virtue ethics might fit into a policy discussion given a view of the good life that is, at least in part, based on an account of virtue as has been suggested by our earlier arguments. I believe that there are two plausible answers to this important question. The first is that policies can be used to promote an environment propitious to the flowering of the virtues that we associate with human flourishing. A piece of political folk-wisdom states: "You cannot legislate virtue." The meaning here is that we cannot dictate the values that people endorse simply by passing laws that prescribe, or proscribe, particular values. Strictly speaking, this is undoubtedly true. At least there is plenty of historical evidence showing laws that do not carry the stamp of legitimacy among those to whom they apply do not work their intended purposes very well. Moreover, in a reasonably well-functioning democracy, proposed legislation that is not perceived to be legitimate does not have a good chance of being executed into law. Still, norms and values are social constructs, and they emerge in a definite social context. Legislation has the capacity to shape the same social context that allows or impedes our understanding of the legitimacy of behaviors. In this way, then, there would seem to exist a potential for policy to influence the development of virtue.

A second way by which policy may conduce to virtue starts by recognizing that the state itself operates as a role model for those in whose service it operates. In this sense it might be thought that people will mimic the virtuous behavior of the state. If the state is seen as acting in the interest of justice, citizens are more apt to act in a just way. If the state is seen as self-aggrandizing, or predatory, people are more apt to act in a self-serving, or predatory, way. At the least, it is likely that people will justify their own selfishness as acceptable or necessary if they are convinced that the state and its agents do nothing to sanction anti-social behavior and actively engages in the pursuit of its own narrow interests.[2] Even in the less extreme case where the state attempts to act in the public interest via an excessive appeal to market incentives, or by altering relative price signals, it runs the risk of signaling that only market values matter and undermines the belief that citizens have civic obligations. I am not arguing that policy appeals to economic incentives (e.g., Pigouvian taxes and subsidies) are never appropriate. I do argue that *how* the state conducts its business can have a larger impact on the public perception of its own sense of its civic obligations. With this in mind let us now return to the question of pathological consumption.

Rational addiction

The first point to note is that from the RCU perspective there is no such thing as pathological consumption. This conviction follows from the underlying assumptions that the perspective takes on the meaning of rational behavior discussed in the previous chapter. Repeating those assumptions in summary form:

1   The economic agent (i.e., consumer) knows her preferences.
2   The agent possesses all relevant information regarding the good.
3   The agent chooses freely.
4   The agent chooses in a manner that maximizes her well-being.

On the strength of these assumptions there is no basis for characterizing any consumption as pathological or, for that matter, rendering any sort of normative judgment on that choice whatsoever. Neither can any consumption choice that may be said to be compulsive, or addictive, be seen as other than welfare maximizing from the agent's perspective. That is to say, even addiction is rational. To appreciate this perspective I shall review here the version of rational addiction offered in the seminal paper by Becker and Murphy (1988).[3]

The Becker and Murphy (B&M) model proceeds from the following assumptions:

1   Instantaneous (marginal) utility from the consumption of an addictive substance is a function of past as well as present consumption.
2   The rational user takes into account all present and future consequences of current consumption. Future consequences are discounted at a rate chosen by the user.
3   The rational user chooses a consumption path that maximizes total utility where this is the sum of present and (discounted) future utility.

Additionally, the addictive commodity is said to possess the following two properties:

P_1: The more of the good's past consumption, the smaller the marginal utility derived from a given quantity of present consumption. That is, the user is assumed to develop tolerance for the good.
P_2: The increase in marginal utility associated with a unit increase in present consumption is greater, the larger is past consumption. That is, past consumption is said to reinforce present consumption as the user, for example, develops cravings for the good.

Following Skog (1999) we can illustrate the logic of the B&M model. Imagine a potential user faced with an initial choice to consume or abstain. If she consumes, she realizes more satisfaction than if she abstains, at least initially. In the following period, faced with the same choice to consume or to abstain, the rational user knows that her welfare will be lower in the second period if she had consumed in the previous period, whatever choice she makes in the second period. This is owing to the tolerance effect identified by P_1.[4] If the user consumed the good in the first period, some of the welfare loss associated with P_1 can be mitigated by consuming in the second period as well. This is the operational significance of P_2. Now, will the rational user, when all is said and done, actually consume or abstain? The answer depends on her rate of discount of future consequences. If she has a very high rate of discount (i.e., is myopic), then she pays no heed to future consequences of current use and will consume the good regardless of what she did in the past. On the other hand, if she has a low rate of discount (i.e., is forward-looking), then she may or may not consume depending on *how low* the rate of discount is and, therefore, the *degree* to which she is forward looking.

An additional complicating factor facing our would-be rational addict is that the discount factor may vary depending on the actual time horizon faced by the addict. As Winter (2011) explains, it is easy to exercise patience (i.e., hold a low rate of discount) between two time periods when each of those periods is quite prospective. It may be harder to exercise patience when the choice between periods is more imminent. We consider a time-consistent rational addict to be one whose discount rate is the same whether or not the moment of choice is imminent or much delayed. A time-inconsistent addict is one whose patience runs out as the moment of choice draws near. For the time inconsistent addict, in other words, reversals in preferences are possible which would seem to be a violation of the rational actor model. At the same time, the truly rational addict, with low discount rate and time consistent behavior, will find it welfare-maximizing to abstain from the addictive good until the very last possible period. But is this really a model of addiction? I would hesitate to describe someone as an addict who leads a life of sobriety and then exits life on a substance-induced moment of euphoria. Similarly, it is difficult to consider a substance user as a *rational* addict who mistakes herself as being time consistent and who, to her regret, discovers *ex post* to be time inconsistent in her behavior. The possibilities that addicts are subject to mistakes in their judgments regarding the time consistency of their preferences, that they sometimes fail to anticipate that current preferences may be a poor guide to future preferences (i.e., projection bias), that they can suffer lapses in self-control, and that they sometimes experience relapses once having overcome an addiction, all have inspired alternatives to the B&M model of rational addiction. One might make an argument that the B&M model could be modified to take into account the imperfect information possessed by the rational addict and consider an alternative model of "bounded" rational addiction. As we saw in the previous chapter, however, even the concept of bounded rationality goes only so far to providing a thick account of how and why people make their consumption choices, and this applies undoubtedly to the consumption of "goods" whose long-term use has potentially ruinous consequences. Let us then consider some explanations of addiction that go beyond the sort provided by the RCU model of standard economics.

Neurobiology of addiction

Neuroscientists have made a great deal of progress in identifying the way in which addictive substances act on the chemistry and circuitry of the human brain that cause people to become addicted in the first place and, importantly, what this suggests for treatment, and how these changes affect the prospects for recovery and relapse. Results from clinical experiments show that animals will self-administer addicting drugs that operate on the brain's pleasure/ reward circuitry at levels higher than would occur in the absence of these drugs. Moreover, they will continue to self-administer these drugs even when it means not attending to other of their needs, and even in the face of simultaneously self-inflicted pain (Gardner and David 1999). What is more, the laboratory evidence suggests that this pleasure/reward principle operates independently of the tendency of addictive substances to induce withdrawal symptoms and in the absence of prior drug use, thus contradicting the mechanism of addiction propounded by the B&M model.

Gardner and David note that treating addicts for physical dependence and withdrawal is relatively easily accomplished via a process of detoxification. They further note, however, that longer term abstinence is made more difficult by "protracted withdrawal" and that long-term, persistent drug craving can be triggered by environmental cues. Drug relapse, a phenomenon that the B&M model provides no accounting for, is especially intractable from a neurobiological perspective. These authors state:

> Thus, a series of virtually insurmountable neurobiological hurdles are erected in the path of drug addicts wishing to stay abstinent: (1) By virtue of their prior chronic drug use, the pleasure/reward circuits of their brains have been forever changed so that they possess heightened vulnerability to addicting drugs … (2) This heightened vulnerability includes a heightened cross vulnerability to other drugs that activate the pleasure/reward circuits of the brain, even to drugs to which the addict may never have been exposed. (3) This heightened vulnerability can be triggered not only by drugs, but by stressors and environmental cues previously associated with drug taking (120).

Recently, the emerging field of behavioral economics has stepped in to combine the insights of economic theory with psychology to provide a more realistic picture of human decision-making than economics alone has managed to provide. From a behavioral economics perspective, in contrast to the RCU perspective, addiction is defined in terms of unwanted consumption and the strategies pursued to quit use of an addictive substance. In this regard Berheim and Rangel (2005) urge that the key to addictive behavior resides not in its hedonic aspects, but in terms of the effect of substance use and abuse on the neurological basis for decision-making. They argue that human beings, similar to other higher life forms, have a basic forecasting mechanism that combines sensory perceptions from the environment with basic cognition to anticipate rewards from particular actions and, on that basis, make decisions. This basic forecasting mechanism they describe as a "gut feeling"-type of decision-making process. At other times, however, a more deliberative process operates wherein higher-order cognitive processes (i.e., cognitive control) intervene. The basic forecasting mechanism has the advantage of speed and for most consumption goods is entirely appropriate. It operates to combine stimuli via the hedonic receptors in the brain (i.e., mesolimbic dopamine system) with prior experience to accurately correlate anticipated outcomes with particular actions (i.e., learning). In the case of addictive substances, however, this mechanism is apt to malfunction. The feedback mechanism may become short-circuited, and the hedonic stimuli will bypass the cognitive processing it undergoes in the normal consumption state. This stimulus then has an outsized impact upon the users' anticipation of pleasure and creates a powerful urge to consume (Berheim and Rangel 2005: 22).

Evidence from clinical psychology suggests that adolescents are especially vulnerable to addiction in two senses. First, because they have yet to reach full neurological development, they often lack the cognitive abilities to assess the risks associated with the use of addictive substances. Moreover, they are more easily influenced by environmental cues and immediate rewards and are therefore apt to engage in impulsive decision-making. Secondly, the use of addictive substances themselves has been shown to affect the development of young brains in ways that suggest cognitive impairment (Wetherill and Tapert 2012).[5] The combination of these tendencies suggest adolescent vulnerability to substance abuse initiation and subsequent addiction – a vulnerability that is exacerbated among those who may have a genetic predisposition to these behaviors.

Addiction as disease

Advances in the neurobiology of substance addiction have given a fillip to the concept of addiction as a disease. The disease model of addiction has been around since the days of the temperance movement that sought to ban the sale and use of alcohol. In its more contemporary version its basic elements include the following assertions:[6]

1   Addiction has a biological basis in the sense that a genetic predisposition is possessed by potential addicts.
2   Addiction is "triggered" by an initial exposure to an addictive substance perhaps abetted by environmental factors.

3   Once activated, the addicted user experiences degeneration to a state of dependency on the addictive substance.
4   Addiction is a chronic disease. No one is ever "cured" of an addiction.
5   Treatment consists of medical interventions that help manage its symptoms.

Not surprisingly, the addiction as disease model, also frequently referred to as the medicalization model, receives strong support from the medical community including the American Medical Association (AMA), the American Psychiatric Association (APA), and the World Health Organization (WTO). The National Institute of Alcohol Abuse and Alcoholism (NIAAA) was created as a result of the passage of the Hughes Act in 1970, and promoted the notion that alcoholism is a medically-based debilitation rather than a moral failing.[7] Similarly, a medically-based perception of tobacco addiction emerged in the 1980s when Swedish pharmacologists began to develop nicotine replacement therapies to treat tobacco dependency (Elam 2012).

The addiction-as-disease model has also encountered considerable resistance (Lewis 2015; Reinarman and Granfield 2015; Schaler 2000). There are two main concerns motivating this resistance. The first is that the medicalization model tends to marginalize other important contextual factors relevant to addiction as a syndrome. These are largely sociological issues and include factors related to family dynamics. Some of these factors are discussed in more detail below. The second broad concern is directed at the ethics of addiction. Here the question is, does the disease model absolve the addict from her responsibility for her addiction? The addict, after all, cannot be held responsible for her genetically predetermined dispositions or vulnerabilities to addictive behavior. Neither can she be held morally culpable for the sequence of neurological events that determine addictive behaviors once they are established. Such an outlook, however, is countered by opponents of the brain disease model of addiction with the argument that the use and abuse of addictive substances is a freely made choice and that the disease model paints too mechanistic a picture of human behavior. The resolution of these conflicting outlooks has important implications for whatever policy approach toward addictive substance use and abuse is taken. It is also clear that there are important fundamental philosophical issues at stake involving the mind–body dichotomy and free will versus determinism, or fatalism. These are, of course, perennial philosophic questions that the ancients contended with and with which contemporary philosophers continue to engage. This includes both ancient and modern stoic philosophers. In sections to follow I shall address myself to how the stoic outlook might reconcile the questions surrounding the ethical content of addiction and the moral responsibility that might attach to addictive behaviors as well as those that might pertain to policy and therapeutic approaches to addiction. For now we shall consider some psychological and sociological considerations as they bear on addiction.

The psychology of addiction

Addiction experts seem to agree that addiction is a profoundly psychological phenomenon even considered apart from the operation of the addictive substance itself on the brain. Consider, for example, the problem of relapse. Why should it be the case that an addict will relapse into addiction once she has managed to free herself in a physiological sense from the effects of the substance in question? We might think that the memories of the emotional and financial hardships wracked by addiction should be incentive enough to avoid re-addiction. This belief, however, offers an oversimplified understanding of the nature of addiction. It fails to account, for example, for the underlying emotional or personality disorders that may drive an addict to substance abuse in the first place. *Co-morbidity* exists when psychiatric disorders co-exist with substance abuse behaviors thereby complicating the treatment of either condition. Mueser et al (2006) point to research that shows people with mental illness are more likely than the population-at-large to have substance abuse disorders. They show that the more incapacitating the underlying psychiatric disorder, the higher the rate of substance abuse, and the more intractable treatment is for either problem. Likewise, Pickard and Pearce (2013) review a literature that suggests that chronic – as opposed to short-term, temporary – addiction is far more likely in the case where substance dependence is compounded by personality disorder.

Another psychological factor complicating addiction is the operation of substance-use cues. This refers to environmental or other associational triggers that, while not sharing in the characteristics of the addictive substance itself, act powerfully to generate cravings in the addict. Barnes (2015: 48–49) describes the functioning of the "dopamine reward system" as being independent of the pleasure/pain-inducing effects of the substance:

> It turns out that the most common explanation for addiction, that dopamine mediates the pleasure of using drugs and the unpleasant effects of stopping use (withdrawal from drugs), is a misleading simplification. The positive rewards of drug use and negative effects of stopping use are certainly involved in the reinforcement for continuing of early drug use, but they do not explain the phenomenon of addiction.
>
> One of the more widely accepted theories is that the dopamine reward pathway represents a process of expectation, learning, memory formation, and relearning, rather than one of pleasure and pain. Dopamine is not involved with the neural circuits that encode the specifics of a reward experience – the enticing odor of that freshly baked cookie or the gorgeous harmonies in Mahler's fourth symphony.

Further on Barnes (2015: 50–51) compares animal and human responses to explain how this reward system may be activated by cues unrelated to the substance itself:

If a cue that the reward is at hand stimulates reward-seeking behavior, just what is the animal responding to? Certainly, not the pharmacological effect of a drug not taken. The animal needs to have a memory of the reward associated with the cue that in itself does not have any of the necessary characteristics of the reward – its taste, dimensions, color. Rather, the cue triggers memory and expectation of how rewarding the goal will be. For an addicted person, persistent maladaptive memories, probably aggrandized by drug-induced distortions of signaling mechanisms, perpetuate compulsive drug-seeking and use. The degree of satisfaction a reward delivers is a function both of properties intrinsic to the reward and of factors specific to the host and the environment.

Cues may be comparatively innocuous sights, sounds, smells, and places such as you might encounter in a bar-room, for example, that trigger a deep craving for a drink. For many drinkers who also smoke, an addiction to one of these substances may act as a cue to consume the other. Cues may also involve emotional trauma or stress. The loss of a job, divorce, death of a loved one can create a powerful desire to self-medicate that results in relapse and re-addiction. If previous motivations to use addictive substances involved a desire to palliate trauma and stress, then it is likely that future stressful and traumatic events will induce a craving for similar self-medication.

Sociological determinants of addiction

Sociological context as a determinant of addictive substance use and abuse logically and temporally predates the recent emphasis on neurobiology. Logically such context matters since a person doesn't qualify as a user, and a user doesn't qualify as an addict, until substance use is initiated. And while genetic science may have something interesting to say about users' susceptibility to addiction, it cannot in isolation explain why anyone would begin to use an addictive substance. In this sense, addiction is clearly a choice uncompelled by any bio-neurological process. And yet this is not to say that all other choices that people make are entirely autonomous of other sorts of strong influences. Social pressures exert strong influences on our choice-making in ways that are both direct and obvious, but also more subtle and complex. They may operate to encourage as well as shield individuals from initial experimentation with potentially addictive substances.

The role of the family is one such focus on the complex role that social institutions may play in the experience of addiction. Families may play an important role in discouraging use of drugs and alcohol by teenagers. Teens seek parental approval, and if strong and negative messages against use are conveyed, then the likelihood of use is reduced. As McCrady (2006: 170) points out, the important factor is the consistency of parental interaction and signaling of the behavior that parents seek to promote in their children. Contrariwise, dis-function in families can operate to induce substance abuse

(Zimić and Jukić 2012). Addiction is often associated with emotional and physical abuse, or emotional detachment of parents from their off-spring. Addiction in children is also more likely in cases where parents are substance abusers themselves (Moos 2006: 185).

Substance abuse behavior is known to be associated with particular subgroup identification, a factor that is known to operate with particular strength among young people to initiate addictive substance use (Battistich and Hom 1997; Duncan et al 2005). Moreover, substance addiction itself is sometimes perceived as a part of a subcultural community and lifestyle that makes overcoming the addiction require that the addict also abandon that subculture's practices and relationships.[8] Biron (2012) explains the appeal of ritualistic behavior that often occurs within particular subcultures where illegal substances are integral to the group's identity. She writes:

> Drug rituals are important for users because of the general lack of social acceptability toward drug use. The rituals associated with substance use help create independent social systems in which drug users find acceptance. These rituals form a common bond and increase cohesion within groups of drug users. Each time a ritual is enacted, the bond among the drug users is strengthened, and their adherence to the beliefs and values that support the ritual is reinforced. Rituals are often comfort inducing, and drug users will return to those patterned behaviors seeking the comfort of their initial use (137).

One of the pernicious effects of drug subcultures is that they are the source of addiction cues referred to earlier. For this reason treatment providers often urge their patients seeking to overcome an addiction to separate themselves from the drug-related subculture and seek sources of support in alternative communities that are dedicated to the on-going sobriety of the addict. Examples of the latter include Alcoholics Anonymous established in 1933 and Narcotics Anonymous established in 1953.

The ethics of addiction

We turn our attention now to an important question raised earlier by the addiction-as-brain-disease model discussion: if addiction is construed as a disease that afflicts its sufferers, then in what sense, if any, can addicts be held responsible for their status as addicts and their consequent suffering? Moreover, how does an answer to this question condition our thinking on issues of therapy and public policy toward addiction as a personal and social challenge? I argue here that Stoicism, in its ancient and modern forms, provides some useful insights through which to think about these questions – insights that in many respects overcome the limitations imposed by the rational choice perspective typically favored by the mainstream economics outlook. Moreover, while ancient Stoicism was "pre-scientific" in the sense that we understand this term today, the theory of knowledge adopted by the ancient school, I argue, lends itself to an interpretation that would find favor among those who regard addiction as a neurobiological adaptation.

An ancient Stoic account of addiction would regard the phenomenon as a failure in the exercise of "right reason." An immediate ethical judgment follows that addiction is a type of vicious behavior and as such is condemned as unworthy in the sage, or would-be sage. Before we get too far into the Stoic ethical implications of addiction, it is useful to begin by examining what the school's theory of knowledge, its epistemology, regards as the source of this failure of reason.

For the Stoics, knowledge of the world begins when objects external to the mind make impressions on the mind.[9] Based on an impression, the agent (i.e., recipient of an impression) must make a decision to assent to the impression, or to withhold assent. By giving assent to an impression, it (the impression) assumes the status of a belief for the agent. Now, impressions are not all alike. Some are strong, and others are weak. Impressions can also be true or false. Correspondingly, beliefs can be either true or false depending on the truth or falsity of the underlying impressions on which they are based as a matter of our assent. Given these contingent qualities of impressions (strong/weak, true/false) our assent to them can also be either strong or weak. The distinction here may involve how well or poorly the belief in question stands up to critical examination. Alternatively, it may depend on how easily it vacillates depending on changes in the personal circumstances of the belief holder. If I hold that the pleasures of consumption pale in comparison to the pleasures of friendship when I am a poor grad student, but then change my mind when I get a high-salaried position, then my assent to the original proposition is weak. The Stoics defined knowledge as strong assent to strong and true (*kataleptic*) impressions. If these contingencies (strong and true) fail, then the result is not belief at all, but rather mere opinion. Strong and true (i.e., *kataleptic*) impressions are common enough. Rarer, however, are strong assents. Strong assents to *kataleptic* impressions are the mark of the sage.[10] That is, the sage is capable of knowledge. The rest of us possess mere opinions.

As a practical matter, beliefs, or opinions, are useful insofar as they result in actions. But intermediating between the two, say the Stoics, is another element: impulses. According to the Stoic account, an impulse is a type of assent that necessarily precedes an action and that also (necessarily) gives rise to an action. For the Stoics, therefore, there is no such thing as a repressed impulse. Moreover, impulses are not necessarily injudicious, though they may be. Impulses are also evaluative. An impulse is that mental event preceding an action that tells us that our action is "good," "beneficial," "the right thing to do," etc. So, an impulse is defined as an assent to an evaluative impression (Brennan 2005: 87).

Furthermore, the Stoics characterized a certain class of impulses as "emotions." As proper impulses, emotions have causal efficacy. Pleasure and desire, for example, are antecedent to certain choices we make, as are fear and pain.

The important thing about emotions is that they are *opinions* and not beliefs. They derive their status as opinions for one, or both, of the following reasons: first, they involve weak assent; and, second, they are assents to non- *kataleptic* impressions. Choices made on the basis of emotionally charged opinions, being unstable and derived from a false understanding of the good, cannot be a part of a life lived according to nature as the Stoics understood the term – that is, a life of virtue.

But Stoic sages have to make practical life choices just like the rest of us. You can't eat virtue after all! Fortunately for them emotions are just one type of (irrational) impulse. Other types of impulses based on true knowledge of the good are called by the Stoics *eupatheiai*. Brennan (2005: 98) identifies these impulses as volition, caution, and joy and describes them as follows:

> Volition is the knowledge that some future thing is a good of such a sort that we should reach out for it.
> Caution is the knowledge that some future thing is a bad thing of such a sort that we should avoid it.
> Joy is the knowledge that some present thing is a good of such a sort that we should be elated at it.

The above list of impulses is fine for the sage, but what about the rest of us who may lack the "knowledge" that they imply? For us, there is still a third type of impulse termed by Brennan as "selections" and described in terms of the "indifferents" discussed in Chapter 2. Recall, a "preferred indifferent" is something that we would choose as instrumental to the realization of virtue while a "dis-preferred indifferent" is something that we would avoid for the same reason. Brennan (2005: 99) then defines "selection" and "deselection" as follows:

> Selection is the belief that some future thing is an indifferent of such a sort that we should reach out for it.
> Deselection is the belief that some future thing is an indifferent of such a sort that we should avoid it.

These definitions once again apply to sages. For versions appropriate to non-sages we would substitute the word "opinion" for "belief." For non-sages then, the ethical challenge, and the key to a well-lived life, is to replace emotions with selections as the kind of impulse that drives their choice-making. There is nothing easy or automatic about the ability to make this sort of substitution inasmuch as the innumerable day-to-day choices that a would-be sage makes are a manifestation of her progress as a sage, but also a process by which her disposition toward virtue is constructed. The ability to do it is what observers mean when they refer to Stoicism as a "character-building" philosophy. That the stoic regards all of us non-sages as vicious does not mean that he believes that we always and everywhere behave in a vicious way. He means rather that until we assent to *kataleptic* impressions in an unwavering way, we will be vulnerable to a false understanding of the good and to vicious choices.

With this brief review of Stoic epistemology (and psychology) in hand, what can we surmise to be the Stoic outlook on the phenomenon of addiction? The first thing we can say is that in contrast to the RCU approach of Becker and Murphy, the Stoic approach would never characterize an addiction as rational. The Stoic belief that the only good consists in the exercise of virtue could hardly be consistent with the use and abuse of addictive substances. The wavering and inconsistent assent that addicts themselves cite with respect to the use of such substances renders them ineligible as candidates to provoke *kataleptic* impressions. Addicts then would never qualify as sages since, as addicts, they could never have more than opinions that the use of addictive substances is in their interest. Interpreted from the pre-scientific perspective of the ancient Stoics, one might say that the ability of addicts to give assent to the impressions associated with consumption of addicted substances is impaired. The result is a loss of self-command and an inability to exercise "right reason." The potential of addictive substances to impair neurological development is well-recognized thus impinging on the addict's ability to have *kataleptic* impressions. Perhaps most significantly, addiction is inconsistent with the Stoic understanding of "right reason" and the pursuit of human flourishing (*eudaimonia*) precisely because it robs the individual of the autonomy that is at the center of a well-lived life.

Whether or not an aspiring sage would ever select to use a potentially addictive substance is another matter. Clearly, many people use alcohol with no ill effects on their health and well-being. In fact, there are many studies that show that moderate alcohol consumption may have some health benefits.[11] Before choosing to use alcohol, however, our would-be sage might attempt to determine her pre-disposition to alcoholism by carefully examining her family history for the condition. If she chooses to imbibe, she will do so only in moderation since the medical evidence to date shows that beyond moderate use, alcohol's expected health risks, even short of addiction, offset its expected health benefits. The aspiring sage would also need to carefully consider the meaning of "moderate" in this context since the actual quantity of alcohol consumed may differ according to a variety of factors such as age, sex, and body type.[12] Certainly the moderate threshold has been breached if the user has become even slightly inebriated since, by definition, a state of inebriation forecloses the possibility of *kataleptic* impressions. Finally the sage and aspiring sage would only consume alcohol while taking into account the place it holds in a life of virtue considered as a whole. The sage would never fall into the trap of addiction. Addiction would never be the result of a mistaken understanding of the short or long term consequences of use. The sage would certainly never engage in hyperbolic discounting of the future. The not-quite-yet sage would not be invulnerable to mistakes of these sorts but, insofar as she is committed to a life of virtue, we can imagine that she will select in a manner that mirrors the sage's knowledge.

The addiction-as-brain-disease model raises some challenging questions regarding the moral responsibility of the addict for his addiction. The primary question of course is, what moral responsibility does the addict have for the disease that afflicts him? We typically consider that a person afflicted by a disease to be the victim of an external agent, like a virus, or a genetic vulnerability. In such cases the diseased victim is considered the passive and unwitting recipient of his condition and we do not normally assign culpability to such an unfortunate individual. In the case of addiction, of course, the problem is not quite so simple since the victim in this case may be said to have invited the disease by initiating use of the addictive substance. Still, as argued earlier, addiction is a complex phenomenon. Initial experimentation with addictive substances does not necessarily entail subsequent addiction. Many people use potentially addictive substances, even highly addictive ones, without becoming addicts. The chances of full-blown addiction may well depend on psychological and environmental factors that are themselves also beyond the ability, or even the consciousness, of the addict to avoid, or alter.

And yet entirely exculpating addicts for their diseases can have counterproductive consequences insofar as it induces a passive attitude on the part of the "patient." The "medicalization of addiction" may unduly and inappropriately narrow the range of policy choices deemed affective for the treatment of addicts. It also presents the addict not only as lacking responsibility for his condition, but also as disempowered in his treatment, yielding control to medical authorities who alone prescribe the course of treatment. The passivity induced by the medicalization model may in fact operate against the chances of recovery via other, perhaps supplementary, treatments that require for their success the active engagement of the addict. The notion embraced by the brain disease model that there exists in many people a genetically-based predisposition to addiction to certain substances may also promote in addicts a fatalistic sense that their addicted condition is unavoidable, and that personal efforts to do so are bound to fail. It is this last assumption in particular that I wish to address from the perspective of Stoic ethics.

As explained by philosopher A. A. Long (1971), at the root of Stoicism's alleged fatalism is the school's understanding of causality, necessity, and fate. Causality is understood as the proposition that all events have antecedent events attached to them as causes. Necessity and fate are a consequence of the Stoic's essentially teleological view of the universe as being directed by a universal *logos* (i.e., god). But man is understood to participate in this *logos* which lends him a degree of autonomy in the causal change of events by which the world unfolds. The implication here is that while it is true that all events have antecedent events that act as causes, and that the chain of events has a certain inevitability as dictated by the universal *logos*, it is not the case that particular events must follow from particular causes when they involve human choice. Some things then are "up to us" as human decision makers.[13] What precisely is "up to us" according to the Stoics are our abilities to give or withhold our assents to impressions. Human beings are determined (or fated) to act as a consequence of things and events that are out of their control. Human acts can hardly be conceived outside of a particular external environmental context. But however compelling are those external events and circumstances, human action does not occur without the exercise of will.

Now, according to the Stoic account, there is another element that must be accounted for in the determination of whether particular human acts are virtuous or vicious. This is the disposition, or character, of the decision-maker. Character, in turn, is partly determined by environmental factors as well as by initial endowment. While environmental factors and initial endowment are predetermined by fate, character is also malleable. It is subject to degradation or improvement by the exercise of the will – man's inner *logos*. Education in particular is an important means of character development. Long (1971: 191) in this context notes the following:

> A subject on which Epictetus dwells constantly is one already mentioned, the need for suitable education. Reason, he argues, in the case of the uneducated, leads to errors of judgment and moral choice. Their vices are a consequence of ignorance, and freedom is incompatible with error.

So, the question of freedom and moral responsibility is a subtle one for the Stoics, but perhaps not more so than it is for us today as Long further notes:

> To be sure, this theory far from solving the problem of moral responsi-bility raises it in a more acute form. The Stoic account of character development requires them, in consistency, to lay down educational minima before making moral judgments, and this they failed to do. But it would be scarcely fair to twit the Stoics for failing to see all the implica-tions of questions which are far from settlement. They were humane as well as precocious when they denied any innate moral determination and traced the causes of wrong-doing to infantile experiences and corrupting environment.
>
> There remains the problem of the causal nexus, and doubtless the Stoics were too ready to keep their cake and eat it. The demands of teleology and providence, combined with pantheism, impose an undeniable strain on the credibility of their ethics. Yet the universal causal principle is present in man, however little, in his own *logos*: he "makes history as well as being history's product." His *logos* is equal in quality to all the divine which is outside. And it constitutes a unique substance whose identity is unaffected by external events. A man can be free, can act as a man, if, and only if, the external movements of his body follow from a decision which reconciles his own will and moral choice to what is necessarily the case (193–194).

Does the Stoic outlook provide us with any help by which to reconcile the brain disease model of addiction with the position that addiction is a choice made by addicts? I think that it does. Environment and genetic endowment, including one's inherited vulnerabilities and disposition to addiction do not consign one to a life of addiction. Certainly there are people with all or most of the known risk factors who avoid that fate. To start on the path to addiction requires that a user of the addictive substance make a choice to use. Moreover, even an initial exposure that modifies the user's neurological disposition does not strictly determine the user to become addicted even as it raises the probability that he will. And, finally, it is sometimes, even oftentimes, the case that an addict can recover and live free of the tremendous costs that addiction imposes. An addict never stops being an addict in that the "externals" he confronts in life now include the disease of addiction. But the addict may still exercise "right reason." The "internal" capacity for this is not extinguished by the addiction. Whether he does or not will depend, in part, on the further development of his character. I argue in the next section that this possibility is increased given appropriate treatment and a public policy environment consistent with successful treatment strategies.

Before we turn to a consideration of policy possibilities, however, there is one point that deserves mention where I believe that Stoic ethics suffers a serious short-coming in matters related to addiction, and may be a more general short-coming in Stoic ethics as a whole. This concerns the "all-or-nothing" feature of Stoic moral assessment. For the early Stoics virtue was considered an absolute and complete ethical state. One could never be "more or less" virtuous. Neither could one be "more or less" a sage. All those who did not reach this high standard were then considered equally vicious. Clearly this is a standard that does not brook moral flexibility and is hardly consistent with any like policy pragmatism. It is worth mentioning as well that it is a position from which later ancient Stoics withdrew and one that contemporary stoics such as Becker (1998: 119) also reject.[14] The "all-or-nothing" perspective when applied to addiction is particularly problematical. The moral responsibility that we are willing to assign addicts will depend on the degree of control that they might be supposed to exercise over their addictions. By dint of endowment or circumstances this will not be the same for all addicts (Sinnott-Armstrong 2013). This is an important consideration as we contemplate the policy and treatment alternatives for what is by most professional accounts a highly complex phenomenon.

Treatment and policy possibilities for addiction

The case for legalization of addictive substances is rarely made in terms of the benefits to be derived from their consumption.[15] Much more likely, the argument is made that the high costs associated with their prohibition imposes an unreasonable burden on society. These costs involve not only those related to the enforcement and legal-judicial systems associated with the apprehension, prosecution and incarceration of those who violate the prohibitions against use of addictive substances.[16] They include as well the actual or potential corruption of these same systems (Burlando and Motta 2016). Moreover, history and popular culture are replete with testimonies of the power of organized criminal organizations that terrorize populations with murder and mayhem in pursuit of the out-sized profits to be gained by the illicit drug trade.

While not discounting the significance of these essentially consequentialist arguments for legalization, there are some other compelling counter-arguments to consider. The first of these is that the legalization of drugs has consequences that extend far beyond those related to the government budget. Among these is the strong likelihood that legalization will result in an increase in the use of highly addictive substances and an increase in the rate of addiction. Correspondingly, we would expect to see an increase in the costs associated with drug use and drug addiction which then must be offset against the budgetary benefits of legalization and taxation. There is historical evidence to support this trade-off from the Prohibition era in the U.S. when consumption of alcohol decreased along with a decrease in the social and health problems that accompanied the decrease in drinking. Both of these increased again when the twenty-first amendment was passed in 1933 repealing prohibition (Blocker 2006). A second, and related, consequentialist argument is that legalizing drug use may have unintended externalities (Waal 1999). The legalization of drugs may have the intended result of fomenting a drug culture that extends well beyond the expected limits of use and abuse following their normalization or "de-stigmatization." Drug use is a social activity wherein users provide positive reinforcement and even social pressure to use drugs (Heath 1999).

Arguments are sometimes made in a libertarian vein that government oversteps its legitimate function in proscribing the pleasures that free adults may engage in a free society. This amounts to a rights-based argument for the freedom to use drugs recreationally. But rights-based arguments do not typically grant to individuals unconstrained liberty to engage in any behavior whatsoever regardless of their consequences. Such rights must, for example, not infringe on the equally compelling rights of other people. To the extent that drug use does, in fact, have unavoidable negative impacts upon others, there exists a compelling case to restrict their use. Even in those cases where these "negative externalities" can be adequately contained, a rights-based argument for recreational drug use may fail where there exists a strong probability of addiction. As noted by Waal (1999: 153), prominent natural rights philosopher John Stuart Mill argued that no person held a natural right to sell himself into, or otherwise submit to, a state of servitude or slavery. But in a manner of speaking this is precisely what addiction amounts to, a condition of self-induced bondage to a chemical master. Neither could a Stoic ethical outlook support a right to recreational drug use.[17] The Stoic stress on the autonomy of the sage and would-be sage from externals would make such a right incompatible with virtue, especially where it contained a serious vulnerability to addiction. Neither would a public finance justification for drug legalization, I contend, pass muster from a Stoic perspective. Such a policy move would be tantamount to surrendering the virtue, or potential virtue, of those who become addicts in the interests of budgetary, or political, expediency. A public policy whose ostensible objective is human flourishing encounters a glaring inconsistency if it relies on relegating a portion of its citizenry to human misery.[18]

If legalization of addictive drugs is inconsistent with Stoic virtue, decriminalization is not. By virtue of her addiction, an addict has made vicious choices. But, according to Stoic lights, this viciousness does not stem from an evil nature, but rather from an impaired, or undeveloped, reason. Thus, from a Stoic perspective, a penal code that follows right reason on addictive substances seeks to correct and redeem rather than to punish merely as a matter of retribution. Certainly, decriminalization does not exclude other policy efforts to reduce the availability of highly addictive drugs and to protect the young from their use, even of those drugs that are known not to necessarily be highly addictive when moderately used. These policy efforts must be supported by the best medical, epidemiological and social scientific research available given what we already know about the complexity of addiction.

It is also worth noting that drug policies and treatment approaches have a far greater potential for success if they recognize the larger social and economic environment in which they operate. It is widely recognized among treatment specialists and other experts that drug use and abuse is often a response to some trauma, or to a sense of hopelessness. A recent widely reported study by Case and Deaton (2015) documents rising rates of mortality for non-Hispanic, middle-aged whites between 1999 and 2013. The rising mortality rates are connected by the authors to deaths caused by drug and alcohol poisonings, suicides, and chronic liver diseases and cirrhosis. They further speculate that the observed rise in morbidity and mortality, unprecedented among Organisation for Economic Co-operation and Development (OECD) nations, may owe to decreased economic prospects and increased feelings of financial insecurity. Recent support for their speculations has been provided by other scholars (C.M. de Goeij et al 2015).

Several commentators have noted what they consider the inappropriate and counter-productive martial rhetoric in relation to the drug abuse problem – to wit, the "War on Drugs." Official rhetoric is, of course, important because it establishes an ideological atmosphere within which policy will be conducted, and broadly shapes the public's understanding of the nature of the challenge and the actors involved, thereby setting limits to what are regarded as acceptable and unacceptable measures to that challenge (Hawdon 2001). At the presidential level the "War on Drugs" began in 1971 with Richard Nixon signing legislation that allocated funding for prevention/treatment and interdiction/enforcement in a 2:1 ratio. These weights were reversed in the 1980s in the Reagan administration (Amundson et al 2014). The war was widened by the creation of the cabinet-level Office of National Drug Control Policy (ONDCP) in 1989 and the appointment of William Bennett as director, or Drug Czar, by President George H. W. Bush. Since 1971 the cost of the war is estimated to be in excess of $1 trillion and its outstanding result is the world's largest prison population. There is a general consensus that the war has been lost.

As Elwood (1994) has noted, the drug problem is complicated and multi-faceted, which is further complicated by war rhetoric. War, after all, pre-supposes an enemy which raises the question: who is the enemy in the war on drugs? There are numerous candidates:

1   foreign drug suppliers (e.g., drug cartels);
2   the foreign states that provide havens for these suppliers;
3   domestic importers of foreign drugs;
4   domestic producers and wholesale distributers of illegal drugs;
5   retail-level distributers of drugs;
6   corrupted and corruptible drug law enforcement agents;
7   illegal drug users including addicts.

Conceived this way the drug problem not only presents its prosecutors with a multifaceted, multi-front campaign, but it generates as many loci of determined opposition. It is not surprising that the war has had little acknowledged success.[19] So, we are left to wonder why the war metaphor persists in the case of drugs when other equally compelling public policy "wars" seem to have been abandoned (e.g., the war on poverty). An answer provided by Elwood is that the war metaphor has proved especially useful to those administrations that employed its rhetoric to essentially political ends.

Other pathological consumption

Pathological consumption is not limited to the use and abuse of dangerously addictive chemicals. It may also involve comparatively benign (e.g., television, internet) and even healthful goods and activities (e.g., food, sex). We might consider any and all of these activities in detail but in the interest of efficiency of presentation, I choose here to focus on one of them – namely, food and eating. The advantage of this particular issue is that it is fundamental activity engaged in by all, and one that has important public health consequences. Obesity and other eating-related disorders weigh heavily on our society and economy. With over two-thirds of Americans overweight, the total direct and indirect costs of obesity are estimated to be in excess of $215 billion annually (Hammond and Levine 2010). These costs include those associated with treating obesity-related diseases such as type 2 diabetes, hypertension, stroke, and cardiovascular disease. They also include those associated with reduced productivity related to absenteeism, "presenteeism", disability, premature mortality, and rising health insurance.

There is *prima facie* evidence that impulsive behavioral disorders share some of the characteristics of substance addictions, though the neurobiological mechanisms involved in the former are still largely unknown (Grant and

Chamberlain 2014). Eating disorders may have more in common with chemical addictions than other types of behavioral disorders inasmuch as they share in common with these addictions the intake of a substance, namely food. Excessive eating then may straightforwardly be considered a kind of substance abuse. Recent scientific research suggests that food, like drugs, activate the dopaminergic and opioid systems in ways that control reward processing and motivation (Lerma-Cabrera et al 2016). Certain foods, moreover, may themselves contain chemicals that are highly addictive. This appears to be especially true of fast foods that are high in sugar, salt, fat, and caffeine (Garber and Lustig 2011).[20] If we ask ourselves why we eat, the obvious answers immediately present themselves: to alleviate our hunger and provide our bodies with necessary energy and nutrients. A moment's reflection, however, will reveal that we also eat for reasons having little or nothing to do either of these primary motivations. Eating is a habitual activity with food preferences and behaviors deeply ingrained from our childhoods. It is also a highly social activity that accompanies a variety of life's important moments. Food is almost essential to any celebratory event. It is also often present to console those who suffer traumatic loss. The term "comfort food" is not accidental.

Eating is often a way that people react to and cope with stress. The relationship between stress and eating may be quite complex (Sominsky and Spencer 2014). On the one hand, the energy we devote to reacting to stressful events and situations in life may reduce our appetites. From an evolutionary perspective, time and energy spent running away from predators, for example, reduces time and energy devoted to seeking food. This is, however, a short run effect. If stress is chronic the body reacts by storing more fat and biochemical processes are activated in the brain that increase appetite and food intake. The manner by which an individual's eating behavior will respond to stress may be determined very early in life and affect their psychological disposition to obesity and other eating disorders.[21]

As is the case for drugs, food cravings are often activated by situational and environmental cues (Stojek et al. 2015). We know, for example, that the mere presence of, or ease of access to, food will prompt food cravings in people that lead to overeating. Food marketers have known this for a long time and there is intense competition for product placement and premium shelf space. Moreover, media are saturated with food advertising, typically for precisely those highly processed, high sugar, high fat foods that are believed to have addictive properties and are related to obesity and its morbidities.

Public policy and eating disorders

At present, as a growing number of critics (Pollan 2006; Moss 2014; Schlosser 2001) have pointed out, our national food and agricultural policies are complicit in the spread of pathological food consumption. Our federal government reversed its policies of supporting small family farms in the 1970s to pursue an alternative policy of cheap food. The major crops involved were corn and soybeans used as feed crops for livestock and as inputs (e.g., high fructose corn syrup) for the manufacture of highly processed foods. The major beneficiaries were the shrinking number of highly capitalized mega-farms who could survive the fall in farm commodity prices as well as the giant agri-businesses who either provided these producers with seed, machinery, and chemicals, or purchased their crops for processing. The result of the policy switch from the consumers' standpoint is a national diet rich in sugar, salt, and fat, the ingredients mostly responsible for our food-related diseases.

Another policy failure related to the goal of the nutritional requirements for human flourishing involves our inadequate response to the problem of food security for millions of Americans. According to the United States Department of Agriculture 14 percent, or 17.4 million households, were food insecure in 2014. Of these food insecure people, nearly 8 million were children.[22] Typically, malnutrition and undernutrition are different types of food-related pathological consumption than the sort we might associate with overweight and obesity. But there is a connection between these conditions. If families do not have sufficient means to purchase high-quality foods, they may have little choice but to fulfill their caloric needs with cheaper sources of high sugar, high fat alternatives. While recent evidence shows that the relation between income and obesity is complicated, the evidence that low socio-economic status is a strong predictor of the incidence of type 2 diabetes is well-established, (Krishnan et al 2010; Connolly et al 2000; Smith 2007). It seems safe to conclude that pathological consumption of food, like drug addiction, is a complex issue requiring complex policy approaches that address underlying social and economic dysfunction in our society. This is not the place to detail the variety of possible specific features of a food policy that would promote human flourishing. There are many extant proposals for such policy reform of our food systems. It is sufficient here to suggest that such reforms will need to overcome established interests that have a strong investment in our prevailing food systems that prioritize profit over human health and well-being.

Mindful consumption

While public policy has an important role in addressing the many incidences of pathological consumption in our society, it would be misleading to suggest that the well-lived life is entirely, or even primarily, a public policy challenge, particularly in a culture such as our own that places a high value on individual autonomy. Individual autonomy presupposes, of course, an equal measure of individual responsibility. What I wish to suggest in this concluding section is that a portion of this responsibility is to re-examine the role that consumption plays in our lives and to ask serious questions about its relationship to our individual and collective flourishing. It is a long recognize piece of conventional wisdom in standard economics that, at bottom, our economy ultimately responds to the autonomous dictates of consumers. There is much to be skeptical about in this assumption, and heterodox schools of economic thought have long called it into question. We have long known, for example, the strong influence that powerful corporations play in molding our tastes through ubiquitous advertising. We also know that these same corporations can themselves influence the course of public policy in ways that dictate and delimit the menu of consumption possibilities that are available to us and foreclose other possibilities.[23] Of course, corporations are not the only kind of social institution that operate to undermine our autonomy as individual consumers. We often feel social and cultural pressure to consume at a standard beyond our means and in ways that fail to satisfy our authentically felt needs.[24] Towards that end I wish to argue for a kind of self-administered therapy that I choose to call Mindful Consumption.

The notion of mindful consumption is derived from what is known as, for lack of a better descriptor, the Mindfulness Movement (MM). Mindfulness has its origins in Buddhist traditions and refers to the practice of being aware on a moment-to-moment basis of one's subjective experience as a means of promoting one's overall well-being. It also refers to a meditative practice that has been demonstrated to have benefits related to a number of clinical psychological applications including eating disorders and weight loss (Kristeller and Hallett 1999; Kristeller et al 2006), stress and anxiety reduction (Miller et al 1995), sleep improvement (Black et al 2015), and addiction therapy (Marlatt 2002). There is also clinical support for the idea that mindfulness training can improve overall cognitive improvement by:

1 activating a metacognitive mode of processing;
2 disconnecting the influence of maladaptive beliefs on processing;
3 strengthening flexible responding to threat; and
4 strengthening metacognitive plans for controlling cognition (Wells 2002).

The idea of "metacognition" is that we focus not only on the challenges of our daily lives, but that we also pay attention to *how* we think about them. Explicit here is the notion that we can have a far greater degree of control over how we think and, indeed, *what* we think about with proper training. Put in Stoic terms, mindfulness meditative practice can be a useful means of processing our impressions before we grant them our assent.[25] Applied to our consumption decisions mindfulness means paying attention to what we consume, how we consume, and why we consume. It means identifying our needs and distinguishing these from our wants. It means considering the various means of satisfying our needs and the implications that follow from these alternatives. It also means interrogating our wants to identify their sources, and asking ourselves if *any* material consumption can ultimately satisfy them. These, I argue, are among the most important questions we can address ourselves to in terms of our flourishing as individuals and as a species. The case for species flourishing, indeed species survival, is made in the next chapter.

Notes

1 As a policy matter it may be difficult to separate out the deontological motive from the virtue-based motive. We may prohibit the practice of slavery, for example, according to the rule that no person is to be used as an instrument for the happiness of another (i.e. deontological motive). Such a rule would hold even if it could be proven that the sum of total utility realized by the slave and slave holder were greater under the slave-holding arrangement (utilitarian motive). At the same time, slave-holding might be prohibited on the grounds that "We are the sort of society that finds the institution of slavery to be morally repugnant" (virtue motive).

2 Relatedly, but ignored in this volume, Bruni (2006) discusses the Civil Economy tradition which he traces back to ancient (Aristotelian) thought and its application to the eighteenth century Neapolitan school and its outstanding exponent, Antonio Genovesi (1731–1769). From the Civil Economy perspective happiness is understood as a relational good recruiting the basic concepts of sociality and reciprocity, each of which is understood in turn as a civic virtue.

3 A less technical and thus more accessible version of the Becker and Murphy model is provided by Skog (1999).

4 As Skog describes, P_1 may also be explained by painful withdrawal effects related to previous consumption.

5 See also the abundant related citations offered by these authors.

6 I draw heavily from Berger (1991) in this description of the disease model of addiction.

7 Details found at http://www.niaaa.nih.gov/about-niaaa/our-work/history-niaaa, accessed 26 December 2015.

8 Moshier et al (2012) in a recent study develop an instrument to assess the strength of drug subculture and its relationship to use persistence, desire to quit, impulsivity, and other user behavior and characteristics. They urge that drug use cultural identification may reduce "recovery capital" and treatment success.

9 I follow the explication of Stoic epistemology provided by Brennan (2005).

10 Brennan notes that even sages are not infallible in that they may assent to an impression that turns out to be false. He cites the case of Sphaerus who reached for a wax imitation of a pomegranate in the belief that it was real. Sphaerus defended his assent on the claim that he assented to the proposition that *it was reasonable* that the object in question was a pomegranate (2005: 75–76). Brennan furthers cites a bit of Stoic doctrine that shows that the Stoics were willing to admit that non-corporeal propositions could also be the cause of impressions as well as physical bodies (2005: 78–79).

11 The definition of moderate given by the United States Department of Agriculture and the Dietary Guidelines for Americans cited in the previous note 7 is one to two drinks per day for men and no more than one drink per day for women. A drink is defined as a beverage containing between 12 to 14 grams of alcohol. By contrast, the recommended levels for "low-risk" alcohol consumption provided by the U.S. National Institute for Alcohol Abuse and Alcoholism (NIAAAA) is no more than four drinks in a day for men up to age 65 and no more than three drinks for women up to age 65 (cited by Barnes 2015).

12 Data provided at http://www.hsph.harvard.edu/nutritionsource/alcohol-full-story/, cited 4 January 2016.

13 The Stoics were the originators of a philosophic outlook that persists to this day called "soft determinism" or "compatibilism." This position has modern advocates such as David Hume and Thomas Hobbes, as well as opponents such as William James and Immanuel Kant.

14 If we consider Stoicism as a philosophy of psychological and ethical *development* then it would seem incoherent not to recognize the possibility of psychological and

ethical *progress* – an option that seems precluded by the hard and fast dichotomy of agents and their behaviors implied by the original Stoics.

15 An exception in this regard is Husak (1992).

16 Miron (2010) estimates that the total government expenditure saved for the United States by the legalization of drugs to be around $48.7 billion annually. He also estimates that taxing illegal drugs at rates comparable to those currently levied on alcohol and tobacco would yield around $34.3 billion in annual revenues.

17 The ancient thinkers, of course, were unfamiliar with natural rights philosophy but could be said to hold views that are precursors to such philosophy. My point here then applies to those who see themselves advancing a contemporary version of the Stoic outlook such as Becker (1998).

18 The question of "sin taxes" in the context of a virtuous public finance is examined in more detail in Chapter 8.

19 Nesbit (2015) cites a CDC report that 2014 saw the highest U.S. annual death toll (50,000) from drug overdoses in history and double the number recorded in 2000. From this perspective it is argued that not only have we not won the war on drugs, we have been routed by them (the drugs).

20 Recent animal studies provide evidence for the addictive properties of sugar. See the review by Avena et al (2008).

21 Sominsky and Spencer (2014: 3) cite research that shows how stress during pregnancy can lead to long-term susceptibility to mood disorders, impaired learning ability, and shape reward pathways that lead to addictive behaviors. Obesity during pregnancy, or even a diet high in fat and sugar, can influence fetus development and the way offspring will perceive fatty and sugary foods throughout life. There is also recent evidence that stress alters the eater's sensitivity to internal hunger and satiety cues and confuses eaters who mistake emotional arousal for hunger (i.e., eating dysregulation), leading to overeating and its associated health problems (Tan and Chong 2014).

22 Of this 8 million, 1 million are deemed by USDA to be *very* food insecure, defined as the condition that normal eating patterns are disrupted and food intake reduced due to insufficient money or resources for food. See http://www.ers.usda.gov/topics/food-nutrition-assistance/food-security-in-the-us/measurement.aspx for details.

23 Consider, for example, the complex of industrial interests that actively promoted the dominance of the automobile in our nation's transportation system to the relative neglect of a mass transportation alternative.

24 Reasonable objections can be made to the expression "authentic needs." How, in practice, it could be asked, are authentic needs to be distinguished from inauthentic ones? Tentatively we might begin with Hursthouse's criteria for "characteristic" human freedoms and enjoyments and the requirements for individual and species survival. We might also include a consideration of Nussbaum and Sen's discussion of capabilities and functionings. See Chapter 4 for more details.

25 While developing from entirely unrelated philosophical traditions, the ethical tangencies that Buddhism and the ancient Greeks share are hard to miss and may be enumerated as follows:

1 The good life is dedicated to the perfection of virtue with virtue understood in terms of virtuous activity.

2 At the moral center of each outlook is the model of the sage.

3 The sources of human suffering are confusion about the good and an inability to subdue the passions, especially the passion of fear.

4 There is rejection of externals as having moral worth.

5 Disciplined practice is the path to virtue.

6 There is a need for virtue to be the result of a virtuous disposition rather than a desire to be, or appear to be, virtuous.

7 Freedom is best understood as the perfection of our autonomous agency.

Garfield (2013) develops this argument by making a comparison between the Buddhist Śāntideva and Aristotle. What he writes about Aristotelian virtue can be equally well applied to Stoicism.

References

Amundson, Kalynn, Anna M. Zajicek, and Valerie H. Hunt. 2014. "Pathologies of the poor: What do the war on drugs and welfare reform have in common?," *Journal of Sociology & Social Welfare*, 41, 1 (March): 5–28.

Avena, Nicole M., Pedro Rada, and Bartley G. Hoebal. 2008. "Evidence for sugar addiction: Behavioral and neurochemical effects of intermittent, excessive sugar intake," *Neuroscience & Biobehavioral Reviews*, 32, 1: 20–39.

Barnes, Henrietta Robin. 2015. *Hijacked Brains: The Experience and Science of Chronic Addiction*, Hanover, NH: Dartmouth College Press.

Battistich, Victor and Allen Hom. 1997. "The relationship between students' sense of their school as a community and their involvement in problem behaviors," *American Journal of Public Health*, 87, 12 (December): 1997–2001.

Becker, Gary S. and Kevin M. Murphy. 1988. "A theory of rational addiction," *Journal of Political Economy*, 96: 675–700.

Becker, Lawrence C. 1998. *A New Stoicism*, Cambridge: Cambridge University Press.

Berger, Louis S. 1991. *Substance Abuse as Symptom*, Hillsdale, NJ: The Atlantic Press.

Berheim, B. Douglas and Antonio Rangel. 2005. "From neuroscience to public policy: A new economic view of addiction," *Swedish Economic Policy Review*, 12, 2: 99–144.

Biron, Denise E. 2012. "Drug use subcultures," in *Substance Abuse, Addiction, and Treatment*, New York: Marshall Cavendish Reference.

Black, D. S., G. A. O'Reilly, E. C. Breen, and M. R. Irwin. 2015. "Mindfulness meditation and improvement in sleep quality and daytime impairment among older adults with sleep disturbances: A clinical randomized trial," *JAMA Internal Medicine*, 175, 4 (April): 494–501.

Blocker, Jr., Jack S.. 2006. "Did Prohibition really work? Alcohol prohibition as a public health innovation," *American Journal of Public Health*, 96, 2 (February): 233–243.

Brennan, Tad. 2005. *The Stoic Life: Emotions, Duties & Fate*, Oxford: Oxford University Press.

Bruni, Luigino. 2006. *Civil Happiness: Economics and Human Flourishing in Historical Perspective*, London: Routledge.

Burlando, Alfredo and Alberto Motta. 2016. "Legalize, tax, and deter: Optimal enforcement policies for corruptible officials," *Journal of Development Economics*, 118: 207–215.

Case, Anne and Angus Deaton. 2015. "Rising morbidity and mortality in midlife among white non-Hispanic Americans in the 21st century," *Proceedings of the National Academy of Sciences of the United States of America*, 112, 49 (December): 15078–15083.

Connolly, V., N. Unwin, P. Sheriff, R. Bilous, and W. Kelly. 2000. "Diabetes prevalence and socioeconomic status: A Population based study showing increased prevalence of type 2 diabetes mellitus in deprived areas," *Journal of Epidemiology & Community Health*, 54: 173–177.

Duncan, Greg J., Johanne Boisjoly, Michael Kremer, Dan M. Levy, and Jacque Eccles. 2005. "Peer effects in drug use and sex among college students," *Journal of Abnormal Child Psychology*, 33, 3 (June): 375–385.

120   *Ethics and public policy*

Elam, M. 2012. "Pharmaceutical incursion on cigarette smoking at the birth of the brain disease model of addiction," in *Critical Perspectives on Addiction, Advances in Medical Sociology*, vol. 14, pp53–75, Bingley: Emerald Press.

Elwood, William N. 1994. *Rhetoric in the War on Drugs: The Triumphs and Tragedies of Public Relations*, Westport, CT: Praeger.

Garber, Andrea and Robert Lustig. 2011. "Is fast food addictive?," *Current Drug Abuse Reviews*, 4: 146–162.

Gardner, Eliot L. and James David. 1999. "The neurobiology of chemical addiction," in *Getting Hooked: Rationality and Addiction*, J. Elster and O. Skog (eds.), Cambridge: Cambridge University Press.

Garfield, Jay L. 2013. "Mindfulness and ethics: attention, virtue and perfection," *Thai International Journal of Buddhist Studies*, 3: 1–24.

de Goeij, Moniek, C. M., Marc Suhrcke, Veronica Toffolutti, Dike van de Mheen, Tim M. Schenmakers, and Anton E. Kunst. 2015. "How economic crises affect alcohol consumption and alcohol-related health problems: A realist systematic review," *Social Science & Medicine*, 131: 131–146.

Grant, Jon E. and Samuel R. Chamberlain. 2014 "Impulsive action and impulsive action across substance and behavioral addictions: Cause or consequence," *Addictive Behaviors*, 39: 1632–1639.

Hammond, Ross A. and Ruth Levine. 2010. "The economic impact of obesity in the United States," *Diabetes, Metabolic Syndrome and Obesity: Targets and Therapy*, Dove Medical Press, Ltd., 3: 285–295.

Hawdon, James E. 2001. "The role of presidential rhetoric in the creation of a moral panic: Regan, Bush, and the war on drugs," *Deviant Behavior: An Interdisciplinary Journal*, 22: 419–445.

Heath, Dwight B. 1999. "Culture," in *Sourcebook on Substance Abuse: Etiology, Epidemiology, and Treatment*, P. J. Ott, R. E. Tarter, R. T. Ammerman (eds.) Needham Heights, MA: Allyn & Bacon.

Husak, D. N. 1992. *Drugs and Rights*, New York: Cambridge University Press.

Krishnan, Supriya, Yvette C. Cozier, Lynne Rosenburg, and Julie R. Palmer. 2010. "Socioeconomic status and incidence of type 2 diabetes: Results from the black women's health study," *American Journal of Epidemiology*, 171, 5: 564–570.

Kristellar, Jean and Brendan Hallet. 1999. "An exploratory study of a meditation-based intervention for binge-eating disorder," *Journal of Health Psychology*, 4, 3: 357–363.

Kristellar, Jean L., Ruth A. Baer, and Ruth Quillian-Weaver. 2006. "Mindfulness-based approaches to eating disorders," in *Mindfulness and Acceptance-based Interventions: Conceptualizations, Application, and Empirical Support*, R. Baer (ed.), San Diego: Elsevier.

Lerma-Cabrera, Jose Manuel, Francisco Carajal, and Patricia Lopez-Legarrea. 2016. "Food addiction as a new piece of the obesity framework," *Nutrition Journal*, 15, 5: 15, http://eds.a.ebscohost.com/eds/pdfviewer/pdfviewer?vid=3&sid=7ee40995-cb52-4dd7-8e32-1c53f34dd6f3%40sessionmgr4002&hid=4205, accessed 21 January 2016.

Lewis, Marc. 2015. *The Biology of Desire; Why Addiction is not a Disease*, New York: Public Affairs.

Long, A. A. 1971. "Freedom and determinism in the Stoic theory of human action," in *Problems in Stoicism*, A. A. Long (ed.), London: Athlone Press: 173–199.

Marlatt, G. Alan. 2002. "Buddhist philosophy and the treatment of addictive behavior," *Cognitive and Behavioral Practice*, 9, 1 (Winter): 44–50.

McCrady, Barbara S. 2006. "Family and other close relationships," in *Rethinking Substance Abuse: What the Science Shows, and What We Should About It*, W. R. Miller and K. M. Carroll (eds.) New York: The Guilford Press.

Miller, John J., Ken Fletcher, and Jon Kabat-Zinn. 1995. "Three-year follow-up and clinical implications of a mindfulness meditation-based stress reduction intervention in the treatment of anxiety disorders," *General Hospital Psychiatry*, 17: 192–2000.

Miron, Jeffrey A. 2010. *The Budgetary Implications of Drug Prohibition*, Cambridge, MA: Harvard University, Department of Economics: 1–39, http://scholar.harvard.edu/miron/publications/budgetary-implications-drug-prohibition-0.

Moos, Rudolf 2006. "Social context and substance abuse," in *Rethinking Substance Abuse: What the Science Shows, and What We Should Do About It*, W. R. Miller and K. M. Carroll, New York: The Guilford Press.

Moss, Michael. 2014. *Salt, Sugar, Fat: How the Food Giants Hooked Us*, New York: Random House.

Moshier, Samantha J., R. Kathryn McHugh, Amanda W. Calkins, Bridget A. Hearon, Anthony J. Rosellini, Meara L. Weitzman, and Michael W. Otto. 2012. "The role of perceived belongingness to a drug subculture among opioid-dependent patients," *Psychology of Addictive Behaviors*, 26, 4: 812–820.

Mueser, Kim T., Robert E. Drake, Win Turner and Mark McGovern. 2006. "Comorbid substance use disorders and psychiatric disorders," in *Rethinking Substance Abuse: What the Science Shows, and What We Should Do About It*, W. R. Miller and K. M. Carroll, New York: The Guilford Press.

Nesbit, Jeff. 2015. "At the edge. We have lost the war on drugs," *U.S. News & World Report*, http://www.usnews.com/news/blogs/at-the-edge/articles/2015-12-21/the-war-on-drugs-is-over-and-we-lost, accessed 22 January 2016.

Pickard, Hanna and Steve Pearce. 2013 "Addiction in context," in *Addiction and Self-Control: Perspectives from Philosophy, Psychology and Neuroscience*, N. Levy (ed.), Oxford: Oxford University Press.

Pollan, Michael. 2006. *Omnivore's Dilemma: A Natural History of Four Meals*, New York: The Penguin Press.

Reinarman, Craig and Robert Granfield. 2015. "Addiction is not just a brain disease: Critical studies of addiction," in *Expanding Addiction: Critical Essays*, R. Granfield and C. Reinarman (eds.), New York: Routledge.

Schaler, Jeffrey A. 2000. *Addiction is a Choice*, Chicago, IL: Open Court.

Schlosser, Eric. 2001. *Fast Food Nation: The Dark Side of the All-American Meal*, New York: Houghton Mifflin.

Sinnott-Armstrong. 2013. "Are addicts responsible," in *Addiction and Self-Control: Perspectives from Philosophy, Psychology and Neuroscience*, N. Levy (ed.), Oxford: Oxford University Press.

Skog, Ole-Jorgen. 1999. "Rationality, irrationality, and addiction – Notes on Becker and Murphy's theory of addiction," in *Getting Hooked: Rationality and Addiction*, J. Elster and O. Skog (eds.), Cambridge: Cambridge University Press.

Smith, James. 2007. "*Diabetes and the rise of the SES health gradient*," Working paper 12905, National Bureau of Economic Research, http://www.nber.org/papers/w12905, accessed 27 January 2016.

Sominsky, Luba and Sarah J. Spencer. 2014. "Eating behavior and stress: A pathway to obesity," *Frontiers in Psychology*, 5, 434 (May): 1–8.

Stojek, Monika Kardacz, Sarah Fischer, and James MacKillop. 2015. "Stress, cues, and eating behavior: Using drug addiction paradigms to understand motivation for food," *Appetite*, 92: 252–260.

Tan, Cin Cin and Chong Man Chow. 2014. "Stress and emotional eating: The mediating role of eating dysregulation," *Personality and Individual Differences*, 66: 1–4.

Waal, Helge. 1999. "To legalize or not to legalize: Is that the question?," in *Getting Hooked: Rationality and Addiction*, J. Elster and O. Skog (eds.), Cambridge: Cambridge University Press.

Wells, Adrian. 2002. "GAD, metacognition, and mindfulness: An information processing analysis," *Clinical Psychology*, 9: 95–100.

Wetherill, Reagan and Susan F. Tapert. 2012. "Adolescent brain development, substance use, and psychotherapeutic change," *Psychology of Addictive Behaviors*, 37, 2: 393–402.

Winter, Harold. 2011. *The Economics of Excess; Addiction, Indulgence, and Social Policy*, Stanford, CA: Stanford University Press.

Zimić, Jadranka Ivandić and Vlado Jukić. 2012. "Familial risk factors favoring drug addiction onset," *Journal of Psychoactive Drugs*, 44, 2: 173–185.

6   Economics, ethics, and the environment

A life according to nature

It is tempting to interpret the Stoic injunction to the would-be sage to "live a life according to nature" to mean that the sage is that individual who lives a life in harmony with his or her natural environment. To do so, however, would be to attribute both too much and too little to the ancient Stoic outlook – too much inasmuch as the Stoics had nothing explicit to say about the environmental challenges faced by their own culture, at least that has survived; too little as the injunction is a general one that encourages a life of right reason broadly considered. It is, in fact, the basis for Stoic ethics as a whole. I argue in this chapter, however, that Stoic ethics does contain some specific content that is particularly well suited to contemporary issues of human–nature relationships and to the long-term prospects of human–environment sustainability. Three of the primary Stoic virtues – wisdom, moderation, and justice – can be shown to have direct relevance to the espoused goals of environmental sustainability: wisdom in the sense of understanding the intricate relationship(s) linking the human species to the rest of nature; moderation in the discipline of our appetites for material goods that make obvious demands on the environment; and justice in our recognition and allocation of the rights and responsibilities of individuals, groups, and nations in regard to their fair and sustainable shares of nature's goods. Before I examine these specific links between ancient ethics and modern environmental concern, however, I would like to provide a brief review of how the ancients themselves considered their relationships to the environment and what environmental challenges they faced.

J. Donald Hughes (2014) notes that the ancient Greeks and Romans understood their relationship to nature in essentially religious terms (i.e., "as the sphere of the gods").[1] Natural phenomena such as fire, air, earth, and water, and the effects of these, were typically interpreted as reflecting the will(s) of the gods. For the ancients, religion did the heavy lifting of explanation which their still incipient science could not handle. This is not to say that an emergent scientific attitude did not develop with the ancient Greeks. Even the pre-Socratic philosophers had developed the beginnings of a materialist view of reality, and with Aristotle the empirical inductive method was well developed. Aristotle, in particular, made the close study of nature a major part of his intellectual program. While his empirical inductive method has moved many to consider Aristotle as the original biologist, his commitment to a teleological and hierarchical view of nature prevents us from considering him as truly scientific in the modern sense of the word. By this is meant that, like most of the deep thinkers of his day, Aristotle believed nature had a purpose, or *telos*, and the specific details of nature existed to serve this purpose. Moreover, the over-riding purpose of non-human nature was to serve human beings in the exercise of their divinely-inspired reason. This is not, it is clear, how science sees nature today, nor is it how science sees reason and rationality.

What ancient societies certainly do share in common with modern ones was a tendency towards environmental abuse and degradation. As Hughes notes, deforestation, over-grazing, soil erosion, and agricultural decline were all tragedy-of-the-commons-type problems confronted by ancient societies.[2] The ancients were able to connect the environmental crises they suffered to their productive practices and out of these connections there emerged, again incipient, a kind of environmental ethos. This was typically often revealed in injunctions to propitiate a particular god or goddess by refraining from certain practices that were environmentally destructive, or by engaging in environmentally compensatory practices. Likewise, certain resources or places came to be considered sacred and off-limits to exploitation (Hughes 2014: 48–52). These prescriptions and prohibitions, however, were on the whole unable to prevent serious environmental damage that contributed to the decline of the ancient civilizations.

If the ancients never developed a fully scientific understanding of the human to non-human environmental relationship, or a satisfying ethical view of the human responsibilities in relation to environmental sustainability, it could be said that their more broadly ethical outlook has much to recommend to modern environmental ethics. Not only do the Stoic primary virtues already noted fit well with a personal life-style and public policy program consistent with environmental sustainability, but the overall Stoic outlook that measures human-thriving in non-material terms is one that modern environmentalists can readily endorse. Something similar can also be said about the Epicurean outlook that rejects the ephemeral pleasure of material consumption in favor of the higher order and more stable pleasures of friendship and fellowship.

William O. Stephens (1994) argues that Stoic naturalism/rationalism provides a firm basis for a social ecology of the type advocated by environmentalist Murray Bookchin. The key element of Stoic doctrine that links their outlook to Bookchin's is social *oikeiosis*. Recall from our discussion in chapter 2, social *oikeiosis* is that tendency originating in human beings' ability to exercise their reason and extend their instinct for self-preservation to an understanding of their obligations to others in ever-widening and inclusive circles of concern. Bookchin's affinity to Stoicism is revealed by this passage quoted by Stephens:

The social bond that human parents create with the young as the bio-community phases into the social community is fundamental to the emergence of society and it is retained in every society as an active factor in the elaboration of history. It is not only that prolonged human immaturity develops the lasting ties so necessary for human interdependence ... . It is also that care, sharing, participation, and complementarity develop this bond beyond the material division of labour, which has received so much emphasis in economic interpretations of social origins. This social bond gives rise to a fascinating elaboration of the tentative parent-offspring relationship: Love, friendship, loyalty – not only to people but to *ideas* and *beliefs*, and hence makes belief, commitment and *civil* communities possible.³

The social commitment derived from social *oikeiosis* is one vital component of a social ecology offered by the Stoics. Another identified by Stephens is Stoic cosmopolitanism. Citing Stoic authorities such as Zeno and Seneca, Stephens argues that human rationality unites the human species in a moral community that extends beyond the borders of nations. This element of Stoic doctrine is especially salient given the manifestly global reach of our environmental vulnerabilities and interdependencies. Our contemporary scientific understanding that meeting the challenges posed by global climate change requires international cooperation, for example, is based on an ethical realization, nascent in Stoicism, that the entirety of humanity, including future generations, has a claim on the goods derived from a sustainable natural environment.

The observation made by Stephens and others that the ancients were anthropocentric in their outlook on nature has frequently been raised against them by contemporary environmentalists. I believe that this charged can be met in two ways. First, a strong defense of the environment, and the values of most environmentalists, can be made from an anthropocentric perspective. The key adjustment to be made in this case requires that we define the human good in terms compatible with the good for non-human nature. While this sort of reconciliation of values may require we jettison the notion of nature's "intrinsic value", nothing else would seem to be lost to those who adopt a strong form of environmentalism including a defense of wildness and wilderness. This is an argument that I shall pursue in greater detail in sections of this chapter to follow. Second, the anthropocentricism of nature associated with the Hellenistic philosophers (e.g., Stoics) is an essentially ethical idea. The Stoic injunction for the sage is a life in accordance with nature. While this was not an explicitly environmental prescription for the Stoics, everything in their doctrine would point in the direction of an environmental virtue ethics assuming that they had possession of a scientific understanding of ecology. In taking this admittedly highly speculative position, I concur with neo-stoic Lawrence Becker that if stoicism had had the benefit of a continuous development up through the modern era, it would have readily incorporated scientific discovery into its ethical worldview. Had this continuity been maintained, the disjunction between science and ethics might not have been as abrupt as it occurred in the period of the Enlightenment. The result might have been a normatively improved conception of science than what we possess now.

Economics and environmental sustainability

The idea of environmental sustainability suffers from such an overabundance of definitions that some commentators have been moved to near despair about the very usefulness of the concept (Sagoff 2002). The multifarious meanings attached to the word "sustainability" owes in part to the many disciplinary, professional, and policy perspectives that consider themselves as having a claim on the concept. The issue of environmental sustainability has certainly captured the attention of economists, including those of a neoclassical persuasion. In fact, a highly prominent neoclassical economist, Robert Solow, has expressed some very definite views on the use and abuse of the term sustainability. For Solow (1991) sustainability cannot refer to any particular component of the environment, nor can it really refer to any particular environmental value. The reason for this is that, in his view, it is presumptuous to believe that the current generation can know with any definiteness what the future holds. We cannot know today, for example, what technologies will develop that will inform future environmental choices and trade-offs. Neither can we claim to know with any certainly the preference functions of future generations.

Solow does allow that environmental sustainability is an ethical issue. The ethical obligation, in fact, cuts along three axes:

1   an intra-generational obligation;
2   an international obligation;
3   and an inter-generational obligation.

The first two of these are overlapping considerations. They encompass an environmental ethic that recognizes the material and environmental needs of the less well-off members of society both at home and abroad. Environmental restrictions have opportunity costs that befall producers and consumers whose incidence must be accounted for in the ethical (to wit, utilitarian) calculus. Regarding (3) we face the especially difficult challenge of representing the interests of the unborn and a lack of information regarding their technical/ material possibilities and, as noted, their preferences. About the best that we can say in this regard concerning our present obligation, says Solow, is that we use resources today in a way that does not diminish future opportunities for equal happiness (i.e., utility). Practically speaking, this ethical obligation centers on making investments in new techniques and new knowledge that either helps to preserve environmental resources and quality for future generations, or that compensates them for their loss. What is morally unacceptable from Solow's perspective is an approach to resource management that reflexively seeks to preserve resources without due consideration of the costs of such efforts to current citizens/workers/consumers. In adopting this particular sustainability ethic, Solow and other neoclassical economists place much faith in the market mechanism to provide appropriate price signals that will guide both consumers and producers in making decisions leading to a socially optimal outcome.[4] As noted, they also invest a great deal of faith in the ability of technological progress to develop synthetic substitutes for non-renewable resources, and otherwise solve problems that arise from our exploitation of nature.

It is worth noting here that the perspective offered by Solow represents a single, though perhaps dominant, strain of economic thinking in regards to the use and abuse of the environment. A second, and perhaps more comprehensive, strain is known as ecological economics (EE). EE is more comprehensive inasmuch as it takes a broader view of what sorts of things ought to count as having value. For example, the ultimate measure of the economy as a whole considered by the conventional economics of Solow is termed gross domestic product (GDP) and includes in its calculation the value of all final goods and services produced in the economy for a determinate period. It neglects to include the value of environmental goods and services which are regarded as simply "gifts of nature." Neither does it make any allowance for the despoliation of the environment that results from conventional economic production. EE takes the position that conventional economics seriously misrepresents the human welfare implications of GDP due to these accounting shortcomings.

These are not the only criticisms leveled at the Solow perspective by EE. The alternative approach takes exception to the claim made by conventional economics that we cannot know with any accuracy, and should not presume to know, the preferences of future generations for environmental goods and services as compared to potential manufactured substitutes. Likewise, it rejects the claim that there does not exist any environmental good/service that could be deemed to be critical. Neither of these claims is credible to EE advocates. It seems certain, for example, that future generations will desire protection from intense ultra-violet light exposure and for this reason will attach a high value to the ozone layer that protects living organisms from these harmful rays. This has required that we reduce, or eliminate outright, the use of chloro-fluorocarbons (CFCs) that have a deleterious effect on the ozone shield. Similarly, we can confidently assume as well that future generations will place a high value on the preservation of the balance of atmospheric gases that mitigate the potential for catastrophic climate change. With regard to other environmental goods, such as species diversity and wilderness, one might imagine that members of future generations could be compensated for their loss with sufficient increases in manufactured alternatives. It could well be counter-argued, however, that the level of unjustified presumption in this case is greater than that which argues for the maintenance of the full menu of environmental values from which they (future generations) might choose. Neither is the EE outlook nearly as confident as conventional economics in our continued ability to find technological solutions to the growing list of environmental challenges. At the least, argues EE, we should adopt a prudential attitude in respect to the conservation, and even the preservation, of our common environmental endowment. Such an attitude, of course, is entirely in line with the emphasis on virtue stressed by the ancient philosophers. With that in mind we turn our attention to the role that virtue must play in environmental ethics.

Environmental virtue ethics

In recent years the notion of virtue ethics has undergone something of a renaissance. Among environmental ethicists this rebirth is referred to as EVE, environmental virtue ethics (Sandler and Cafero 2005). A compelling argument for EVE is provided by Sandler (2010), who argues that other ethical traditions are inadequate to the theoretical and practical task of addressing what he calls "longitudinal collective action problems." These he describes as arising from "the cumulative unintended (and often unforeseen, or unforeseeable) effects of a vast amount of seemingly insignificant decisions and actions by individuals who are unknown to each other and distant from each other spatially, temporally, and socially" (168). Sandler goes on to describe the difficulties that arise from such problems:

> Longitudinal collective action environmental problems are likely to be effectively addressed only by an enormous number of individuals each making a nearly insignificant contribution to resolving them. However, when a person's making such a contribution appears to require social, personal, or economic costs the *problem of inconsequentialism* arises: given that a person's contribution, although needed (albeit not necessary), is nearly inconsequential to addressing the problem and may require some cost from the standpoint of the person's own life, why should the person make the effort, particularly when it is uncertain (or even unlikely) whether others will do so (168, italics in original)?

This description is a very good illustration of the limits of rational choice utilitarianism as it applies to environmental problems. It suggests that consideration of the cost-benefit type, typical of standard economic logic, will weigh against environmental protection/conservation when the benefits to individuals are slight and uncertain and the costs are immediate and real. Rational choice utilitarians might counter that this is not necessarily so insofar as decision makers incorporate environmental goods into their preference functions and, moreover, insofar as they incorporate the welfare of future generations into their preference functions. Such an argument has force, however, only insofar as it can provide an accounting for why an agent would include environmental goods in her preference function given the problem of inconsequentialism described above. Such an accounting would assume a disposition to environmental virtue. Public policy that hopes to be effective in promoting environmental sustainability, in turn, would be the sort that is successful in promoting just this disposition.

Cafaro (2005) believes that one effective way to promote EVE involves a close examination of the lives and writings of certain men and women who are felt to exemplify models of virtuous environmental behavior. Among these models Cafaro includes Henry Thoreau, Aldo Leopold, and Rachel Carson. Cafaro sees in the writings of each of these individuals certain commonalities that EVE must manifest. Among these are:

1 an attitude towards economic life that understands it as a support for comfortable and decent human lives, rather than as an engine driving unlimited material accumulation and consumption;
2 a commitment to science combined with an appreciation of its limits;
3 non-anthropocentrism;
4 an appreciation of the wild and support for wilderness protection.

The last two of these are worth additional comment, especially in light of our earlier discussion of Solow on sustainability.

The first of these characteristics, non-anthropocentrism, is a requirement that is frequently identified by advocates of EVE. It amounts to the requirement that we recognize the "intrinsic value" of nature considered apart from whatever value it affords the human species.[5] Holmes Rolston III (2005) is one such commentator who supports such a view. For Rolston III the only appropriately EVE outlook is one that views nature's value as non-relational; that is, it regards such value as an absolute deserving of our moral and practical consideration. It would require then that we ascribe to nature a value that transcends our own existence.

I must confess that I find this position to be a difficult one to accept, if not a completely unintelligible one. I submit that the concept of "value" is a relational one. That is, if the term is meaningful, it presupposes both a subject (an evaluator) as well as an object evaluated. Moreover, I would submit that the act of evaluation is by definition an inherently rational one. If we accept these presuppositions, then it is difficult to avoid the charge of anthropocentrism, or even "speciesism". I would further submit, however, that none of the other elements of the EVE catalog is at risk by a rejection of non-anthropocentrism. This is so when we take an appropriately wide view of what is of value for human welfare in relation to nature and the environment. Take the matter of "wildness," for example. It is not hard to come up with reasons why it is important for human beings to value wildness and to take steps to preserve and protect wilderness.

First, and most obviously, wild areas are repositories of natural resources and environmental services that are materially related to human welfare. This is the familiar argument for the protection, for example, of rainforests that maintain biodiversity, sequester carbon, and help regulate weather and the hydrology cycle. Second, wild places act as laboratories within which natural processes may be observed, studied and learned from. Without these places, and the opportunities they provide to gain knowledge, our chances for long-term survival as a species will be diminished. Third, wilderness has cultural value. It has direct aesthetic value and is the direct and indirect source of much artistic inspiration. Even those of us who are not intrepid enough to venture into wild places derive cultural benefits from their existence, and human flourishing (i.e., *eudaimonia*) would be diminished in their absence.

Finally, and perhaps most importantly, the maintenance of wilderness places limits on human prolificacy considered not just in terms of biological reproduction, but also in terms of production and consumption more generally. Consider, for example, the designation of rainforests as "off limits" to the development of industrial agriculture. This preserves the forest for its ability to produce vital environmental services while also requiring of us to consider a more balanced and equitable approach to social and economic development that addresses the needs of the landless poor. We know, for example, that poor people will push into rainforest to earn a subsistence living if they are provided no other option. We also know that if we can reduce poverty and increase education (especially of women), then birth rates fall and this is necessary for sustainability. This is not to say that designating wild reserves by itself accomplishes all this. But it does help force us to exercise better judgment about how we develop. Wild places provide the natural bounds that support the virtues of temperance, moderation, and prudence essential not only to EVE, but to the well-lived life more generally. Seen from this perspective it may be said that not only does environmental integrity rely on the development of human virtue, but human virtue is itself an outcome of environmental integrity. Given this dialectical relationship I do not see that anything is at risk in adopting a humanistic view of EVE. It remains for us to show that the ancient Hellenistic philosophers offer something important to the development of EVE.

Eudaimonism and EVE

The argument to be made here is not that the Hellenistic philosophers provide us with a fully adequate and sufficient environmental ethical argument. That is certainly not true. In fact, they had little to say on the issue of the natural environment at all as we understand it today.[6] The argument I wish to advance, rather, is that these philosophers made ethical arguments whose elements support an environmental ethic better than does the narrow utilitarianism of modern economic theory. Looked at another way, it might be said that any adequate environmental ethic can find more inspiration in the works of the Hellenistic philosophers than in the writings of modern economic welfare theory. They do this precisely insofar as they provide superior guidance for living "the good life." Furthermore, I believe it can be argued that the Hellenistic philosophers provide us with ethical insights that allow us to contend with the challenge of sustainability along the three dimensions identified by Solow (i.e., international, intra-generational, and intergenerational).

Here is one key aspect of this. The point is frequently made that a sustainable economy will require a change in consumers' attitudes away from the standard perception that individual welfare is a constantly increasing function of material consumption, and that our collective social welfare is similarly a constantly increasing function of the growth in gross domestic product. While the Epicureans share with modern economic utilitarians the view that the good life is a matter of increasing pleasure and decreasing pain, the ancient Greeks were willing to assert a hierarchy of pleasures, while modern economic utilitarians are not willing to make any such assertion. The insistence of modern economic theory on the commensurability of all values, and their representation in terms of market prices, makes such a hierarchy inadmissible.

Recall that for Epicurus pleasures were to be disaggregated into those that are natural and those that are unnatural. Natural (necessary) desires, he argued, are easy to satisfy, and superfluous desires are difficult to satisfy and they rob people of the time for the best pleasures which require leisure and repose. In the matter of consumption as we saw in Chapter 2, by comparison with modern economic theories of welfare, the Epicureans were virtual minimalists. While the Epicureans endorsed the view that a good life was a pleasurable one, they saw pleasure emanating not so much from consumption, but from their relationships with like-minded friends. Crucially, as an empirical matter, this is precisely the conclusion reached by recent hedonic research (Layard 2005).

Notwithstanding the primacy of pleasure in their ethical system, the Epicureans also paid important attention to such qualities of character as prudence, temperance, moderation, etc. What separated them from their philosophical opponents and contemporaries, the Stoics, was that they viewed these virtues as having instrumental, rather than intrinsic, or final, value in their pursuit of pleasure. While these values could be said to play an important role in the outlook of the classical economists, especially for Adam Smith, they, or anything like them, are virtually absent in the normative content of the rational choice theory that informs modern economic models and theories. Character traits as prudence, temperance, moderation are effectively moot for neoclassical theories that rely on market prices in a system of voluntary exchange to guide resources to their optimal uses based on contemporaneous utility maximization.[7] These same traits, however, would seem essential in a system that attempts to achieve sustainability into an indefinite future.[8]

For the Stoics, *eudaimonia* was entirely a matter of leading a life of virtue. Virtue itself consisted in "a life in accord with nature." As noted above, it would be tempting to argue that this concept of virtue implies a life consistent with the goal of environmental sustainability in the strong sense.[9] There is nothing in the writings of the Stoic philosophers that makes this explicit claim. As Kimpel (1985: 135) argues, however, the most cogent interpretation of the Stoic use of the term "nature" as a term of moral approbation involves whatever is sufficient for the survival and health of a human being. The term nature as it is employed by the Stoics at the same time is interpreted as that which appeals to our beings as rational creatures. Clearly, there is quite a lot of room for interpretation of these conceptions of "nature" and "natural." What seems unambiguous is that for the Stoics virtue is valued for its own sake and is not a means to some other end such as utility.

And yet, there is much in Stoic writings that points in the direction of a sustainability ethic. Like the Epicureans many of the Stoic philosophers were consumption minimalists (Mills 2002). Seneca went as far as to declare that "nature craves only bread and water." He further enjoins us to "despise everything that useless toil creates as an ornament and an object of beauty." In fact, Stoic *eudaimonia* insists on the irrelevancy of consumption altogether and locates it instead in virtue understood as "right reason." Right reason, in turn, is understood according to the Stoic account as consistent with the natural unfolding of the universe. Living in accord (harmony) with nature is the essence of Stoic rationality. This involves a consistency between human nature and the larger cosmos of which it is a part. In an exegesis of the Stoic philosopher Chrysippus, Long (1996: 190) illustrates this consistency as follows:

> First, the two natures are so related that the "human" is "a part of" the universal one. The thought is not, or merely not, that our lives are unavoidably conditioned by the physical structure of the world. Human nature is "a part of universal nature" in a much more comprehensive sense, a sense we could capture by expressing the relation as one of "active participation", sharing in and contributing to the world's divine organization. That thought in turn fits a second notion stated by Chrysippus – the notion of community governed by law. We achieve life in agreement with nature by conforming ourselves to the rules prescribed by a deity who governs the universe according to right and rational principles.

The interpretation of "nature" in the previous paragraph is expressed in a theological rather than in a scientific way. But for the ancients this distinction did not exist. It doesn't require a heroic stretch of the imagination to believe that for the Stoics the "rules prescribed by a deity" would be accord with the rules necessitated for environmental sustainability. Moreover, Stoic ethical writings are replete with injunctions to live moderately and prudently, characteristics that are entirely consistent with a sustainable lifestyle. The virtue of moderation serves to reign in our individual and collective appetites to a level that is less likely to have harmful impacts on the natural environment, as well as to allow us to focus on the non-material aspects of human flourishing. The virtue of prudence serves to guide our decision making in ways that pays due respect to the limits of our knowledge and our dependence on environmental integrity.

A second important intimation given in the above paragraph that carries significant implications for an ethics of sustainability is the stress laid on "active participation." Unlike the recommendation of the Epicureans that *eudaimonia* could be found in a retreat from the world at large into "the Garden," the Stoic conception requires an active engagement with it as a matter of duty. The late (Roman) Stoics including Cicero, Seneca, and Marcus Aurelius, were themselves actively engaged with the politics of their time, often to their own detriment.

It is worth noting that in contrast to Aristotle's view of the requirements for citizenship, the Stoic emphasis on human rationality is a highly democratic one and is not limited to a particular segment of the populace (e.g., free males). Women and even slaves were considered by Stoic thinkers as capable of the potential for "sage" status. Epictetus was himself a slave.

The Stoic emphasis on the public welfare dominates individual self-interested behavior. Cicero is explicit about this in *De Officiis* where he writes:

> To deprive another man of something, to increase your own comfort by making another man miserable, is more against nature than death, poverty, pain and other misfortune that can happen to one's body or possessions. In the first place, such an act does away with human society and social cooperation. [If we are so demoralized that a man will rob or injure another man to achieve a private advantage, it necessarily follows that what is preeminently "according to nature," the social structure of the human race will disintegrate.]
>
> (Cicero 1974: Book 3, 21)

Not only does Cicero enjoin the "good man" from taking from others to benefit himself in the interest of social stability, he also positively urges him to work on behalf of the common welfare. There can be no doubt as to the communitarian commitment implied by Cicero's position. Moreover, this commitment extends beyond the borders of one's own nation as the following makes clear:

> By the same argument, it is more "according to nature" to take upon yourself enormous work and trouble in order to preserve and aid all the nations ... . These actions are preferable to living for yourself, not merely apart from every trouble, but also in the midst of all kinds of delicacies, amid the most refined pleasures, surpassing all others in beauty and strength (25).

It seems clear that the Stoic sage in Cicero's light does not seek a life of hedonic pleasure and certainly not in the circumstances that such a life denies others, both those close to us and those far away in place, the necessities of life.

If there is any confusion about Cicero's ultimate commitment to the social good, he does us the favor of simplifying the Stoic imperative for virtue:

there ought to be one single rule for everyone: that which benefits each individual and what benefits all mankind should be identical. If any individual seizes an advantage for himself, the whole of human society will break apart (26).

The Stoic emphasis on impartiality would seem to provide us with a basis to advocate for a wide distribution of environmental benefits as well as an equitable sharing of the costs of preserving and conserving environmental resources.[10] His "single rule for everyone" seems to morally preclude the private appropriation of critically important environment resources by any individual or group if the risk of "human society will break apart" occurs.

Finally, are there any grounds for believing that Stoic ethics takes into account inter-generational claims that are also central to our concerns with sustainability? The answer is "yes" and once again it comes from Cicero (citing Stoic authority):

It is thought wicked and inhuman to profess indifference about whether the world will go up in flames once one is dead (the sentiment is usually articulated in a familiar Greek verse). And so it is undoubtedly true that we must consider on their own account the interests of those who will one day come after us.

(Cicero 2001, Book 3, 64)

The relevance of Cicero's admonition to our contemporary environmental challenges is evident. It is neither permissible to allow the world to "go up in flames once one is dead" nor to permit future generations to contend with the violent climate change that science has tied to our present use of fossil fuels. The potential dislocations and suffering associated with anthropogenic climate change imposes on us an unavoidable moral responsibility that will not wait years to reveal itself. They are already becoming manifest.

Beyond Cicero's assertion, I believe there are two additional entry ways by which Stoic ethics leads us to intergenerational commitment. The first is the Stoic emphasis on the universality of our obligations to other people. There would seem to be no compelling *a priori* reason to bring human beings of a different place within the orbit of our ethical concern but to exclude human beings of a different time. There would seem to be no logically or ethically compelling reason then not to consider the needs of future generations for environmental values as we do the needs of people here and now, at home and abroad. The other avenue involves the Stoic emphasis on reciprocity and solidarity as guiding ethical principles. Here we may argue that we have an obligation to pursue a sustainable future precisely because as citizens of a "cosmic city" we would expect our forebears to do the same in our own interest. We meet our obligations to those virtuous forebears for their contributions to our welfare with a like degree of consideration for those who are to follow.[11]

The economics and ethics of recycling

A useful case study to consider for its relevance to the questions raised in this chapter concerns the question of recycling as a "green" consumer practice and as a public policy choice. Like many practical environmental issues, recycling has inherent economic and ethical complexities. These complexities are compounded by the fact that the U.S. has no national mandatory recycling requirements, and such policy is largely determined at the state and local levels. While most states have some sort of disposal bans, on e.g. acid containing batteries and other toxins, only 19 states have mandatory recycling law of at least one commodity, and only 11 states have bottle bills (NERC 2011). This "federalist" approach is typically rationalized with the argument that the individual states have different capacities and needs as they pertain to waste management and that a national, uniform recycling policy would be economically inefficient and an imposition on states' rights. This position has an understandable appeal inasmuch as states are differentially endowed with both population and space available for landfill. If the case for recycling rests on its environmental and economic attractiveness as an alternative to dumping wastes in landfill, then it makes sense to allow states to set their own policies in relation to the relative price of landfill in their localities. It might even seem that some states have a comparative advantage in landfill-intensive waste management relative to others and import (for a fee) solid wastes from higher-priced landfill states, rendering recycling less urgent even in those states where landfill capacity has reached its limits and prices are high. This is precisely the argument made by very pro-market economists such as Michael C. Munger (2013) who takes exception to several of the core beliefs of those who hold fast to their almost religious conviction in the environmentally redemptive powers of recycling. Among these beliefs is the notion that *everything* that can be recycled, should be recycled. As Munger points out, this attitude does not make good economic sense for all potentially recyclable commodities, and in some cases, it doesn't make environmental sense either.

Much of the economic case in favor of recycling depends on the prices that the market is willing to pay for recycled commodities. Currently, some recycled commodities like aluminum and steel have high re-sale prices due in part to the high costs of mining and processing the raw materials out of which they are made. The same cannot currently be said of many plastics given low oil prices. Consideration must also be given to the costs associated with the processing of the recyclables themselves. Plastics, once again, are a complicated case. They are far from homogenous having differences in chemical composition, molecular structure, and manufactured/molding characteristics that have implications for their potential as recyclables. The different commodities must be sorted and cleaned, and then decomposed into resin before they can be manufactured back into new plastics, (MacBride 2012). All of these processing costs must be evaluated in relation to the cost of disposal into a landfill and/or the cost of production of new plastics from virgin materials. Consequently, some plastics (e.g., polyethylene terephthalate, or PET) have high-value as recyclables, while others (e.g., polyvinyl chloride, or PVC, polystyrene, or PS, low-density polyethylene, or LDPE) have lower recovery prospects based on standard economic considerations (Hopewell et al 2009). The economic case for plastics recycling is further undermined by the fact that oil and gas prices are currently quite low. Since these fossil fuels are the prime feedstocks out of which virgin materials for new plastics may be produced, it may be more economical to send used plastics to the landfill. At least this is the argument advanced by Munger and others.

I would argue that Munger underestimates the case for recycling, and this underestimation applies with force to the recycling of plastics. A part of the failure of his argument is in the narrowness of his economic logic. For Munger the results of any production can be categorized as *resources* or *waste*. A resource, says Munger, is anything that someone is willing to pay for. Everything else is waste, and should be disposed of as efficiently as possible. To his credit Munger recognizes that our decision-making in this respect should be based on "correct prices" in order to be socially optimal. Correct prices would necessarily include those associated with environmental goods and services. The problem with Munger's analysis is that it is not at all apparent that he understands what to count as an environmental good or service, and how this accounting will affect "correct prices." In the case of plastics it would seem that we need to recognize the fact that these materials are non-biodegradable, long-lasting and often contain chemicals of known toxicity. We also need to be cognizant of the environmental cost of producing new plastics out of virgin materials. Not only are plastics made from materials derived from fossil fuels, but their manufacture is highly energy intensive. An important benefit of recycling is the reduced carbon footprint and the reduction of greenhouse gases it entails as compared to that associated with new production. It is not apparent that Munger considers such environmental costs and benefits precisely because it is difficult, maybe impossible, to assign them prices. How do we price, for example, the costs of changing concentrations of greenhouse gases in the atmosphere? The strong balance of scientific opinion is that global climate change due to anthropogenic factors is the reality we face for the foreseeable future. And yet our understanding of precisely how to measure the economic impact of these changes is far from clear. Munger himself recognizes the difficulty of "getting the prices right" when environmental costs and benefits enter the calculation. He makes clear, however, his preference for relying on market signals even in the face of this imprecision as opposed to making recycling a "moral issue." He states:

> Now, perhaps we need to use moral arguments to compensate for the fact that we have to charge "too low" a price for landfills. But moral arguments are blunt. Prices allow contingent imperatives: recycle when, but only if, it's cheaper. Moral claims about recycling cannot be modulated: if recycling is good, more recycling is better. And the ideal is to recycle

everything. The problem is that, from economic perspective, from the perspective of balancing resource use, that's just not true.

(Munger 2013: 11–12)

It seems that Munger gives the market too much credit and the moral out-look too little. He is willing to embrace the signals provided by imperfect prices, but considers the moral perspective to be too "blunt" to provide operational guidance. Perhaps Munger's difficulty is that he understands only a deontological type of environmental ethics (e.g., "recycle everything").[12] If he were to adopt a virtue ethics approach of the Stoic type (i.e., "right reason") he might say "recycle the right things, at the right time, in the right place, for the right reasons." I do not believe that such an approach would amount to "recycle everything." It would not, for example, endorse recycling if this required taking measures that undermined the over-riding goal of human sustainability, or if it degraded the environment for future generations of human beings, or if it threatened the non-human elements of the environment required for human flourishing.

The exercise of right reason in the context of the recycling question would also recognize that there are alternatives to recycling and disposal in a landfill. "Reduce and reuse" are two such alternatives. An environmentally mindful consumer will take environmental consequences into account in making purchasing decisions, thereby sending price signals to firms to also take such consequences into account. Public policy also has a necessary and vital role to play. Some municipalities (e.g., New York, San Francisco, and Sacramento) have banned the use of single-use plastic bags and there is a statewide referendum for November 2016 that would extend the prohibition in California. Extended producer responsibility (EPR) legislation would force producers to take opera-tional and fiscal responsibility for the costs of collecting, separation, sorting, and cleaning of the myriad types of plastics that enter the waste stream. Fees, or outright prohibitions, on plastics of known toxicity would provide incentives to industries to redesign efforts to reduce their introduction into the waste stream. Such policy initiatives are bound to encounter political opposition from industry groups resistant to the idea that they internalize the negative environmental externalities of their production and commercial activities (MacBride 2012: 195). There is reason provided by the strong positive response of consumers to recycling programs themselves to suppose that such resistance to EPR can be overcome. An important step in crafting an effective environmental policy in the matter of plastics use and recycling must begin by educating the public on the potential benefits and costs of particular pro-grams where these benefits and costs are understood not in the narrow terms of standard economics considerations but in terms of the larger scope of ecological economics.

This last point gets us to another important short-coming in Munger's position that recycling should be framed strictly as an economic rather than an ethical issue. His argument that market prices provide an adequate guide to our decision-making and, therefore, in most cases to our public policy choices places a great deal of faith in the ancillary assumption that those prices reflect the public will. But as most economists will readily recognize, at best, market prices reflect the public will contingent on a particular distribution of income and purchasing power. Changes in income distribution imply changes in the pattern of market demand and quite possibly changes in the relative valuation of environmental goods and services versus manufactured goods and services. This shortcoming is all the more obvious when we turn our attention to the question of sustainability and our obligations to future generations. The reason for this is that the beneficiaries of the services of nature do not register their preferences in any market or market-like process. They must rely on the good faith and beneficence of their forebears. As explained above, whether this faith is well-founded is entirely a matter of the latter's virtue as both Sadler and the Stoics contend.

Virtue, markets, and the environment

Environmental economists, like most economists generally speaking, set great store by the ability of the market mechanism to provide efficient outcomes in the allocation of goods, services, and resources. Thus, for example, it is often argued that markets for pollution rights, also known as "cap-and-trade," are an efficient way to address the challenge of environmental protection. Markets for pollution rights are efficient in the sense that they enable high-cost pollution abaters to transfer a disproportionate share of the burden of pollution reduction to low-cost pollution abaters. Achieving a given level of environmental cleanliness, thereby, comes at a lower cost than it would if no such discrimination occurred. The approach also has the advantage of enabling the polluters themselves to devise the most cost effective technological means of meeting the chosen environmental standard. Objections to cap-and-trade include the argument that there is something illegitimate about the creation of markets that encourages us to use nature as a sink for our wastes. Another objection is that tradeable pollution rights seem like a mechanism wherein some wealthy people and firms are able to avoid an obligation to protect the environment that is in fact, or at least should be, a universal one. In general and in its operational particulars, marketable pollutions rights would seem to have little in common with environmental virtue. I wish to argue that this is not necessarily the case.

There are a couple of points at which environmental virtue ethics gains entry into the discussion of marketable pollution rights. The first and most obvious entry point involves the question of pollution cap. Applied to the issue of atmospheric carbon, to take one important example, it is estimated that a sustainable future will require that we reduce carbon to a level of 350 parts per million (ppm) from its current level of 385 ppm (Hansen et al 2008). Achieving this target will require a substantial modification of how we produce and consume energy. A re-conception of the good life along the lines outlined by the Hellenistic philosophers would provide a starting point for this modification. A second demand placed on our virtue involves the initial allocation of pollution rights. A workable global agreement on climate change will need to recognize the asymmetries of need and responsibility that attach to the nations of world as well as the recognition of existing inequalities of opportunity within every nation. The ends of environmental and distributive justice would seem to require that a global auction mechanism be established that enables the value of pollution rights be captured and distributed to those nations and subnational social groups to whom an environmental debt is owed. An additional role for virtue would be played by those global environmental agencies charged with monitoring and enforcing the limits established by the emissions cap. The point here is not to spell out in detail the specific design of the institutions required for environmental virtue. It is only to illustrate that as a matter of principle there is no inconsistency in a marriage of market instrumentality with a commitment to environmental virtue given the design and operation of virtuous institutions.

Notes

1 Hughes's book was previously published in 1994 under the title *Pan's Travail Environmental Problems of the Ancient Greeks and Romans*.
2 "Tragedy of the commons" refers to the tendency of users of open, common resources to overexploit those resources since none of them individually has an incentive to exercise moderation, and all are aware that each other user is similarly motivated. Garrett Hardin (1968) is credited with popularizing these ideas.
3 Bookchin (1994: 119–120) (emphasis in original).
4 It is important to note that Solow himself is aware of the problem of market failure as it relates to the natural environment and advocates government policy to correct its welfare-reducing distortions.
5 The genesis of the argument for the intrinsic value (IV) of nature probably begins as early as White Jr. (1967). An early anthropocentric rejoinder was provided by Passmore (1974). Norton (1991) provides very useful discussion of the IV-anthropocentric debate from both a practical political as well as philosophical perspective. Norton argues that the case for the IV view ultimately rests on an "intuitionalist" apprehension of nature's intrinsic value.
6 Hughes (2014: 66) provides an overview of ancient Greek and Roman thought on environmental issues and concludes, "it is almost impossible to identify a general pattern of environmental effects deriving from the competitive philosophies of the ancient world."
7 Bruni and Sugden (2013) have recently made an appeal for a consideration of virtue ethics as applying to standard economics. This appeal will be considered in the concluding chapter of this book.
8 This is especially so given the primacy of the so-called "precautionary principle" (PP) that holds such a prominent position in environmental policy discussions. PP is the recommendation that the burden of proof falls on those wishing to exploit natural resources to show that no harm to the ecology will result.
9 Irwin (2003: 347, n. 6) argues that the Stoic commitment to a life in accord with nature refers to both human nature as a rational animal as well as cosmic nature more generally.

10 As I argue elsewhere (Richards 2017), an equitable sharing of environmental costs and benefits may require a reconceptualization of global environmental property right.
11 See Gill (1998) for a discussion of reciprocity, solidarity, and altruism in ancient Greek ethics.
12 Munger's truncated understanding of ethical understanding is shared by his market co-religionist, Steven Landsburg (2013) who states:

> When you cast policy issues in moral terms, you degrade the character of public discourse. You lead people to see conflicting priorities as an occasion for battle, rather than an occasion for compromise. You send the message that policy is best decided by appeals to one's inner conscience (or, more likely, to the polemics of demagogues), rather than by appeals to impersonal cost-benefit analysis.

Apparently, Landsburg's taste for compromise includes no basis for policy discussion between the alternatives of "polemics of demagogues" and "impersonal cost-benefit analysis."

References

Bookchin, Murray. 1994. *The Philosophy of Social Ecology: Essays on Dialectical Naturalism*, Montreal: Black Rose Books.

Bruni, Luigino and Robert Sugden. 2013. "Reclaiming virtue ethics for economics," *Journal of Economic Perspectives*, 27, 4 (Fall): 141–164.

Cafaro, Philip. 2005. "Thoreau, Leopold, and Carson: toward an environmental virtue ethics," in *Environmental Virtue Ethics*, R. Sandler and P. Cafaro (eds.), Lantham: Rowman & Littlefield.

Cicero. 1974. *De Officiis/On Duties*, translated by H. G. Edinger, Indianapolis, IN: Bobbs-Merrill Company, Inc.

Cicero. 2001. *De Finibus/On Moral Ends*, edited by Julia Annas, translated by Raphael Woolf, Cambridge: Cambridge University Press.

Gill, Christopher. 1998. "Altruism or reciprocity in Greek ethical philosophy?" in *Reciprocity in Ancient Greece*, C. Gill, N. Postlethwaite, and R. Seaford (eds.), Oxford: Oxford University Press.

Hansen, J., M. Sato, P. Kharecha, D. Beerling, R. Berner, V. Masson-Delmotte, M. Pagani, M. Raymo, D. L. Royer, and J. C. Zachos. 2008. "Target atmospheric CO2: Where should humanity aim?," *Open Atmospheric Science Journal*, 2: 217–231.

Hardin, Garrett. 1968. "Tragedy of the commons," *Science*, 162, 3859 (December): 1243–1248.

Hopewell, Jefferson, Robert Dvorak, and Edward Kosior. 2009. "Plastics recycling: Challenges and opportunities," *Philosophical Transactions of the Royal Society B*, 364: 2115–2126.

Hughes, J. Donald. 2014. *Environmental Problems of the Greeks and Romans, Second Edition*, Baltimore: Johns Hopkins University Press.

Irwin, T. H. 2003. "Stoic naturalism and its critics," in *The Cambridge Companion to the Stoics*, B. Inwood (ed.), Cambridge: Cambridge University Press.

Kimpel, Ben. 1985. *Stoic Moral Philosophies: Their Counsel for Today*. New York: Philosophical Library.

Landsburg, Steven E. 2013. "Don't cast recycling as a moral issue," *Cato Unbound*, June 11, http://www.cato-unbound.org/2013/06/11/steven-e-landsburg/dont-cast-recycling-moral-issue.

Layard, Richard. 2005. *Happiness: Lessons from a New Science*, New York: Penguin Books.

Long, A. A. 1996. *Stoic Studies*, Cambridge: Cambridge University Press.

MacBride, Samantha. 2012. *Recycling Reconsidered: The Present Failure and Future Promise of Environmental Action in the United States*, Cambridge: MIT Press.

Mills, Stephanie. 2002. *Epicurean Simplicity*, Washington, DC: Island Books.

Munger, Michael C. 2013. "Recycling: Can it be wrong, when it feels so right?," *Cato Unbound*, June 3: 1–21, http://www.ewp.rpi.edu/hartford/~ernesto/S2014/SHWPCE/Papers/SW-Preprocessing-Separation-Recycling/Munger2013-Recycling.pdf.

NERC. 2011. "Disposal bans & mandatory recycling in the United States," The Northeast Recycling Council, Inc., June 24, https://nerc.org/documents/disposal_bans_mandatory_recycling_united_states.pdf.

Norton, Bryan G. 1991. *Toward Unity among Environmentalists*, New York: Oxford University Press.

Passmore, John. 1974. *Man's Responsibility for Nature.* New York: Scribner's.

Richards, Donald G. 2017. "Ecological economics, property rights, and the environmental 'meta-commons'", in *Exploring Property Rights in Contemporary Governance*, S. Zavattaro, G. Peterson, and A. Davis, (eds.), New York: SUNY Press.

Rolston III, Holmes. 2005. "Environmental virtue ethics: Half the truth but dangerous as a whole," in *Environmental Virtue Ethics*, R. Sandler and P. Cafaro (eds.), Lantham: Rowman & Littlefield.

Sagoff, Mark. 2002. "The hedgehog, the fox, and the enviroement," in *The Moral Authority of Environmental Decision Making*, J. M. Gillroy and J. Bowersox (eds.) Durham, NC: Duke University Press.

Sandler, Ronald. 2010. "Ethical theory and the problem of inconsequentialism: Why environmental ethicists should be virtue-oriented ethicists," *Journal of Agriculture and Environmental Ethics*, 23, 1–2: 167–183.

Sandler, Ronald and Philip Cafero. 2005. *Environmental Virtue Ethics*, Lantham: Rowman & Littlefield.

Skidelsky, Robert. 2010. *Keynes: The Return of the Master.* New York: Public Affairs.

Solow, Robert. 1991. "Sustainability: An economist's perspective," 18th J. Seward Johnson Lecture to the Marine Policy Center, Woods Hole Oceanographic Institution, Woods Hole, MA, June 14.

Stephens, William O. 1994. "Stoic naturalism, rationalism, and ecology," *Environmental Ethics*, 16, 3 (Fall): 275–286.

White Jr., Lynn. 1967. "The historical roots of our ecological crisis," *Science*, 155: 1203–1207.

7   Reason, ethics, and the end of life

Death is a comparatively unmined research area for economists though it hasn't been completely overlooked by the discipline. Economists and other social scientists have certainly conducted research on the determinants of mortality. It is fairly central to studies of such issues as life insurance and risk, bequests, and certain forensic matters. Studies of life-cycle behavior are also implicitly concerned with human mortality. A seemingly important lacunae in economic research as it bears on the monumental fact of human mortality, however, concerns welfare theory. There does not seem to be much examination of the normative content of either economic behavioral assumptions, nor of policy questions, related to our ultimate end. The areas of economics that do touch on human mortality seem as dedicated to the normative/ethical tradition of rational choice hedonism as any other part of the discipline's mainstream research program.

The position I take in this chapter is that the discipline can and should do better in its approach to the implications of human mortality for human choice-making, and that its limitations are precisely due to the thinness of its normative-ethical presuppositions as discussed in Chapter 4. I further propose that insights for fleshing out the ethical foundations of economics useful for policy formulation may be obtained through the study of ancient philosophy and particularly that of the Hellenistic period of Greek and Roman civilization. The Epicurean and Stoic schools of ancient ethical thought, in common with their classical ancient Greek predecessors, emphasized a eudaimonic conception of the good life. *Eudaimonia* recall basically translates to human flourishing or, even more simply, human happiness and provides a superior normative-ethical foundation than the narrower, hedonic tradition that underlies mainstream economic theory and policy. Moreover, the Hellenistic philosophers in developing their ethical principles paid explicit attention to the role played by human mortality. As I shall argue, this again contrasts to the comparatively superficial, added-on treatment it tends to receive in the hands of mainstream economic thought. This contrast, I shall further argue, has potentially important relevance to some public policy issues related to end-of-life concerns that are of contemporary urgency. Among those given close attention here are palliative health care and physician-assisted suicide.

Each of these issues has been the focus of intense and often emotional debate in recent years.

Ancients ethics and mortality

Epicurus believed, like most other Greek philosophers, that *eudaimonia* was to be pursued via the application of correct reasoning. What distinguishes Epicurean rationality from other Greek ethics, however, is the belief that "right reason" leads people to a life dedicated to the pursuit of pleasure. Epicurean ethics, then, is hedonic in its orientation. In this it has something in common with the normative basis for modern, mainstream economic theory with its emphasis on utility maximization as its driving behavioral assumption. However, as argued in Chapter 4, this similarity is a superficial one. Whereas the standard economic story sees all sources of utility as being fully commensurate with one another, the Epicurean view argues for a hierarchy of pleasures and urges those who seek *eudaimonia* to pursue "genuine pleasures."

The Epicurean philosophy is frequently summarized in terms of four basic truths (Bergsma et al 2008):

1 Don't fear the gods.
2 Don't worry about death.
3 What is good is easy to get.
4 What is terrible is easy to endure.

Let us briefly examine the basic arguments that support (1), (3), and (4) and then take a more detailed look at those used to rationalize (2). Epicurean theology asserts that while god exists, s/he does not take an active, interventionist role in our lives. Having created the universe god seems content to allow it to unfold as it will. Thus, people have no reason to fear the gods on this count. Likewise, in Epicurean theology there is neither heaven nor hell to which the soul is consigned after death, a position that has obvious consequences for the second of the above-listed truths. The important point is that human beings need not fear eternal damnation (nor the withholding of eternal bliss), and have no reason to fear the gods on these grounds.

As noted, Epicurean ethics is hedonist in its approach and argues that "the good" is to be understood as that which provides pleasure and avoids pain. Good choices are correspondingly understood as those that increase pleasure and reduce pain. These beliefs provide us with the perspective from which to appreciate truths (3) and (4). The Epicureans envision a hierarchy of pleasures with those associated with consumption accorded a lower position on the hedonic (i.e., pleasure) scale. Contrary to the modern perception of Epicureanism, as well as that of their own contemporary critics, the school did not emphasize sumptuous living. The Epicureans in fact are said to have practiced a minimalist standard of consumption. They believed that desires could be divided into natural and necessary, natural and unnecessary, and "groundless" (i.e., those based on false opinion). Necessary desires could be satisfied with minimal effort.[1] The attempt to satisfy groundless desires was a waste of time and effort as well as a cause of much avoidable error and hardship. Among the worst consequences of the pursuit of groundless desires is that it operates to distract the Epicurean sage from the higher-order pleasures associated with the pursuit of philosophy among like-minded friends.

The Epicureans recognized that life included the possibility of physical decline, disease, and pain. They believed, however, that these unfortunate circumstances could be managed. Most pain could be tolerated, and they proposed techniques to help people accomplish this. One such technique encouraged those in pain to focus their imaginations on previously experienced pleasures as a way to block out pain. Moreover, most ordinary pain was likely to be short lived, and physical recovery would provide relief. Intensely felt pain that did not find relief in recovery was also likely to be short-lived, with death providing the means of escape. This provides support to truth number two, "Don't worry about death," which is of particular relevance to the rest of this chapter and is for that reason deserving of close attention.

Central to the Epicurean conception of *eudaimonia* is its emphasis on the removal or avoidance of pain, both bodily and mental. The pleasure that the Epicureans seek has far more to do with tranquility and peace of mind (*ataraxia*) than it does with sensual delight. As death and dying are instinctive sources of anxiety for most people, Epicurean ethics is keen to reassure people that such anxiety is unnecessary and will not occupy the enlightened (i.e., rational) mind. For the Epicureans, "death is nothing to us." It is natural to ask, what are the sources of Epicurean confidence in the face of death? The argument in broad outline is straightforward: death is not an issue until it arrives, and until it arrives the business of the rational person is to live well. When death does arrive, the person, rational or otherwise, is no more, and does not (cannot) feel anything. Death then has no sentient object on which it can exercise any pain or evil. Better put, the critical assumption is that pain and evil require a subject; yet death removes the subject. Therefore, death presents no pain or evil for the deceased, and should not then be feared by the living. We shall consider some objections to this argument in a latter section.[2] For now let us recognize that the Epicurean outlook on death follows from their views on physics and theology. Namely, human beings are material things composed of atoms and subject to the fate of other material objects in the universe. After death human bodies decompose and return to the elements out of which they are constituted in the first place (i.e., "ashes to ashes; dust to dust"). Neither does the human soul survive after death. If this prospect is a source of anxiety for people, Epicurus advises that they consider that before they came into existence, they suffered no pain or evil. Why should the prospect of death invoke such anxiety of pain or evil when they simply resume their preexistent status as non-beings?

Stoic *eudaimonia* lay in possession of "the good." "The good" according to the Stoic account is entirely a matter of the embrace of virtue and the avoidance of vice. Virtue is seen as that which is in accord with nature. An understanding of this begins early in life as individuals select those things that serve them well (i.e., are in accord with their natures) and reject those that do not serve them well (i.e., are contrary to their natures). These things, however, are not in themselves virtuous, nor are they "goods" strictly speaking. External values such as health, wealth and good reputation are in accord with human well-being, but are not in themselves constitutive of the final end, which is virtue. They are neither necessary nor sufficient for virtue. A wealthy, healthy, individual with a sound reputation is capable of acting viciously. Likewise, a poor, sick person held in disrepute by his neighbors may behave virtuously. External benefits then are *preferred* by the Stoic sage; they are selected when their selection does not interfere with the pursuit of virtue; but they are morally indifferent to their opposites.

The Stoics maintain an outlook regarding life and death that is very similar to that of the Epicureans. That is, the Stoics do not regard the loss of life as the greatest of evils and is not to be feared by those who aspire to wisdom. Thorough-going rationalists, the Stoics enjoin the rational individual to recognize her own mortality and that of others, and to be prepared for the end of life. Like the Epicureans the Stoics do not believe that the afterlife holds any particular terrors or promise. The afterlife for all livings things is experientially the same as "pre-life," which is to say nothingness. If it makes no sense to fear pre-life, then it makes no more sense to fear the afterlife according to Stoic logic. In the words of Seneca (1969: 104):

> Death is just not being. What that is like I know already. It will be the same after me as it was before me. If there is any torment in the later state, there must also have been torment in the period before we saw the light of day; yet we never felt conscious of any distress then. I ask you, wouldn't you say that anyone who took the view that a lamp was worse off when it was put out than it was before it was lit was an utter idiot? We, too, are lit and put out. We suffer somewhat in the intervening period, but at either end of it there is a deep tranquility.

However limited is Seneca's analogy between human consciousness and a lamp, if we accept his metaphysical priors, his position on the "terrorlessness" of our non-existence seems quite reasonably argued. This particular fear, however, does not exhaust the grounds for human anxiety regarding their mortality. Some additional concerns will be addressed in sections below. A particularly salient issue to be discussed concerns the choice of suicide. The Stoics believed that suicide could be rational and in taking this position they stood at odds with the conventional wisdom of their day. The question of suicide in the ancient era was no less controversial and contentious than it is today. To understand the Stoic position and its possible relevance to the contemporary question of physician-assisted suicide, it will be helpful to review again the ancient conception of "rational" and how it departs from the "thin" understanding of this concept typical of modern analysis.

Mainstream economics and ancient accounts of mortality

As noted above, economics as an academic discipline has tended to shun the topic of death. Recognition of mortality in economics research typically has been limited to considerations of life-time optimization wherein the economic decision maker is assumed to be a fully rational inter-temporal maximizer of one objective function or another. Very few research efforts have been undertaken to determine the plausibility, or even meaning, of this strong underlying assumption of rational behavior in the face of death, or of the consequences of its violation. It may be that the comparative dearth of death studies by economists owes precisely to the discipline's strong preference for the standard rationality assumption. This militates against economics studies that focus closely on a consideration of mortality inasmuch as death is an issue on which many, maybe even most, people would rather not engage in thinking about deeply. If people are unable or unwilling to engage the fact of their mortality and its consequences, modeling their rational behavior in this respect becomes difficult or impossible.

An alternative approach available to economists, however, is to examine the implications of a departure from the standard rationality assumption as it bears on the prospect of death, or to investigate the consequences of death anxiety. The latter approach is taken by Kopczuk and Slemrod (2005), who posit the existence of an inter-temporal utility maximizing individual who is rational in the standard economic sense, but fears death. This fear is assumed to be a source of disutility. When confronted with signals of her mortality the individual has the option of repressing the information, or using it to inform the discount rate which in turn dictates the allocation of resources between present and future consumption. The consequence of such repression is that the decision-maker is operating on the basis of a deliberately reduced information set that results in an overly optimistic estimation of longevity and a misallocation of resources between present and future consumption. That is, such an individual will over-save, under-consume, and leave excess wealth upon her demise. The authors consider some variants of their basic model in which some individuals may be aware of their tendency to repress signals of mortality, and correspondingly adjust their resource allocation to mitigate this time inconsistency problem. They may even make a distinction between strong and weak signals of mortality. Appropriate reactions to these signals may suggest a type of optimally-repressive, death-denying behavior.

The approach developed by Kopczuk and Slemrod is in every important respect standard in its normative implications. Welfare is chiefly a function of the utility derived from consumption, though in this case utility is also derived (or disutility reduced) from the ability to avoid facing up to the important fact of one's mortality, at least for a while. Decision makers are assumed to be utility maximizers. Death itself is taken to be "a bad" only insofar as it places a limit on the utility derived from consumption. The "thinness" of this normative account is apparent.

Of the two Hellenistic schools of thought under consideration the one that is closest in spirit to the utilitarianism that underlies rational choice hedonism of modern economic theory is Epicureanism. It will be useful then to start with the Epicurean defense of its infamous position that "death is nothing to us." On the face of things, it would seem difficult to square the Epicurean position that the good life is one that is based on the enjoyment of pleasure and avoidance of pain with its equally committed position that death is not a harm. The economic argument embraced by Kopczuk and Slemrod suggests that death is indeed a harm inasmuch as it involves a deprivation of utility to the deceased. The Epicureans confront precisely this argument to demonstrate the contrary position. The Epicurean rejoinder to the economic argument that death deprives the deceased of additional opportunities for utility is a variant of the more general argument that death represents a harm. That is, death cannot deprive the deceased because the deceased does not exist as a sentient being capable of suffering the pain of deprivation.[3]

Green (1982: 105) offers a challenge to the Epicurean position, and a variant of the death as deprivation argument, when he defines fear as "an emotional response to expected disutility under conditions of subjective uncertainty." He goes on to describe a "rational" fear of death in the following way:

> It is natural to suppose that if this man fears that he will not live much longer, he fears death. After all, if he thinks he may not live long, this is presumably because he believes he may die soon. *And surely, if he wants to live longer, he would rather not die soon.* This being the case, it is hard to see how it could be rational for the man to fear that he hadn't long to live but not to fear death (105, italics added).

The problem with Green's logic is that he implicitly assumes that the Epicurean maxim, "death is nothing to us" amounts to an additional maxim, "life is nothing to us." Nothing could be further from the truth. In dismissing death fear the Epicurean sage does not turn her back on life. The Epicurean sage in fact exercises the virtues of prudence, moderation, and temperance in her decision-making precisely to enjoy the pleasure that life affords. Green's mistake is to interpret the exercise of these virtues as being motivated by a fear of death. The Epicurean, rather, sees the exercise of these virtues, along with study of the school's doctrine, as the key to the equanimity in the face of unavoidable death that aids her in the pursuit of the highest good. A well-lived life and a "good" death spring from the same well-developed habits of thought.

The very idea of a "rational fear" would be not be admissible in a Stoic courtroom. The whole point of reason for the Stoics is to bring the passions under control and fear, for them, is a kind of passion, or untethered emotion. Far from denying death as a means of minimizing the disutility of its fearsomeness, the Stoics enjoin us to confront it head on as a necessary part of a well-lived life. The Stoics believed that the habit of recognizing and paying close attention to our mortality would have a salutary effect on how we coped with the disturbances of life. They did not underestimate the challenge that consciousness of mortality represented to the human imagination. They recognized that all living things had an innate fear of death and this instinct was necessary to their survival. Kopczuk and Slemrod (2005: 1) give explicit account of this instinct in their economic analysis when they write:

> Fearfulness in the presence of a danger is a natural phenomenon that can be easily explained on evolutionary grounds: fear forces an individual to fully concentrate on its source and, therefore, facilitates survival. Fear arises when and if an immediate danger is perceived and leaves no room for manipulating it. If generalized death anxiety is a consequence of an evolutionary-grounded fear coupled with a fully rational understanding that one is mortal and therefore constantly endangered, cognitive strategies that lead to ignoring non-preventable risk play an important role.

Once again, this "rational fear" approach emphasizes repressing considerations of human mortality in the interests of utility related to present versus future consumption possibilities. The normative implications of this approach are in stark contrast to those of the Stoic view. Recall that for the Stoics what distinguishes adult human beings from other living organisms, at least potentially, is their rationality. The "at least potentially" qualifier recognizes that there is nothing automatic about an individual's ability to confront her mortality rationally. It takes practice. Thus, Epictetus (1995) urges us:

> Day by day you must keep before your eyes death and exile, and everything that seems terrible, but death above all; and then you will never have any abject thought, or desire anything beyond due measure (fragment 25: 293).

For the Stoic death seems terrible to the unwise, but this impression is related to a *failure* of rationality. The Stoic view is that everything that is good is under our control. This is the meaning of virtue. The things that are not under our control, those that are subject to fortune, including our lives, are not in themselves good. They may in certain circumstances be preferred, but they are not themselves constitutive of the good. The Stoic sage then would never say that life is good and death is bad. What the sage would assert is that how we live life and face death is either good or bad, virtuous or vicious, a matter of right reason or wrong reason. Undoubtedly, for most of us this outlook would be considered severe. It is highly counter-intuitive to our modern imaginations, just as it was for the many contemporaries of the ancient Stoics themselves, not to regard life as a good and death as an evil. And yet it is not hard to find examples in which people have set aside life in favor of something they regard as more fundamentally important than themselves (e.g., a belief, a cause, another person, a tribe or nation). Neither is it hard to find less heroic instances in which people have voluntarily set aside life in favor of dignity. At the same time it is not difficult to identify instances wherein people cling to life beyond the point at which it would offer any hope of pleasure, or even the exercise of anything approaching normal human functioning. This behavior is especially typical in consideration of what we may call "end-of-life" decisions to which we turn next.

Health care and the "end-of-life"

It has become a part of the conventional wisdom that U.S. healthcare is serviced by a high technology, high cost, and inefficient system.[4] This is especially true of so-called "end-of-life" care defined as treatments for chronic illnesses suffered in the last two years of life which are estimated to account for 32 percent of total Medicare spending (Wennberg et al 2008). The authors of the previously noted study argue that the source of much inefficiency in end-of-life health care is related to what they term "supply-sensitive care." This is the statistical tendency for expenditures on particular treatments for chronic diseases to correlate with the availability in a given region of resources (e.g., medical specialists, medical technology, hospital beds) to treat those diseases (Wennberg et al 2008: 3). These same authors further argue that there is no direct relationship between the amount of medical services provided and the quality of outcome.

The "more is better" approach is part and parcel of standard economic theory that emphasizes a direct relation between inputs and outputs as embodied in the concept of the production function. In the case of medical care, the presumption is that an increase in medical resources (inputs) will lead to an increase in health and longevity (output).[5] This attitude finds expression in the actual allocation of resources insofar as practitioners will seek to utilize their productive capacity to its fullest potential. This is especially true of the American healthcare system where specialists are compensated on a "fee for service" basis. Hospitals and health centers compete with one another by seeking to acquire the latest diagnostic and treatment technologies, and they have an incentive to recover their costs by making maximal use of the techniques.

A great deal of inefficiency also occurs in an attempt to address the preferences of patients who are faced with chronic illness and from which they have little chance of survival. Such patients are confronted with the dilemma of choosing between treatments intended to extend life as long as possible and having a degree of control over the terms and circumstances of their demise. Wennberg et al (2008: 16) note that a study of patient advance directives indicating a preference to die at home showed that a majority of these (55 percent) actually died in a hospital, while less than half (46 percent) of patients who wished to die in a hospital did not. Not surprisingly perhaps, they note that the chances of a patient dying in a hospital are directly related to the availability of hospital beds in the patient's region. The authors state, "The available evidence thus suggests that patients prefer a more conservative pattern of end-of-life care than they actually receive.

The capacity of the local health care system often trumps patient preference" (Wennberg et al 2008: 17).

The Patient Self-Determination Act (PSDA) of 1991 was passed to give patients more rights to dictate their course of treatment, to refuse particular treatments, and to formulate Advanced Care Directives (ACDs), including Do Not Resuscitate (DNR) orders. Hospitals (though not individual doctors) are required to provide patients with the necessary information to exercise these rights and to include the relevant documentation in their medical records and files. The decades of the 1980s and 1990s also saw an increased use of hospice and palliative care options as ways to more effectively address the needs of patients with life-threatening illnesses and to hold down the cost of end-of-life health care. Research on these measures show them to have been largely successful on the first of these objectives, but a much less clear picture on the latter objective has yet to emerge.

In his review of several randomized and non-randomized trials of the effectiveness of hospice and ACDs in generating cost savings, Emanuel (1996) describes the methodological obstacles involved. These include:

1   patient self-selection bias in the use of the interventions;
2   varying time frames of assessment which affects the types and period range over which costs are considered;
3   the kinds of costs that are considered (e.g., Medicare Part A, hospital-related costs versus Part B, out-patient costs);
4   different methods of reporting savings; and
5   differences in the types of patients and illnesses considered.

Where savings are detected, argues Emanuel, they appear to originate from Part A expenditures in the last months of life. More recently Gade et al (2008) in a multi-center, randomized study find that palliative care is associated with greater patient satisfaction, a lower rate of ICU admissions, and lower total health care costs following hospital discharge, with average costs equal to $4,855 per patient.

There seems to be general agreement among medical and health economics researchers that much more study on the economic impact of such alternative courses of treatment, such as hospice and palliative care and interventions such as DNRs and ACDs, is needed. It is repeatedly noted in the literature (SUPPORT 1995; Schneiderman et al 1992) that the failure of such approaches to result in unambiguous cost savings is the lack of systemic coordination in end-of-life care courses of treatment as well as inadequate prior preparation and communication on the parts of both patients and health care providers, including physicians.

Notwithstanding the mixed findings regarding the cost savings effects of hospice, palliative care, and ACDs, Emanuel (1996: 1914) argues that such measures should be actively promoted by policy makers insofar as they are found to at least not increase costs while addressing patients' needs more effectively and respecting their autonomy. To achieve the desired cost savings will require more. He writes:

> This does not mean that we cannot achieve huge medical savings near the end of life. Such savings would require Americans to drastically reduce their use of medical tests and technology over many months before death. And this, in turn, necessitates a radical transformation in American culture and values about the importance of youth and health toward the acceptance of death as a natural and inevitable part of life.[6]

Physician-assisted suicide (PAS)

The question of suicide as a response to deterioration in the quality of life has received heightened attention in recent years. Relatedly, the issue of the role played by the medical industry in relation to suicide has also been a focus of increased debate. Five states have established by statute or court decision the right of physicians to assist their patients in taking their own lives, and the issue has been actively considered in several others.[7] In most other states PAS is treated as a felony with punishment involving heavy financial penalties and/ or prison terms of up to 15 years. The Supreme Court of the United States has considered arguments to establish a right to PAS and has thus far rejected those based on the Due Process and Equal Protection Clauses of the Constitution (White 2015).

Generally speaking, opposition to PAS rests on a number of objections and concerns. Primary among these is fear of exploitation wherein it is argued that many of those who might consider PAS are near the end of their natural lives. They are often sick and/or disabled and unable to provide for their own care. They may also be under overt or subtle pressure from third parties (including relatives) to end their lives. Essentially, this is an argument that recognizes the potential of loss of autonomy and the need to protect individuals who might be victimized by removing the possibility of a choice to end their lives. Another argument in opposition to PAS is that people who are considering suicide are by definition under extreme physical and/or mental duress, and are therefore unfit to make such a final and irrevocable decision. By this argument it is denied that suicide can ever be a rational choice and that people should be protected from this sort of irrationality. A third argument offered in opposition to PAS is that it establishes a "slippery slope" precedent. That is, once a legal right to PAS has been established, it has the potential to evolve into a kind of generalized cultural expectation. Once again, the underlying logic to this type of argument is based on a fear of a lack of true autonomy among vulnerable populations. A fourth argument is that it is unreasonable to expect medical professionals, who have devoted their professional lives, and taken an oath, to promote health and life to be part of a process that is contrary to those same ends. Moreover it is argued that palliative care offers an alternative to PAS. The anticipated pain and suffering that those who might choose PAS can be successfully mitigated to a far greater extent than is commonly realized rendering suicide an inferior and unnecessary choice. Finally, it is frequently argued by some opponents of PAS that no one has a right to choose death under any circumstances as a moral matter. This is a position adopted by many religious groups, especially the Catholic Church which is actively organized in opposition to extending the right to PAS in states where it currently does not exist (Gummere 2014; Doerflinger and Gomez 2016).

In states where PAS is legally established by statute, enabling legislation has been crafted that meets several of the above-listed objections. In Oregon, where PAS has legally operated since 1997, and therefore has the longest record of experience, the law requires that a prescription for a lethal dose of medication for a patient who suffers from a terminal illness must stipulate he is not likely to survive more than six months. The prognosis must be confirmed by two physicians including the one writing the prescription. The patient must be examined by a psychiatrist or a psychologist to establish that he does not suffer from impaired judgment stemming from mental illness such as depression. The patient must be judged not to be making an impulsive decision or to be under some external compulsion to end his life. In order to minimize risk of an impulsive decision, the patient must submit both a written request and two oral requests for the prescription within a fifteen day period. Patients must also be informed of alternative care treatments such as hospice (Ganzini 2016).

The slippery slope argument (SSA) against PAS has been criticized both as a general form of argument and in its specific details as it applies to PAS. In the first of these it is noted that the SSA is less a cohesive argument than a form of rhetorical fallacy wherein a critic of practice A admits the provisional acceptability/legitimacy of A, but as a practical/political matter resists A on the grounds that enabling it will set the stage for its extensions into unacceptable/illegitimate domains. Implicit in the SSA is an unacknowledged assumption that the decision-making/legislative apparatus is incapable of assessing potential extensions of A into other domains on their merits. It argues rather the momentum of A's success will establish additional, noxious extensions of the practice.[8] Applied to the question of PAS, evidence in support of the SSA is said to adduce from the case of the Netherlands where initially the law permitted PAS in the case of terminally ill patients, but over time has been extended to permit the practice to those who are chronically ill, whose suffering is psychological, and for incompetent patients, including children (Benatar 2011). Whether or not we would wish to establish a PAS law identical in all respects to the Dutch law is a debate worth having on its merits.[9] The SSA, it must be recognized, is an effort to forestall such a debate.

Palliative care advocates are typically among the strongest opponents of PAS (Radbruch et al 2016). The consensus opinion among palliative care proponents is that such care can successfully mitigate end-of-life physical pain and suffering while tending to the spiritual and psychological needs of terminally ill patients. Under the most extreme cases of such distress, it is argued that palliative sedation offers a clear alternative to PAS in the final days and hours of life. Those who advance the argument for the legalization of PAS rejoin that this does not go far enough in granting to the patient the requisite autonomy and self-determination that we would connect to a fully human and well-lived life. As Benatar (2011: 207) notes:

> Not everyone agrees about just how bad life must be before it ceases to be worth living. However, the fact of that disagreement provides no more reason for prohibiting euthanasia than it does for requiring it. To force people to die when they think that their lives are still worth living would be an undue interference with people's freedom. It is no less a violation of human freedom to force a continuation of life when people believe that their continued life is worse than death.

The legalization of PAS and normalization of palliative care, of course, are not only medical, that is to say technical, matters. They are also highly charged ethical ones. As I have argued in this book the normative basis of standard economic theory is limited in its ability to account for some important issues involving human choices. So-called end-of-life choices would seem to fit into the category of those questions beyond the scope of standard economics to handle well. The very lack of economics literature on such issues is telling in this regard. With that in mind we might consider what insights from the ancients might provide us concerning the relationship between the well-lived life and the end of a well-lived life.

Hellenistic philosophy and end-of-life problems

Even if we hesitate to embrace the Epicurean claim that "death is nothing to us," there is much in the Hellenistic perspective that can contribute to the cultural transformation that Emanuel recommends.[10] The Epicurean injunction that severe pain is necessarily short-lived may also not necessarily be true, but a major objective of hospice and palliative care is to manage pain. It is far truer today than it was in ancient times that the physical pain associated with chronic illness and dying is manageable via drugs and other therapies. Moreover, if we can accept the Epicurean argument that the fact of our inevitable demise holds no terrible prospect of pain and suffering in the afterlife, this would further remove a substantial portion of the terror associated with death. While this will not be an easy transformation for many people, it would seem that their chances are enhanced to the extent that death and dying become less taboo subjects for reflection and discussion. This, it seems to me, is where the Hellenistic philosophies potentially provide their greatest contribution to our current health care dilemma as it relates to the end of life.

The ability of caregivers to communicate patient preferences, coordinate care, and reduce inefficiency in the health care system begins with patients themselves and their families. To the extent that the latter begin the discussion at an early enough stage, before they are confronted with the difficult decisions that the end of life represents in an urgent, pressing way, these very decisions are more likely to be honored. Costly and futile tests and treatments are then likely to be avoided. An ethical orientation that acknowledges death honestly and explicitly, as does the Hellenistic tradition, indeed as does ancient philosophy in general, provides an important starting point for such reflection even for those who are reluctant to accept all of its premises. The Stoic emphasis on the values of autonomy and dignity (Long 2002) are well within the concerns of many people at life's end. Conscious and early acknowledgement of our unavoidable end can serve to prepare people in ways that enable them to have some control over the circumstances of their leave-taking, and alleviate to some extent their own anxiety and that of their survivors.

An acquaintance with the Hellenistic normative arguments would also be valuable for medical practitioners and administrators. A study by Gwen Prigerson (1992) of terminally ill patients in California hospitals shows that their physicians are often reluctant to disclose their terminal conditions. The same study shows that a doctor's willingness to openly and unambiguously disclose a terminal condition to a patient positively correlates with the acknowledgement of that condition by the patient and the type of treatment they seek. Gwen Prigerson also finds that physicians working in teaching/research hospitals are more likely to pursue curative rather than palliative courses of treatment for terminally ill patients even when patients themselves have indicated a preference for palliative care.

The benefits of life planning that include an explicit contemplation of one's demise are not limited to cost savings with result to health care. It is well known that relatively few people make provisions for the possibility of their untimely deaths. They tend to under-provide themselves and their survivors with life insurance. Relatively few people opt to become organ donors.[11] Rational reflection on death can add to the peace of mind that the ancient Greeks identify with *eudaimonia* while also contributing to the positive externalities identified with modern economic theory. The other-directedness of such foresight in the face of death is entirely in keeping with the Stoic emphasis of a well-lived life whose greatest possession is volition in service to honor, dignity, and integrity. In other words, an understanding and adherence to Stoic principles suggests the possibility of a virtuous death as much as it does a virtuous life.

Stoic philosophy may also fruitfully contribute to the ethical discussion of physician-assisted suicide. The ancient Greeks and Romans themselves were also highly conflicted about the moral acceptability of suicide, though they were not as burdened by guilt feelings regarding the act as their Christian counterparts. In contrast to Christianity, the ancient outlook did not regard death as a consequence of man's fallen state, but rather as a transition from one world to the next (Garland 1983: 33). Many prominent citizens of ancient Greek and Roman societies in fact met their demise at their own hands including Lycurgus, Charondas, Zeno, Cleanthes, Cato, and Seneca. We could also include on this list Socrates who on being condemned to death and, faced with the choice of fleeing Athens, made the principled decision to kill himself.[12] In several of these cases the motivations were a heightened sense of patriotic duty combined with an acute desire to avoid dishonor.

To take up again the question left at the end of the previous section: Is suicide morally permissible? From a Stoic perspective the answer to this question is "yes" insofar as we reject the argument that life is intrinsically valuable (Tomasini 2014). If the quality of life is sufficiently low then suicide is a morally permissible alternative. Again, from a strictly Stoic perspective as a matter of fact, suicide may under some circumstances be a moral imperative. This would be so in the case where a continued existence conflicts with the requirements of virtue. Recall, for the Stoics life itself is not intrinsically good. The only intrinsic good is virtue. If the requirements of virtue conflict with a continuing life, then the Stoic sage will exit life. How would the Stoics address the question of suicide in cases where virtue is not at stake? Brennan (2005: 40–41) takes the position that the Stoic attitude to suicide depends entirely on the availability (or not) of "preferred indifferents" such as health, food shelter, family, friends, etc. As life itself is a preferred indifferent, the decision to continue living or to exit life depends on the sage's ability to procure enough of these ancillary resources to justify life. He adds that the same calculus applies to non-sages.

Such a calculus, argues Tomasini, is not a simple utilitarian cost-benefit exercise as standard economics might understand things, but requires that a distinction be made between "regular (non-rational) suicide" and "rational suicide":

> That is, there is little point in medical professionals acting as gatekeepers, preventing non-rational assisted suicides, if rational suicide is merely to assist those technically sane individuals who can weigh up the pros and cons of continued life, and then decide in favor of death. This leaves the door open for suicide on demand; a possible choice for anyone who is autonomous, without a mental illness and reasonably responsible, but perceives for one specious reason or another, their life turning out badly.
>
> (Tomasini 2014: 106)

Regular suicide by this understanding may be rationally intelligible in the sense that it can provide a consistent set of reasons for ending a life. But a "rational suicide" is one that includes a moral point of view involving the requirements for human flourishing (Mayo 1986). Among these requirements are included the exercise of the individual's autonomy. One could reasonably argue that an individual incapacitated by a drug-induced stupor to relieve otherwise unendurable pain and suffering has had this autonomy violated to an unacceptable extreme. Another requirement is that a rational suicide be motivated by the individual's long-term, deeply felt interests (i.e., the individual's values). This requirement would not license suicide in the case where the motivations were episodic, transitory, or ephemeral. It would require an examination of the decision to exit life via the exercise of "right reason" in the manner urged by the Stoics.

Conclusions

The argument has been made here that Hellenistic ethical precepts provide a firmer foundation for individual choice and public policy than does the narrow hedonic approach that is the standard for much modern (mainstream) economic analysis. To accept this conclusion is not to accept every ethical or metaphysical assertion made by the Hellenistic thinkers. To do so would certainly entail logical difficulties inasmuch as these philosophers held to positions that were on some important points mutually inconsistent. The Stoics, for example, would not likely take the position that "death is nothing to us." At the very least, they held it to be a dis-preferred indifferent. That is, death was to be avoided, albeit not at the cost of one's virtue. Neither would I personally embrace the Epicurean view that a premature death represents no harm to the deceased or his survivors.

These qualifications aside I find much in the Hellenistic philosophies that represent a significant improvement over the standard economic normative perspective. The Hellenistic notion that rationality is a human characteristic that people have a moral obligation to develop represents a radical improvement over the neoclassical economic assumption that rationality is a given and fully complete endowment of the human personality. Put another way, whereas the Hellenistic philosophers seek to educate would-be sages, modern economic theory seeks to describe *homo economicus*. As a basis from which to search for the good life, and to formulate good policy, I find the former more appealing and, at least potentially, more useful.

Where the specific purpose of finding answers to the problems presented by the end of life is concerned, including those related to health care and its associated costs, a careful study of Hellenistic philosophy provides advantages that the rational choice, maximizing tradition does not. The most salient of these is the emphasis it gives to a willingness to think frankly and seriously about human mortality. This emphasis is part and parcel of the Hellenistic, and more general ancient Greek, concern with providing guidance to a well-lived life rather than focusing on anything as narrowly construed as utility, or profit, maximization.

A final question remains as to how probable is a conversion of popular thinking to a Hellenistic view of end-of- life issues, or, more generally, of an embrace of its *eudaimonism*. The ancients themselves had no illusions regarding the popularity of their teachings and implied lifestyles. Is there any reason to anticipate that people in the twenty-first century are any more prepared to embrace the non-material values that the Greeks attached to *eudaimonia*? Is there any reason to expect that people in the twenty-first century could become accustomed to treating their mortality as a non-taboo topic available for dispassionate deliberation and discussion? While I would not dismiss out of hand anyone who responded with skepticism to the suggestion that such cultural transformations are in the offing, it must also be admitted that there exists strong demographic and economic pressures that work in their favor. It is projected that the portion of the U.S. population over age 65 will reach 20 percent by the year 2030.[13] This represents an enormous increase in the portion of society that will need to confront the choices raised in this chapter and, as has been argued above, an equally daunting challenge to our public finance. If we are to meet these challenges it would seem that we need to begin to replace at least some of our prevailing mental models.[14] A return to the classics may provide sources of inspiration for replacement models.

Notes

1 To illustrate the Epicurean argument, my desire to satisfy my thirst is both natural and necessary. My desire to satisfy my thirst with orange juice is natural and unnecessary, since water will do. My desire to satisfy my thirst with 1964 Dom Perignon is groundless. Discussion can be found in Diogenes Laertius, *Letter to Menoeceus*, 10, 127–128, included in Inwood and Gerson (1994).

2 See Green (1982) and Warren (2004) for a discussion of several such objections.

3 It does not help to claim that the fact of the deceased non-existence is the source of harm since this would introduce a logical contradiction that a non-existent subject suffers the fact of its non-existence (Warren 2004: 45).

4 Skinner and Fisher (2010) estimate that between 20–30 percent of U.S. Medicare spending represents waste. In fact they regard this as a lower bound estimate that does not include the inefficiency found in the best hospitals due to (1) elective surgeries chosen by ill-informed patients and (2) the underuse of effective and low-cost treatments.

5 An explanation for this inverse relationship involves the risks associated with invasive medical procedures and hospital stays where patients may be exposed to antibiotic resistant infections. Increases in diagnostic tests may reveal issues that suggest additional treatments even in cases where those same issues present no real threat to the patient. Multiple consultations on the part of multiple specialists frequently raise the complexity of a patient's care that also increases its associated risks (Wennberg et al 2008: 13).

6 Maksoud et al (1993) in a study of DNR orders among 852 hospital death records conclude that total hospital and professional charges are significantly lower when a patient is admitted with an established non-resuscitation order compared to those who establish such an order while in the hospital.

7 States that have enacted PAS with legislation are Oregon (1994), Vermont (2013), Washington (2008), and California (2015). Montana's Supreme Court made the practice constitutional in 2009. For details see http://euthanasia.procon.org/view.resource.php?resourceID=000132.

8 Those who make use of the SSA may even suspect that the proponents of practice A are seeking to establish a juridical beachhead from which to launch a more ambitious (and nefarious) program of action which must be resisted in the interest of the larger social welfare even if A itself carries some limited social benefit.

9 Evaluating an SSA-type argument to proscribe PAS "on its merits" may require that we consider both necessary and sufficient conditions to allow its practice, and not merely a single identifiable qualifying standard (e.g., quality of life, patient

autonomy). For discussion of this view, see Smith's (2005) treatment of Keown's (2002) SSA position.
10 The Epicurean assertion "Death is nothing to us" is not a boast. It is rather a cognitive claim about the nature of death.
11 According to the U.S. Department of Health and Human Services, over the period of 1989 to 2009 the total of living and deceased organ donors increased from 5,927 to 14,630 in 1989, a percentage change of 147, while the waiting list grew from 17,917 to 105,567, or 489 percent. For more details consult http://www.organdonor.gov.
12 The principle at issue for Socrates was less his love for Athens than his love for virtue as a citizen. The latter could not be served, he felt, by fleeing his sentence.
13 This ratio now stands at approximately 13 percent according to the U.S. Census Bureau: http://www.census.gov/population/www/projections/projectionsagesex.html.
14 A good place to begin might urge low tolerance for political rhetoric that characterizes necessary discussion of policy-supported end of life options as "death panels."

References

Benatar, David. 2011. "A legal right to die: responding to slippery slope and abuse arguments," *Current Oncology*, 18, 5: 206–207.
Bergsma, Ad, Germaine Poot, and Aart C. Liefbroer. 2008. "Happiness in the Garden of Epicurus," *Journal of Happiness Studies*, 9, 3 (September): 397–423.
Brennan, Tad. 2005. *The Stoic Life: Emotions, Duties, and Fate*, Oxford: Oxford University Press.
Doerflinger, Richard M. and Carlos F. Gomez. 2016. "Killing the pain not the patient: Palliative care vs. assisted suicide," United States Conference of Catholic Bishops, http://www.usccb.org/about/pro-life-activities/respect-life-program/killing-the-pain.cfm.
Emanuel, Ezekiel J. 1996. "Cost savings at the end of life: What do the data show?," *Journal of the American Medical Association*, 275, 24 (June 26): 1907–1914.
Epictetus. 1995. *The Discourses: The Handbook, Fragments*, Christopher Gill (ed.), Robin Hard (translated). Everyman: London.
Gade, Glen, I. Venohr, D. Conner, K. McGrady, J. Beane, R. Richardson, M. Williams, M. Liberson, M. Blum and R. Penna. (2008) "Impact of an inpatient palliative care team: A radomized control trial," *Journal of Palliative Medicine*, 11, 2 (March): 180–190.
Ganzini, Linda. 2016. "Legalised physician-assisted death in Oregon," *QUT Law Review*, 16, 1: 76–83.
Garland, Robert. 1983. "Death without dishonor: Suicide in the ancient world," *History Today*, 33, 1 (January): 33–37.
Green, O. H. 1982. "Fear of death," *Philosophy and Phenomenological Research*, 43, 1 (September): 99–105.
Gummere, Peter J. 2014. "Opposing assisted suicide in Vermont," *Ethics & Medicine: A Commentary of the National Catholic Bioethics Center on Health Care and the Life Sciences*, 39, 1 (July): 1–4.
Inwood, Brad and L. P. Gerson (eds.) 1994. *The Epicurus Reader: Selected Writings and Testimonia*, Indianapolis, IN: Hackett Publishing.
Keown, John. 2002. *Euthanasia, Ethics and Public Policy: An Argument against Legislation*, Cambridge: Cambridge University Press.

Kopczuk, Wojciech and Joel Slemrod. 2005. "Denial of death and economic behavior," *Advances in Theoretical Economics*, 5, 1: 1–24, Berkeley Electronic Press, http://www.bepress.com/bejte.

Long, A. A. 2002. *Epictetus: A Stoic and Socratic Guide to Life*, Oxford: Clarendon Press.

Maksoud, Alfred, Dennis W. Jahnigen and Christine I. Skibinski. 1993. "Do not resuscitate orders and the cost of death," *Archives of Internal Medicine*, 152 (May 24): 1249–1253.

Mayo, David J. 1986. "The concept of rational suicide," *The Journal of Medicine and Philosophy*, 11, 2 (May): 143–155.

Prigerson, Holly Gwen. 1992. "Socialization to dying: social determinants of death acknowledgement and treatment among terminally ill geriatric patients," *Journal of Health and Social Behavior*, 33, 4 (December): 378–395.

Radbruch, Lukas, Carlo Leget, Patrick Bahr, Christof Müller-Busch, John Ellershaw, Franco de Conno, and Paul van den Berghe. 2016. "Euthanasia and physician-assisted suicide: A white paper from the European Association for Palliative Care," *Palliative Medicine*, 30, 2: 104–116.

Schneiderman, Lawrence J., Richard Kronick, Robert M. Kaplan, John P. Anderson, and Robert D. Langer. 1992. "Effects of offering advance directives on medical treatments and costs," *Annals of Internal Medicine*, 117, 7 (October): 599–606.

Seneca. 1969. *Letters from a Stoic*. New York: Penguin.

Skinner, Jonathan and Elliot S. Fisher. 2010. *Reflections on Geographic Variations in U.S. Health Care*, The Dartmouth Institute for Health Policy & Clinical Practice, http://www.dartmouthatlas.org/downloads/press/Skinner_Fisher_DA_05_10.pdf, 31 July 2011.

Smith, Stephen W. 2005. "Fallacies of the logical slippery slope in the debate on physician-assisted suicide and euthanasia," *Medical Law Review*, 13 (Summer): 224–243.

SUPPORT. 1995. "A controlled trial to improve care for seriously ill hospitalized patients," *Journal of the American Medical Association*, 274, 20 (November 22/29): 1591–1598.

Tomasini, Floris. 2014. "Stoic defense of physician-assisted suicide," *Acta Bioethica*, 20, 1: 99–108.

Warren, James. 2004. *Facing Death: Epicurus and his Critics*, New York: Clarendon Press Oxford.

Wennberg, John E., Elliott S. Fisher, and David C. Goodman. 2008. *Tracking the Care of Patients with Severe Chronic Illness: The Dartmouth Atlas of Health Care 2008*, The Dartmouth Institute for Health Policy and Clinical Practice, Center for Health Policy Research, http://www.dartmouthatlas.org/downloads/atlases/2008_Chronic_Care_Atlas.pdf, accessed 3 August 2011.

White, Christina. 2015. "Comment: Physician aid-in-dying," *Houston Law Review*, 53, 2: 595–629.

8   Towards a virtuous public finance

It would be hard to conceive of an area of economics that is more fraught with ethically charged decisions and consequences than that of public finance. At its most fundamental level public finance is concerned with the role that government should play in the allocation of goods, services, and productive factors in the economy. The mechanisms of public finance – taxes, government expenditures, transfer payments, etc. – have unavoidable distributive implications. The structure and magnitude of taxes have clear implications for economic incentives either directly for their impacts upon disposable income, or more indirectly via their effects on relative prices. Large-scale government expenditures can also have important impacts upon the long run structure of the economy, causing whole new industries to emerge and develop and others to fade into irrelevance.

In posing the question of the ethical/normative content of public finance, there are numerous directions in which to turn. One might raise the question, for example, of our ethical responsibility to contribute to the public good by paying taxes. Taxes, of course, are not voluntary contributions to the public purse. They represent instead an act of official coercion. They often raise the prospect on the part of the tax-payer of either avoidance (considered ethically neutral or benign) or evasion (considered ethically objectionable or illegal). Some libertarians have gone so far as to declare any and all taxes as theft. Another approach to the ethics of public finance focuses on the tax administration itself. An effective tax system presupposes an efficient and honest bureaucracy. Tax compliance is far more likely if the system is perceived to possess legitimacy, and the latter requires the bureaucracy to be perceived as competent and not susceptible to corruption. Still, a third aspect of public finance with clear ethical/normative content considers the use of taxes and/or subsidies to shape the behavior of citizens. Taxes may be levied on particular commodities (e.g., tobacco, soft drinks) to discourage their consumption and to promote good health. Subsidies may be provided to other goods deemed to have public goods aspects such as education or vaccines to reduce the spread of communicable diseases. It is easy to see then that the ethical dimensions of public finance are multiple and varied. Moreover, there are circumstances in which they can work at cross purposes. Consider the case of so-called "sin taxes" – so-called since they are levied against goods or activities considered by one criterion or another to have some negative consequences for their consumers or for the public at large. If the purpose of such taxes is to discourage the activities to which they are applied, then they will not be successful in generating revenue for the state. If the state becomes dependent on the revenues from sin taxes to fund other projects, then the taxes serve one objective while failing at the other. At the very least policy makers need to be very clear about the objectives they are pursuing in the structure of their public finance strategy both in terms of its economic and social objectives.

In this chapter I wish to examine the ethics of public finance in a eudaimonistic context. That is, I wish to consider the meaning of an approach to public finance that takes as its aim what the ancient Greek thinkers understood as the goal of the well-lived life, *eudaimonia*. As we have seen from previous chapters, *eudaimonia* cannot be reduced to utility conventionally understood in standard, modern economic thought. For the Cynics and Stoics, a eudaimonistic existence was wholly a matter of virtue. For the Epicureans, it was a matter of pleasure, but a highly qualified sort of pleasure that was also informed by virtue. The purpose in this chapter is to pose and address the question, "What does a virtuous public finance consist of?" Moreover, *virtue* in this sense is to be understood in terms of several of the above-listed connotations.

It is important to remember once again that the ancient Hellenistic philosophers/statesmen themselves had very little to say about the state and public policy itself, let alone public finance. As noted in Chapter 2, the period during which the Hellenistic empire prevailed was one of considerable political and economic turmoil and the philosophical schools often recommended withdrawal from political life. This was not uniformly true, however, and the Stoics in particular considered public engagement to be a duty of the sage. Even given the limited view of the remaining schools regarding active civic engagement, I have argued in this book that their ethical perspective as a whole provides guidance to contemporary policy formulation. This is no less true, I believe, for public finance questions than it is for other areas of policy concern already addressed in this volume. Their virtual consensus on the desirability of a minimalist approach to consumption, for example, suggests a possible policy approach to taxation in the form of a consumption tax. This particular proposal, in fact, will be given detailed attention towards the end of the chapter.

As the range of possible ethical aspects to public finance is quite broad, I undertake here only a limited set of issues to examine in detail. Two particular policy areas to be examined concern:

1   education finance;
2   the suitability of "sin taxes" and gaming for a virtuous public finance.

A third, more general, issue is the overall structure and burden of tax incidence. The particular concerns with respect to (1) include both the adequacy of resources for public education as well as their distribution. The underlying and driving assumption is that the pursuit of *eudaimonia* pre-supposes the exercise of our mature, rational potential and this, in turn, requires the pursuit of education. An examination of sin taxes would seem to be a natural consideration for an investigation of how public finance interacts with the question of public and private morality as it is clearly concerned with what many would consider "vicious" behavior. What makes the pairing of sin taxes with gaming especially interesting is that the two sorts of measures have, in most cases, diametrically opposite objectives. Typically, the purpose of a sin tax is to discourage a behavior, such as smoking. Gaming schemes, or state-sponsored gambling, on the other hand, while also considered by many to be a vicious practice, are designed to raise state revenue. The coincidence of these public finance instruments raises the question of ethical inconsistency, among other problems. The third question casts a wider net, but is focused on the question of the reach of our civic responsibility collectively and as indivi-duals. I shall invoke here, as I have done in previous chapters, the Stoic principle of *oikeiosis* (familiarization) to justify an approach to public finance and the state that promotes "capabilities" as the term is employed by Nussbaum and Sen (1993). Before I turn to the discussion of the policy issues themselves it would be useful to explore what the Hellenistic thinkers have to say about how the would-be sage understands his or her civic responsibilities.

Hellenistic views on justice and community

We can make inferences about the application of Hellenistic ethics to public policy issues, including those related to public finance, by considering what the ancient philosophers had to say about the concepts of justice and community. It would seem at a fundamental level that questions about the appropriate role of government as an allocator of economic resources are intimately bound up with precisely these concepts. While the Hellenistic philosophers were primarily concerned with virtue as it applies to the individual's prospects for *eudaimonia*, public finance issues imply a concern with the virtue content of institutions.

Julia Annas (1993: 292) suggests the following interesting questions: do institutions derive their justice from the virtue of individuals? Or do individuals derive their just characters by conforming to just institutions? Annas argues that the Epicurean account of justice provides a sort of "two stage" process by which a contractual theory of justice (institutional justice) creates conditions propitious for the development of virtue in individuals. The account starts, as it always does for Epicurus, with pleasure. How is justice a source of pleasure? In two ways: first, individuals gain peace of mind (*ataraxia*) in the knowledge that they have acted in a just way towards others. Second, the knowledge that others may be relied upon to act in a just manner towards us is also a source of our tranquility. The second of these motivations suggests a contractural theory of justice. Such theories are common approaches to explaining how our justice-related institutions (e.g., laws, courts, enforcement apparatus) come to be established. The underlying assumption is that in the absence of these institutions, people are likely to act strictly in their narrow self-interest. To prevent people from acting solely and always in this way, and to defend themselves from the self-interested behavior of others, societies have established institutions that operate in the interest of justice. Part of the Epicurean account of justice recognizes this motivation. But Epicurus, Annas reminds us, also has a far more optimistic view of human nature that sees it as having the potential to develop a "taste" for justice independent of such contractural motivations. Indeed, as Annas points out, such a purely defensive position as suggested by the contractural approach is hardly consistent with the tranquility that Epicureans see as the highest good. Moreover, one's commitment to justice based on the contractural motivation is unlikely to be stable inasmuch as it is contingent on circumstances related to such considerations as the probability of defection from the contractural understanding. This instability is inconsistent, argues Annas, with the commitment to justice properly understood as virtue of character.

So how can these apparently conflicting motivations for just behavior be reconciled? Annas (1993: 298) suggests that the answer lies in seeing the two concepts of justice, (1) social justice and (2) justice as a virtue of individuals, as having different motivations. Social justice requires a contract to discourage mutually depredatory behavior. But the motivation for justice as a virtue may arise in the individual entirely out of a love for justice (and other virtues). The key, says Annas, is to link these motivations somehow. This is accomplished by observing that contracts can have educative and social developmental functions as well as a disincentive function, strictly understood. These educative and developmental functions may operate over time to inculcate in individuals the love of justice that is a virtue and a source of pleasure.

Phillip Mitsis (1988) also addresses the tension that arises when Epicurus provides a theory of justice grounded in *ataraxia* as well as in a contractural account. The peace of mind that the Epicurean sage derives from not inflicting injustice on another is sufficient reason to avoid doing just that. Mitsis (1988: 83), citing Epicurean doctrine, notes the following that is of especial interest to the so-called economic problem:

> A wise man, like the gods, is not disturbed; nor does he disturb others, since the necessities of life are easily obtained and there is no need for a life of struggle. Accordingly, individuals have no natural need to engage in troubling pursuits and have no reason for harming others. Desires for harming others arise only from a mistaken estimate of the nature and limits of human desires.

For Epicurus, evidently, the economic problem of scarcity only arises in the circumstance in which man loses sight of his natural desires and begins to reach to satisfy those that are unnatural and unnecessary. This will not occur in the case of the sage, but, as Mitsis points out, the Epicurean must allow for the fact that society has not evolved to the point where everyone has reached sagehood.[1] The contractural motivation for the Epicurean sage differs in an important way from that identified by other contract theorists such as Rousseau and Hobbes, however. For the latter theorists, when people enter into social contracts they give up the option of harmful or unjust behavior towards others in exchange for the assurance by others that they will exercise similar restraint. But the Epicurean sage harbors no such aggressive dispositions, and they do not enter into a consideration of his self-interest in any way. The sage is willing to abide by the contract knowing that a commitment to justice contributes to *ataraxia*. The sage is also hopeful that the contract will serve the socially useful purpose of educating all to limit their desires to those that are natural and thereby also attaining *ataraxia*.

An especially salient aspect of the Stoic theory of justice begins with an account of *oikeiosis* which roughly translates from the Greek to mean "familiarization" or "akin to." The English language antonym would best be understood as "alienation." The term applies to nature in the following two ways: (1) *primary oikeiosis* occurs when nature familiarizes a living thing with itself. That is, the organism recognizes what is good for its constitution and what it therefore should appropriate to itself. This recognition is fundamentally motivated by self-love. Similarly it will select against what is detrimental to its well-being. Primary *oikeiosis* is considered present in living organisms from birth and is grounded in an even more fundamental innate capacity of self-perception (Long 1996). (2) *Social oikeiosis* occurs when nature familiarizes a living thing with others of its species.[2] This occurs most fundamentally between a parent and its off-spring. Moreover, it is characteristic of both non-human as well as human animals. What separates the latter from the former, however, is its capacity for rational thought, a capacity that develops over time in the individual. The object of our appropriation turns from a concern for the basic means of our sustenance to an appreciation for, and desire to appropriate the "products" of, our rationality itself. Annas (1993: 263) describes this development in the following terms:

> Finally, we come to a point when, if our reason develops properly we appreciate that the value of our getting things rationally is crucially different from the value of our rational activity itself; it is the reasons we act on that matter, not the consequences of acting on those reasons. To realize this is to realize the distinct value of virtue.

Annas then notes that this development amounts to a full–blown ethics insofar as social *oikeiosis* requires that the familiarization that is extended to one's closest relatives must as a matter of logical consistency be further extended to one's more distant relatives, and then to one's neighbors, countrymen, and, finally, to humanity as a whole. That is to say, social *oikeiosis* taken to its logical and rational limit entails utter impartiality in our moral choices. One could raise reasonable doubts regarding the psychological plausibility of this demand in a world of non-sages, or even of aspiring sages, (Annas 1993: 267–275). Impartiality of moral choice, however, would seem to be the essence of institutions and policy in a democratic society committed to the rule of law. The demands placed on social *oikeiosis* in this regard would not seem to be greater than those that govern legislation following Benthamite utilitarianism or Rawlsian "fairness," for example.

Long (1997: 23) notes the economic aspect of *oikeiosis* in Cicero (*De Officiis*, I.22):

> But since, as Plato has admirably expressed it, we are not born for ourselves alone but our country claims a share of us and our friends too, and since, as the Stoics hold, all the products of the earth are created for human use; and since human beings are created for the sake of human beings, so as to be able mutually to help one another – in this we should follow nature as our guide, to contribute to the common interest by an exchange of functions, by giving and receiving, and so by our skills, work and talents cement the community of human beings with one another.

Long is careful to point out that there is nothing in the Stoic theory of justice that proscribed private property and economic competition. He cites Stoic authorities Panaetius and Hecaton, in addition to Cicero, and suggests a line of influence that reaches up to Locke's defense of private property (1997: 18–19). Long (2007: 256), however, is keen to emphasize what he considers to be the over-riding target of Stoic justice:

> I propose that notwithstanding our natural impulses and needs for material goods and services (which Stoic philosophers acknowledged but lacked the power or motivation to actively campaign for on an egalitarian scale), Stoicism challenges us to consider that rationality and mutual reverence are not only values of a categorically higher order but are also integral to our sheer survival as a civilized race. Is it the case that these higher-order values are at risk precisely because our cultures have placed so great a premium on the supposed necessity of nonessential material goods?

Virtue-based theories of justice enjoy an additional advantage over consequentialist theories such as utilitarianism in that the former are not vulnerable to certain paradoxes that plague the latter. One of these is referred to by philosophers as "Repugnant Conclusion." Derek Parfit (1984) illustrates the issue this way:

> For any possible population of at least ten billion people, all with a very high quality of life, there must be some much larger imaginable population whose existence, if other things are equal, would be better even though its members have lives that are barely worth living.

The difficult question of course is how, on utilitarian grounds, do we choose between these two outcomes? I argue that virtue-based ethical theories such as we associate with the ancient thinkers, including the Stoics, do not confront this problem. This is so for at least two reasons:

1   Stoic *eudaimonia* can never be conceived in terms of an "adding up" of experiential outcomes based on "externals."
2   Stoic *eudaimonia* is not, in fact, resource-constrained. The "production" of virtue does not depend on the injection of externals, scarce or otherwise. In fact, it might be said that virtue is "self-developing" inasmuch as "sages" provide role models for others.

In the present case I argue that properly conceived policy choices ought to play this role. The Stoic expectation is that in this way over time virtuous behavior becomes an end in itself. Under these circumstances we ought not to limit our focus to the "opportunity cost" of the good since nothing is really sacrificed in the exercise of virtue. In this way Stoic pursuit of *eudaimonia* can be seen as providing a firmer foundation for our social and economic lives and our policy choices.

Having set out here an outline of Hellenistic ethics and its concepts of justice, I now undertake an examination of three contemporary public finance issues and argue the case for reform based on an expanded normative/ethical basis derived from the ancient views. The three issues are as follows:

1   education finance;
2   the use of so-called "sin taxes";
3   the overall structure of public finance.

Ethics and education finance

That education was central to Greek ethics is undeniable given the stress they placed on reason as the road to ethical understanding. All the Greek philosophers were in essence educators with some such as Aristotle and Plato establishing formal institutions of learning and others such as Socrates, Diogenes, and the Sophists operating on an informal and/or itinerant basis. While the latter teachers confined their instruction to ethics, the former grounded their ethical outlooks on a broader curriculum that included physics, metaphysics, and logic. The institutions founded by Plato (the Academy) and Aristotle (the Lyceum) are considered forerunners of today's universities. They were distinctive for their time from other competing schools, such as that established by Pythagoras, in not requiring their students to make any special commitments as a requirement for study. While there were expenses incurred to study, and not all families could afford to send their offspring, education was available to the middle class.[3] The Hellenistic philosophers in particular were concerned to make their teachings as accessible as possible taking inspiration from Socrates who considered it unseemly to accept fees for his instruction (Capes 1977/1922: 39).

Recall from Chapter 4 Nussbaum's (2011) notion of "central capabilities" defined as a (minimum) specific list of "areas of freedom" without which a life is bereft of human dignity. In developing her ideas she makes use of two other concepts borrowed from Wolff and De-Shalit (2007) termed "fertile functioning" and "corrosive disadvantage." A fertile functioning is an ability that helps to catalyze a broad spectrum of central capabilities, while a corrosive disadvantage is a set of circumstances that operates to inhibit their development. Poverty, for example, might be a corrosive disadvantage that inhibits such central capabilities as bodily health, bodily integrity, and control over one's environment.[4] Education is a fertile functioning that provides an important means by which this corrosive disadvantage may be overcome to enable disadvantaged persons to realize these and other important central capabilities. Nussbaum (2011: 152) is quite explicit on this point:

> At the heart of the Capabilities Approach since its inception has been the importance of education. Education (in schools, in the family, in programs for both child and adult development run by nongovernmental organizations) forms people's existing capabilities into internal capabilities of many kinds. This formation is valuable in itself and a source of lifelong satisfaction. It is also pivotal to the development and exercise of many other human capabilities: a "fertile functioning" of the highest importance in addressing disadvantage and inequality. People who have received even a basic education have greatly enhanced employment options, chances for political participation, and abilities to interact productively with others in society, on a local, national, and even international level.

Once again, and not coincidentally, Nussbaum cites philosophical inspiration for her capabilities approach from Aristotle and the Stoics. From Aristotle Nussbaum takes the insight that human beings are vulnerable to the vicissitudes of economic life and that sometimes they need assistance. From the Stoics she appropriates the motivating belief in "human dignity." While the Stoics themselves did not employ that particular expression, an important ethical contribution of theirs is that all humankind are united by "a share in the divine" and that is true regardless of race, gender, class, or national origin.

So what are the public finance implications of an approach to justice that recognizes the importance of education as an avenue to *eudaimonia* conceived in terms of capabilities combined with the recognition of entitlement based on human dignity? At a minimum it would seem to establish an imperative for government to provide minimally sufficient educational resources to enable every citizen to realize their central capabilities. In absolute terms this might mean that those who suffer corrosive disadvantages (e.g., poverty, as termed by Nussbaum), would receive more resources to reach this minimal standard than those not similarly afflicted. Beyond this standard, however, we might expect that social justice conceived in terms of equality of opportunity befitting common human dignity would urge policies to promote equality of educational opportunity.

And yet there is abundant evidence to suggest the absence of equal educational opportunity in America. The Education Law Center (2014) published a "report card" on the nation's performance for the 2007–2011 period in delivering adequacy and equity in school funding. The results of this report are troubling. It finds flat or declining overall levels of school funding as states were forced to reduce expenditures in the face of generalized economic contraction. Even more troubling, the report card shows more states have become more "regressive" in their distribution of state resources with districts with lower levels of poverty accounting for more resources and districts with higher poverty receiving less. In addition, the report finds that enrollment rates in early childhood education programs for low-income families lag behind those for children from high-income families in nearly all states, and that states with lower overall funding levels offer teacher salaries that are below those for states with higher funding levels.

The standard presumption is that educational funding disparities reflect the method of public educational finance which typically depends on local property taxes. This is only partially true. As Baker and Corcoran (2012) have pointed out there also exists a number of "stealth inequities" in school funding that actually have the effect of moving state resources in the direction of the wealthiest school districts in some states. The mechanisms of these stealth inequities are a consequence of the provisions of states' general aid formulas that are politically driven. Thus, they include, for example, minimum aid provisions that stipulate any district will receive a minimum allocation regardless of its need. A variant on this is a so-called "hold harmless" provision stipulating that in the event of a change in the funding law, any particular district will not suffer a loss of aid under the prevailing formula, again notwithstanding its local tax capacity (25). Yet a third mechanism involves granting property tax relief to local school districts irrespective of their tax capacity. When states compensate local school districts for lost revenue tied to lower property tax rates, the higher-valued property associated with wealthier districts guarantees a disproportionate allocation of state aid, thus enabling wealthier districts to increase per student education funding above the levels available in poorer districts (34). As the authors put it, there occurs a kind of inverse equalization rather than an equalization process. Other stealth mechanisms operate by punishing poorer districts on the basis of "performance." For example, some state aid is tied to average daily attendance. But it is well-known that students from poorer backgrounds have more school absences than those from wealthier, and more stable, backgrounds. Overall, the authors of this study find the several states they study have a tendency to reallocate state resources toward more well-off school districts, contrary to the goal of providing school districts with less income and wealth, and greater educational need, more assistance. To take one example, the authors estimate that the state of New York in the period studied reallocated state taxes to its richest school districts of more than $2,000 per pupil (51).

Several other studies (Hoxby 2001; Schmidt and Scott 2006; Roy 2011) have examined education finance reform initiatives that have been undertaken in recent years. They find a trade-off between the goals of educational finance equality and educational resource sufficiency. This trade-off is a consequence of a continuing commitment to local school finance tied to property tax rates. Typically this involves setting property tax rates by a formula such that a school district wishing to increase education spending must increase its tax rate more than proportional to the spending increase. The surplus revenues generated thereby are put into a common pool that is shared with poorer school districts. The increased "tax-price" of education spending in richer districts may, however, act as a disincentive to their spending. If spending is reduced, so may the available revenues to fund the common pool leaving poorer districts with fewer resources than they had pre-reform. This "leveling down" approach to education spending equalization can be, therefore, counter-productive to the joint intended objective of increasing educational access. A preferred approach to reform would "level up" educational spending for poor school districts. This could be accomplished by a reform that would de-link school funding from local taxes altogether and allocate resources out of general state revenues to schools according to their particular needs. Such an approach, of course, would be contingent on a reconsideration of fiscal federalism as it applies to public education.

The failure of public finance to support the fertile functioning that we expect from education is not limited to the K-12 levels. Public finance for early childhood and higher education must often compete with one another at the state level for declining overall levels of resources. Higher education has responded in recent years with increases in tuition that outstrip the rate of inflation leaving students of limited means to borrow in order to finance their educations. Students then are graduating with high levels of debt that impede their abilities to launch careers. Changes made to public assistance programs to low-income families that require they work has raised the need not only for early childhood education programs such as Head Start and Early Head Start, but also for affordable daycare programs more generally.

A public finance commitment to enable central capabilities and promote the human flourishing associated with an ethics rooted in a eudaimonistic conception of the good life must make educational access, adequacy, and equity a priority. While there is some recent evidence that school finance reform has a beneficial effect on educational performance (Roy 2011), it is well known that a variety of factors outside the school, including the quality of a child's home life, are important determinants of school success. It can hardly be supposed then that an education policy designed to promote human flourishing can be successfully separated from public policy more generally concerned with the same objective.

Are "sin" taxes virtuous?

The question posed in this section title is a complicated one, as previously noted, for a variety of reasons. First, it is ambiguous in terms of specifying *whose* virtue is being called into question. Are the taxes in question designed to promote the virtue of the tax payer? That is, is the sin tax levied strictly with the object of providing disincentive to the taxed activity? Alternatively, the purpose of the tax might be to generate revenue for the tax collector. Thus we might ask, can virtuous states appeal to the vicious behavior of their constituents in order to fund their activities?

The answer to this last question might depend on the particular content of the activities funded by the taxes. Suppose the proceeds of the sin tax are used to fund an educational initiative to discourage the taxed activity. A tax on tobacco might, for example, generate revenues to finance an anti-smoking educational effort. Such "ear-marked" benefits linked to taxes designed to discourage a particular consumption activity such as smoking would seem to enjoy the advantages of ethical consistency. Such moral advantages are lost, however, in those cases where sin taxes are simply motivated as alternatives to other sources of revenues to fund government and its activities. Moreover, even in the former case where there is a consistent connection between the tax and the disposal of its associated revenue, we cannot overlook the fact that sin taxes, and sales taxes more generally, are typically regressive in their incidence. That is, they take a larger share of income from low-income tax-payers than they do from high-income tax payers. This by itself may be contrary to the goals of a state committed to justice and to the other requirements for human flourishing.

Sin taxes have played a shifting role in state finances in the second half of the twentieth century. In 1950 state taxes on alcoholic beverages, tobacco products, and motor fuels combined to account for 31 percent of state revenues. By 1993 this ratio had fallen to less than 10 percent. In the case of alcohol and tobacco alone the drop was from 11.5 to 2.86 percent (Holcombe and Sobel 1997). The decline in the relative importance of these sources of revenue may be tied to changing consumers' tastes in favor of a healthier life-style combined (in the case of fuel taxes) with increasing energy efficiency.[5]

In contrast to fuels, alcohol and tobacco, the profile for gambling-related revenue has grown considerably. In 1988 only two states, Nevada and New Jersey, permitted casino gambling. Today twenty-three states operate casinos and state-sponsored lotteries operate in all but seven states. Of the top ten states with the highest rates (ratios) of sin taxes to total revenue in 2011, nine of these rely on casino or lottery revenues as the largest source of fiscal revenues (Sauter et al 2013). We might argue that the decrease in alcohol and tobacco-related taxes is evidence of their success in discouraging consumption that has adverse health consequences. But, this could hardly be said of state revenues derived from gambling. In this case the state acts as an active promoter of a "vicious" activity not only by granting licenses in the case of casinos, but by waging advertising campaigns to encourage people to participate.

It is not hard to appreciate the political attractiveness of "gaming."[6] Unlike paying taxes no one is coerced into purchasing a lottery ticket or inserting money into a slot machine. Gambling is strictly voluntary and, arguably, the gambler derives some pleasure from playing independent of its payoff. In fact, lotteries, casinos, and para-mutual betting are typically marketed as a form of entertainment (along with the standard caveat that players "play responsibly.") It could also be argued that state-sponsored gaming provides a social benefit by drawing players away from illegal gambling alternatives often run by syndicates that are a source of violence and other mayhem. Not only is the public spared the negative externalities associated with organized crime, but taxpayers avoid the burden of apprehension, prosecution, and incarceration of the criminals. It is useful to consider in this context the reasons why illegal gambling may inspire violence. One reason is that gamblers who use the services of illegal bookmakers frequently enter into informal credit relationships with them (i.e., "loan sharking"). Combine this with the frequently impulsive character of wagering and the gambler can easily get into deep debt on extremely unfavorable terms. The gambler may be forced into desperate asset liquidation or other measures to meet his obligations.

While the publically sponsored gambling apparatus does not include such predatory lending behavior, compulsive betting in casinos and on lottery drawings certainly does occur. Volberg (1994) notes that in states where legalized gambling has existed for more than twenty years, the incidence of pathological gambling is three times as high as in states where legalized gambling has existed for less than ten years.[7] Volberg's evidence also shows that gambling problems begin early in life as young people have ready access to legal forms of betting. She also shows that women and minorities (especially Native Americans) are more vulnerable to pathological gambling than is appreciated by their numbers who enter treatment programs. As new forms of gambling, including "instant" games and on-line forms of betting, gain popularity there is concern that pathological betting will increase since these activities are particularly addictive (Malanga 2012). Economists Grinols and Mustard (2006) in a study of over 3,000 U.S. counties have noted an increase in a variety of categories of crime in 167 counties shortly after the introduction of casino gambling.

As noted previously, the motives of policy-makers who embrace sin taxes are typically conflicted inasmuch as arguments on behalf of such taxes point to their ability to reduce the taxed behavior as well as their ability to generate needed revenues for the state. In the case of gambling, state-sponsored gaming might be considered virtuous, it is argued, if it could be shown that it replaced more socially toxic alternatives. Kearney (2005) notes, however, that this is not the case. Rather, she finds that the introduction of a state lottery reduces overall household non-gambling expenditures by 2.4 percent per month. This substitution effect is even greater (2.5 percent) for low-income households. Moreover, these effects are still larger for instant games which are disproportionately played by low-income households. Sauter et al's (2013) data suggests the alternative motivation that states resort to gaming revenue as a politically painless alternative to direct taxation. Among the top ten states that rely on sin taxes, the most important source of which are gambling revenues for nine, the average income tax rate is 3.97 percent. The average income tax rate for the other forty states is 5.64 percent.[8] It appears then that sin taxes do indeed play the politically attractive function of enabling some states to lower rates of direct taxation. The substitution of regressive forms of taxation for proportional or progressive forms, however, is questionable from the perspective of social institutional virtue.

Eudaimonia and the overall structure of taxes and public spending

At this point it will be worthwhile to take a "big picture" look at what the structure of public finance might look like in a society committed to a eudai-monistic conception of the good. We might begin by asking what the broad characteristics of this structure might be. Taking a cue from Nussbaum, we can say that it should support the realization of the central capabilities of all. This requires, at a minimum, a sufficiency of public goods (e.g., security, public health) and quasi-public goods (e.g., education, cultural goods), and the resources necessary for their provision. Among the important public goods required for human flourishing are those afforded by a healthy natural environment. As argued in Chapter 6, "a life in accord with nature" as per the Stoic recommendation should be taken to mean to live according to the requirements of a thriving natural environment. It is hard to conceive what human flourishing could mean absent its participation in a flourishing natural environment. Moreover, given the inequality that presently characterizes the distribution of income and wealth in our economy, a eudaimonistic conception of justice requires that the tax structure also work to achieve an adequate redistribution of resources sufficient for enabling all to have access to the essential material requirements for achieving their central capabilities. Our present federal income tax has a progressive structure with rates ranging from 10 to 39.6 percent. But rather than apply such a progressive rate scheme to income, I would suggest it could be applied to luxury consumption.

It is often noted that as Americans we are a consumption-oriented culture. Similarly it is frequently noted that consumption spending is the engine of our economy. And yet there is no evidence that our sense of individual well-being stands in a consistently direct relationship to our absolute consumption. Moreover, evidence from behavioral economics suggests that while relative improvements in standards of consumption are a source of happiness, such pleasure is ephemeral. The striving consumer who moves from a 2,000 square foot house into a 3,000 square foot house experiences an immediate increase in satisfaction. This lasts as long as it takes her to realize the comparative puniness of her new abode when she sees the truly magnificent McMansions up the street.[9] The reason that even relative gains in consumption produce only temporary increases in perceived well-being has to do with the ability of human beings to constantly psychologically adapt to their changed material circumstances (Brinkman et al 1978). This phenomenon works in the opposite direction as well. Human beings have a remarkable ability to adapt to relative material deprivation. One is struck by statements of people who survived the Great Depression who note that while they *were* poor as children, they didn't *know* they were poor. Meeting the prevailing standards of consumption of one's immediate social group goes a long way to removing the sting of relative poverty. Contrariwise, the experience of relative deprivation, while receiving a constant barrage of media messages extolling luxury consumption, creates a sense of social alienation and inadequacy. None of this is to minimize the real pain of absolute material need that many people in America feel. Inadequate nutrition, housing, and health care are the lot of millions of Americans and hundreds of millions of others around the world. It is, rather, to make the case that taxing the superfluous consumption of the well-off in order to provide for the necessary consumption of the poor seems like a first approximation to a virtuous public finance.

Advocacy of consumption taxes has a long and diverse intellectual lineage going at least as far back as Hobbes who argued in *Leviathan*: "It is fairer to tax people on what they extract from the economy, as roughly measured by their consumption, than to tax them on what they produce for the economy, as roughly measured by their income." John Stuart Mill advocated the taxation of luxuries while maintaining tax free the necessities of life. He proposed an exemption from taxation for low incomes but not for articles of luxury consumption even if purchased by the poor. To avoid the double taxation of savings, once as principal and the second time as the returns from investment, he urged taxation on incomes allocated to expenditures (i.e., consumption).[10] Twentieth-century proponents of the progressive consumption tax include Irving Fischer, Nicholas Kaldor, and James Meade (Seidman 1997a).

Several advocates of the consumption tax have cited the difficulties in its implementation and administration as major drawbacks. These difficulties have to do with calculating either total savings or total consumption expenditure at the level of the individual household. More recently, Seidman (1997a, 1997b) argues that the practical difficulties of the personal consumption tax are overcome in the form of the proposed unlimited savings allowance, or USA tax. Under this scheme households would submit an income tax return that provides for standard deductions and a level of exempt income. It would also, as the name implies, allow for the deduction from taxable income of an unlimited amount of savings. Taxes on net income would be applied on a graduated scale which, along with the standard deduction and exemption, ensures that the overall incidence of the tax is progressive. In essence, the tax is a levy on what amounts to luxury consumption without the need to identify particular goods and services as luxury items.[11]

Seidman and others argue that the fundamental benefit of the progressive consumption tax is to increase the rates of savings, investment, and economic growth. Economic growth is, by the standards of conventional economic

thinking, desirable precisely because it enables a higher future standard of
living conceived in the final analysis in terms of a higher level of per capita
consumption. Neoclassical growth theory, in fact, argues that policy-makers
might seek to pursue an optimal savings rate that will allow society to achieve
a long run (steady state) growth rate that maximizes long run per capita
consumption. This "virtuous" outcome may require an increase in the actual
savings rate in order to attain the optimal (steady state) value for the capital
stock. As such, current generations may be asked to sacrifice in order that
future generations reap the benefits of a maximum level of per capita
consumption.[12]

There is, undoubtedly, a kind of virtue in such a policy choice. It should be
clear, however, that this notion of virtue may fall well short of the standard
defined in this book as "the exercise of right reason in pursuit of the well-
lived life." This is so inasmuch as there is nothing in the neoclassical model
that makes provisions for environmental sustainability.[13] The neoclassical
economic growth model fails as a guide to human flourishing for the same
reasons that neoclassical economics itself fails. These reasons include its
championing of consumption as the ultimate purpose of economic life and
the sole source of human satisfaction. It also fails by not taking into account
any consideration of income distribution. The focus on (maximum) per capita
consumption makes no necessary allowances for either the content or distribution of output in a manner that would address, for example, the
imperative of promoting universal central capabilities.

The point then is that a virtuous approach to public finance must do more
than tax the right things, the right people, and in the right amounts. It must
also take into account the state's role in providing the necessary access to
basic goods and services that enable all citizens to meet the minimum necessary
needs for their flourishing. It must also take into account the needs that
people have for services provided by nature. Moreover, virtue requires that
such services be provided to future generations into an indefinite future. Thus,
the goal of consumption taxes, properly understood, must be to actually
reduce production and consumption tied to a currently unsustainable of level of
material throughput. Finally, a properly virtuous approach to public finance,
and public policy, more generally, ought to promote what Frank (1999: 222)
terms *inconspicuous consumption*. By inconspicuous consumption, which we
might also term Epicurean consumption, we understand to be those largely
non-material-intensive uses of our time from which we derive meaning and
pleasure and whose value we recognize independently of market processes.

Conclusion

It is undeniable that policy is necessarily consequentialist in its aims. Policy
aims to produce effects on society. A virtuous public policy does not aim
merely to increase social welfare as it is narrowly conceived in traditional
economic terms. It aims rather to influence the growth of the citizenry. In this

light the means of policy are as important as its ends. Policy that appeals to the vicious impulses of its citizenry cannot be expected to promote virtuous ends.

It must be recognized that much here depends on our conceptions of virtue and vice. In this chapter I have urged a view of these evaluative terms as they might have recommended themselves to the ancient Greek philosophers including Socrates, Plato, and Aristotle, but even more particularly to Diogenes, Epicurus, Seneca, and Epictetus. For the Hellenistic thinkers, human flourishing could never be confused with utility maximization centered on consumption. They all believed, above all else, it consisted in freedom[14] and friendship. For at least some of them, it also required a commitment (i.e., duty) to serve the broader social good. Finally, they also believed that human life was endowed with a developmental end, a *telos*. A virtuous life, a well-lived one, was one that promoted the human *telos* guided not just by reason, but by "right reason."

Notes

1 Mitsis provides a discussion of the Epicurean poet Lucretius's views on the stages of human development and their implications for social justice. Mitsis adds, however, that Lucretius does not suggest that a contract approach to social peace will emerge (1988: 86).
2 I refer the reader to Chapter 4 where the concept of social *oikeiosis* is employed to develop the Stoic understanding of collective rationality and social justice.
3 Capes (1977/1922) speculates that colleges in ancient Athens may even have provided financial aid to families of moderate means.
4 In addition to these Nussbaum (2011: 33–34) lists and describes seven other central capabilities that include life; senses, imagination and thought; emotions; practical reason; affiliation; other species; and play.
5 They may also reflect the operation of Engel's law which argues that certain goods have low income elasticity and, therefore, demands for such goods do not grow proportionately with income.
6 Seelig and Seelig (1998: 93) suggests that the term "gaming" supplanted "gambling" once government entered the business. "Gambling" they argue carries negative connotations the state would rather avoid whereas "gaming" is suggestive of "fun, playfulness, and innocence."
7 Pathological gambling is defined by the American Psychiatric Association (1980) as that which results in a loss of control over gambling leading to the chasing of losses, lies and deception, disruptions of family and job, financial bailouts, and illegal acts.
8 Oregon is an outlier in the sense that it is included in Sauter et al's (2013) top ten and yet still maintains the highest maximum state income tax rate in the nation at 9.9 percent. If Oregon is exclude from the sample, the average top income tax rate for the remaining nine most sin tax dependent states is reduced to 3.3 percent, thus further increasing the gap between this group and the rest of the nation.
9 See discussion of this phenomenon by Frank (1999) and Skidelsky and Skidelsky (2013).
10 Book V, Chapter II, "On the general principles of taxation," *Principles of Political Economy*.
11 Seidman's discussion of the USA tax also allows for the taxation of business via the use of a value-added tax.
12 Growth economists refer to this as the "Golden Rule" model of economic growth so-called after the biblical injunction to "do unto others, etc.". For details see, for example, Mankiw (2016).

13 The primary author of the neoclassical growth model is none other than Robert Solow. This is the same Robert Solow that is identified with Solow (weak environmental) sustainability.
14 "Freedom" here requires further qualification. From the eudaimonistic perspective of the ancient Greeks this refers primarily to freedom from undue fear and anxiety in preference to tranquility and peace of mind rather than any positive freedom to act. There is nothing, of course, that would require us to embrace one of these interpretations of freedom to the exclusion of the other, though we would need to exercise "sage-like" judgment to reconcile their conflicting demands.

References

American Psychiatric Association. 1980. *Diagnostic and Statistical Manual of Mental Disorders, 3rd Edition*, Washington, DC.

Annas, Julia. 1993. *The Morality of Happiness*, New York: Oxford University Press.

Baker, Bruce and Sean P. Corcoran. 2012. *The Stealth Inequities of School Funding*, Center for American Progress, https://www.scribd.com/doc/106159743/The-Stealth-Inequities-of-School-Funding, 9 October 2014.

Brinkman, Phillip, Dan Coates, and Ronnie Janoff-Bulman. 1978. "Lottery winners and accident victims: Is happiness relative?," *Journal of Personality and Social Psychology*, 36, 8 (August): 917–927.

Capes, W. W. 1977/1922. *University Life in Ancient Athens*, Reprint, London: Folcroft Library Editions.

Education Law Center. 2014. *Is School Funding Fair? A National Report Card*, http://www.schoolfundingfairness.org/, 8 October 2014.

Frank, Robert H. 1999. *Luxury Fever: Weighing the Cost of Excess*, Princeton, NJ: Princeton University Press.

Grinols, Earl L. and David B. Mustard. 2006. "Casinos, crime, and community costs," *The Review of Economics and Statistics*, 88, 1 (February): 28–45.

Holcombe, Randall G. and Russell S. Sobel. 1997. *Growth and Variability in State Tax Revenue*, Westport, CT: Greenwood Press.

Hoxby, Caroline M. 2001. "All school finance equalizations are not equal," *The Quarterly Journal of Economics*, 116, 4 (November): 1189–1231.

Kearney, Melissa Schettini. 2005. "State lotteries and consumer behavior," *Journal of Public Economics*, 89: 2269–2299.

Long, A. 1996. "Hierocles on oikeiōsis and self-perception," in *Stoic Studies*, A. A. Long (ed.), Berkeley, CA: University of California Press.

Long, A. 1997. "Stoic philosophers on persons, property-ownership and community," *Bulletin of the Institute of Classical Studies, Supplement*, 68: 13–31.

Long, A. A. 2007. "Stoic communitarianism and normative citizenship," *Social Philosophy & Policy*, 24, 2 (July): 241–261.

Malanga, Steve. 2012. "The state gambling addiction," *City Journal*, http://www.city-journal.org/2012/22_3_gambling.html, 23 October 2014.

Mankiw, N. Gregory. 2016. *Macroeconomics, 9th edition*, New York: Worth.

Mitsis, Phillip. 1988. *Epicurus' Ethical Theory: The Pleasures of Invulnerability*, Ithaca, NY: Cornell University Press.

Nussbaum, Martha C. 2011. *Creating Capabilities: The Human Development Approach*, Cambridge, MA: The Belknap Press of Harvard University Press.

Nussbaum, Martha C. and Amartya Sen. 1993. *The Quality of Life*, Oxford: Clarendon Press.

Parfit, Derek. 1984. *Reasons and Persons*, Oxford: Clarendon Press.

Roy, Joydeep. 2011. "Impact of school finance reform on resource equalization and academic performance: Evidence from Michigan," *Education Finance and Policy*, 6, 2 (Spring): 137–167.

Sauter, Michael B., Alexander E. M. Hess, and Thomas C. Frohlich. 2013. "States profiting the most from sin," *24/7 Wall St*, August 16.

Schmidt, Stephen J. and Karen Scott. 2006. "Changing incentives in education finance in Vermont," *Education Finance and Policy*, 1, 4 (Fall): 441–464.

Seelig, Michael Y. and Julie H. Seelig. 1998. "Place your bets! On gambling, government and society," *Canadian Public Policy – Analyse de Politiques*, 24, 1: 92–106.

Seidman, Laurence S. 1997a. *The USA Tax: A Progressive Consumption Tax*, Cambridge, MA: MIT Press.

Seidman, Laurence S. 1997b. "A progressive consumption tax," *Challenge*, 40, 6 (November/December): 63–84.

Skidelsky, Robert and Edward Skidelsky. (2013). *How Much Is Enough: Money and the Good Life*, New York: Other Press.

Volberg, Rachel A. 1994. "The prevalence and demographics of pathological gamblers: Implications for public health," *American journal of Public Health*, 84, 2 (February): 237–241.

Wolff, Jonathan, and Avner De-Shalit. 2007. *Disadvantage*, New York: Oxford University Press.

9 Final thoughts on virtue, the market, and policy

It will not be lost on the reader that an important element in the ethical vision that I am proposing for public policy is virtue. As I made clear in the Introduction, this will appear to many as an odd position for a policy advocate, and an economist at that, to assume. After all, virtue is a characteristic of people, not policies. And economic policies, normally considered, aim to produce consequences, not virtues. Even when economists and economic policy-makers do engage in normative, or welfare, discussions, the point of departure of these discussions is bound to be some measure of social utility. Economists have long been far more comfortable with the utilitarian tradition in ethics when they have bothered to discuss ethics at all.

In recent years, however, we have witnessed a resurgence of interest in virtue ethics (Cafero 1998). This interest has extended to economics as well. Bruni and Sugden (2013) have argued that virtue ethics has an underappreciated relevance to the standard (i.e., classical/neoclassical) model of economics. Their argument is premised on the notion that the market is a kind of practice with a *telos* (i.e., an end in itself). This *telos*, they describe, is the objective of enabling mutual beneficial exchanges. The supporting virtues that advance this end are listed to include: universality, enterprise and alertness, respect for the tastes of trading partners, trust and trustworthiness, acceptance of competition, self-help, non-rivalry, and stoicism about reward. I do not wish to challenge here the meaning or relevancy of these "market virtues" as identified and described by Bruni and Sugden. I do, however, wish to challenge what I take to be a highly questionable metaphysical assumption at the heart of their argument. There is a certain unspoken providentialism inherent in the authors' treatment of "the market" as a kind of historical subject characterized by a *telos* (i.e., an ultimate end or purpose). The authors' treatment of flesh and blood human beings seems to consider them to be agents/subjects in service to this larger historical principle and its *telos*. Thus, those human agents who exhibit the above-listed virtues help in the realization of the principal's (the market's) over-riding *telos* (i.e., the efficient allocation of resources via voluntary and mutually beneficial exchange).

Moreover, it should be clear that Bruni and Sugden have a highly stylized and ideal understanding of "the market." It is identical to the model of perfect competition of introductory economics textbook fame. It assumes a world of small, price-taking firms who confront each other and their customers on *free and equal terms* (emphasis added). It is a model in which no informational asymmetries exist. Now, there is nothing wrong with positing an ideal type model. The Stoic sage is just such an ideal. But there *is* something wrong with confusing this model with the world as it actually works. Bruni and Sugden are guilty of precisely this confusion when they make certain claims about this model's relevance to the lives we lead including ascribing to it "normal market transaction" (2013: 158). I submit that normal market transactions rarely occur under the conditions of the perfectly competitive market. I further submit that flesh and blood human beings rarely enter into market transactions with firms on "free and equal terms." This is especially so in terms of the labor market, perhaps the single most important market relationship that most people must negotiate. Neither is it the case that buyers of consumer goods have full information on the various products that they buy. Moreover, they are less likely to have critical information in the absence of government oversight of the firms and industries involved. Informational asymmetries are particularly pernicious when they involve such essential goods as food, drugs, and health services.

In fact, Bruni and Sugden more generally ignore the possibility that actual market relationships are just as often as not a species of *power* relationship entered into by the contracting parties on very unequal terms. Consider a worker who has lost a job due to the off-shoring decision of its employer firm. The firm has embraced the "virtues" of universality and enterprise and alertness by seeking to locate in a market abroad and has advanced market efficiency by doing so. Can the authors say with straight faces that *the market* has thereby advanced in its mission to serve its *telos* of enabling mutual beneficial exchanges? Are the now unemployed workers enjoined to exercise the virtues of acceptance of competition, self-help, and stoicism of reward in order to serve the same *telos*? I submit that anyone inclined to accept this account of virtue ethics is embracing, to use a familiar term, a very thin, and perhaps distorted, notion of virtue.

Bruni and Sugden admit that a filial adherence to market virtues does not constitute by itself a recipe for a well-lived life. They insist, however, that virtues are defined in relation to a particular practice. Thus, we would infer by their account that market virtues can be separated from other kinds of virtues that pertain to other spheres or practices. An individual who would be considered highly virtuous as an agent of the market could conceivably conduct himself in a highly vicious way in terms of non-market practices. To illustrate, there would be no necessary contradiction between a highly virtuous business owner/executive who is simultaneously a highly vicious parent, spouse, friend, and citizen. As a matter of empirical fact, it might not be hard to identify many plausible cases where this result holds. As a satisfying picture of the role of virtue in human flourishing, however, it leaves much to be desired. This is so inasmuch as it is not easy, if at all even possible, to compartmentalize our lives according to market and non-market issues and concerns. Bruni and Sugden will counter that some market virtues are transferable to other social realms. The important point at issue is the desire to promote mutual benefit. But this is a virtue, supposedly, of *the market* as a historical subject, a metaphysical idea to be sure. It is not a perquisite virtue of the human agents that constitute the market. As is frequently pointed out, including by Bruni and Sugden (2013: 151), Adam Smith argued that the gains realized by market exchange were not the result of individual beneficence. They were the result of the pursuit of individual self-interest.

Certainly, the ancients did not imagine that virtue could be separated according to distinct practices. A sage was that person who exercised virtue in *all* actions. Courage, temperance, moderation, and justice were expected of the sage in all her dealings. Virtuous actions for them were "all things considered" matters. Moreover, the *telos* that operated at the center of the ancient ethical outlooks was the *human telos*. We can ask, in what did the concrete content of this purpose consist? Depending on which of the ancient schools respond, we might get different answers (e.g., *ataraxia*: tranquility; *eudaimonia*: happiness; *logos*: reason). I can see merit in each of these as contributing to human thriving. And, as we've seen, several contemporary commentators friendly to the ancients have also emphasized that the human *telos* can also be convincingly linked to the exercise of the autonomy of the individual, or to the exercise of capabilities.

So, the question remains, does public policy have a role to play in the promotion of the human *telos*? An important objective of this book has been to demonstrate that appropriately conceived policies can serve to promote the human *telos* in direct and indirect ways. Policies that promote the central capabilities of human beings help to develop in them the positive freedom required for full participation in the economic, political and cultural lives of their communities and nations. A public policy commitment to increasing access to quality education may be the single most important means of accomplishing this objective. Measures that provide vulnerable segments of the population to basic goods and services, however, must be regarded as a supplementary function of public policy. Public policy fails in the promotion of human flourishing, and fails to model virtue, if it chooses the wrong instruments. The requirements for human flourishing at times may conflict with narrowly considered economic efficiency and/or political expediency. Defending the rights of the marginalized and dispossessed, advocating for environmental protection, overcoming deeply ingrained fears and prejudices require what at times seem like extremely binding shortages of political virtue. One suspects that to the extent our political and policy making processes tend to mimic our market-dominated economic processes, these shortages will be difficult, maybe impossible, to overcome. Contrary to the hopes of Bruni and Sugden, there may not be a great deal of overlap in the virtues that inform market virtues and those that operate in political practice, if the challenge to political practice involves the promotion of non-market virtues.

Bruni and Sugden are fairly clear, for example, that the concept of self-sacrifice is not among the list of character traits they define as market virtues. Self- sacrifice, they argue, contradicts the *telos* of the market which resides in *mutual* benefit from exchange. And yet it is not hard to come up with cases where public policies designed to promote human flourishing makes demands that imply a redistribution of resources among individuals and households. The very notion of civic *duty* is pregnant with the suggestion of accepting a smaller share of individual benefit in favor of some larger purpose. On some level people in general derive a great deal of satisfaction in meeting obligations that involve a transfer of material benefits to others. Think, for example, of the sacrifices that parents make for their children, to take a very common case. The important question is, can the disposition to derive a sense of well-being from self-sacrifice involved in the support of those near and dear to us be extended to those who are not so near and dear? The Stoics as we've seen, believed this to be the meaning of social *oikeiosis*, a developmental objective of the sage. It hardly needs observing that we have not yet evolved to be a nation of sages. There is plenty of reason to be pessimistic about the prospects for a massive outbreak of altruism that inspires those of us who live among the materially privileged strata of the global population to accept a reduction in our material consumption that enables the materially deprived to better their lives. There exist similarly substantial doubts about the power of altruism to generate the self-sacrifice required to meet our global environmental challenges. It may be, however, that Bruni and Sugden are correct that altruism and self-sacrifice are the wrong notions on which to hang our hopes. Our salvation as a species may depend on the development of a world-view that understands our essential nature as a *species being*, to borrow a phrase from Marx. Such an innovation in human consciousness would reveal that a precondition for individual human flourishing is the flourishing of all.

"Easy goods," "hard goods," and the good life

This book has argued that standard economic theory is incapable of providing useful guidance for a certain class of economic choices and their corresponding policy challenges. We might consider the defining characteristic of this class of choices with the help of a distinction between the kinds of goods involved. I submit that this distinction be termed "easy goods" versus "hard goods." Easy goods are what most of understand by the word "goods." They are easily identifiable as the things that provide us with pleasure, or utility. They are the stuff of Epicurus's and Mill's lower-order pleasures and Hirschman's wanton preferences. Choice-making regarding easy goods is reasonably well-described by the RCU approach of standard economic theory. By contrast, hard goods are precisely "hard" because they may in the first place be difficult to identify as goods at all, and not merely because they may be costly to acquire. Virtue considered as a good, the only final good for the Stoics, is a case in point. Indirect evidence that virtue is an intrinsic good, and not just an instrumental one, is provided by the things we often urge on our children (e.g., "Do your best!"; "Don't worry about what you can't control"; "Do the right thing"; "Share," etc.). Undeniably, we impress this sort of advice on our young because, in the end, we want them to be "happy." For most of us, though, this doesn't go far enough. We do not want them to be happy fools, or happy criminals, after all. We want them to be happy, but happy in the right way. Towards that end we try to cultivate in them a taste for the hard goods of life, including virtue. We try to impress on them the meaning of *eudaimonia*.

At the beginning of the Great Depression John Maynard Keynes wrote an essay in which he predicted that 100 years hence humankind will have solved the economic problem.[1] By this startling assertion he meant that we will have reached such a state of advanced productivity, and population growth will have been mitigated to such a degree, that we will be able to satisfy all the absolute material need of the globe's population.[2] The real challenge, Keynes speculated, will be the readjustment in human habits and instincts in negotiating the transition from a world in which the economic problem is the driving force of human existence to one in which this compulsion is no longer appropriate. Less than 20 years out from Keynes's deadline, it is clear what a remarkably prescient thinker he was. It seems both true that the world possesses the technical capacity to satisfy its reasonable needs, and that the requisite changes in our habits and instincts remain bound to a period when toil and trouble was the *sine qua non* of our daily existence. That is, we seem technically capable of leading lives worthy of the Epicurean Garden, but we seem incapable of making the corresponding psychological and ideological commitments. It would seem that a beginning to such a necessary shift of mental model would entail moving away from an emphasis on a narrow utilitarian basis for our economic choice making and toward a eudaimonic basis. This shift needs to enter our thinking on an individual as well as on a collective policy level.

Notes

1   "Economic possibilities for our grandchildren," in Keynes (1963).
2   Keynes makes a distinction between "absolute" needs and "second class" needs. The latter he regards as those related to the desire for social status. Keynes qualifies his prediction with the proviso that there occur no disastrous wars or population surges over the 100-year interval. Anyone tempted to argue that Keynes failed to anticipate World War II should consult his *The Economic Consequences of The Peace*.

References

Bruni, Luigino and Robert Sugden. 2013. "Reclaiming virtue ethics for economics," *Journal of Economic Perspectives*, 27, 4 (Fall): 141–164.
Cafero, Philip. 1998. "Virtue ethics (not too) simplified," Twentieth World Congress of Philosophy, Boston, August 10–15, https://www.bu.edu/wcp/Papers/TEth/TEthCafa.htm.
Keynes, John Maynard. 1963. *Essays in Persuasion*, New York: W.W. Norton & Co.

Index

addiction: behavior 9; rational 97–9;
neurobiology of 99–100; as disease
100–1, 108–9; psychology of 102–3;
sociological determinants of 103–4;
ethics of 101; treatment and
policy 104, 110–112; drugs and
legalization 112
Alexander the Great 5–7, 30, 35
Ambrose 40
American Historical Association 5
American Medical Association 101
American Psychiatric Association 101,
75n7
Annas, Julia 162–4
anthropocentrism: economics and the
environment 10, 125–6; and ethics 125
Antisthenes 19, 31n5
Apollodorus 20
Aquinas, Thomas 3
Aristotle: 3, 5, 7–9, 17–19; compared to
Plato 17; *Politics*/economic ideas 18;
phronimos (practical man); on nature
124; and education 166
Ashley-Cooper, Anthony: *see*
Shaftesbury
ataraxia: 23, 41, 55, 78; in the face of
death 144; and justice 162–4; 180
autarkeia 20
autonomy: and rationality 73; 78, 107–8;
and individual responsibility 115–116;
and death 151, 153–5

Bacon, Francis 81
Barnes, Henrietta Robin 102–3
Becker, Gary 97–9
Becker, Lawrence 81–2, 89 89n7, 90n12,
90n13; 125
Benatar, David 153
Bennett, William 112

Bentham, Jeremy: 3–4, 8, 52, 81;
reductionist view of human nature 68
Bhagavad Gita 31n2
Biron, Denise 104
Bodin, Jean 41
Bookchin, Murray 124
Brenkert, George G. 60
Brennan, Tad 105–6, 117n9, 117n10
Bruni, Luigino 178–81
Buddhism: 73; traditions 116
Bush, George H. W. 112

capabilities 180
cap-and-trade: 138; objections to 138
Carson, Rachel 129
Catholic Church 152
Cato 154
Center for Disease Control 118n19
character 131
Charondas 154
chlorofluorocarbons 127
Christ as a stoic model 39
Christianity: 35–7; philosophy 37;
literary forms; consistency with
ancient thought 40, 154
Chrysippus 81
Cicero: 28 39, 41, 85; rejection of
emotion as a virtue 46, 63n19;
public engagement of the Sage
133–4
civic duty 181
civil economy 117n2
civil society 43
classical economics 34, 46–7, 131
classical philosophy 38
Cleanthes 81
Clement 37, 40
co-morbidity 102
consumer sovereignty 73

consumption: 13, 96; pathological 96–7,
113–114; mindfulness 116; minimalism
132, 143, 161; and welfare 131; and
taxes 161; as economic engine 172;
luxury 173; inconspicuous 174
contract theory of justice 84, 163–4
Coornhert, Dirck 43
Crates 21
Cynics/Cynicism: 19–21, 161; asceticism
20–1; cosmopolitanism 21

Dante 62n5
Darwin, Charles 81
David, James 99
death: rational denial of 11–12; fear of
23, 146–1; as an evil 39; and economic
research 142, 146
democracy: Plato's hostility to 16;
Hellenistic outlook 30
de Quevedo, Francisco 40
Del Rio, Martin 40
De-Shalit, Avner 167
Descartes, René 81
determinism (*see also* free will):
Epicurean 22; Stoic 32n13
dialectical materialism 57
Diderot, Denis 43
Diogenes Laertius 20–1, 23, 26–9, 31n5,
41, 157n1
Diogenes of Sinope 19
Dobbin, Robert 21
drugs: legalization of 111
Dudley, Donald R. 19–20

eating disorders 114–115
eclecticism: philosophic 12; ethics 30;
Smith 62n16
economics: 3; as a scientific discipline 5,
69; ethical presuppositions of 8,
142–3; influence of 9; policy 11;
behavioral 99; ecological 127; and
death 146–7
education: 162; finance 161; and ethics
166; "stealth inequities" in 168
Education Law Center 168
egalitarianism 7
Elster, John 72
Elwood, William 113
Emanuel, Ezekiel J. 150, 153
Engel's Law 175n5
Enlightenment: 8, 38; Scottish 42, 44, 47
environment: ethics 10; sustainability
124, 129; virtue ethics 125, 128–9
Epictetus 109

Epicurus/epicurean: pleasure 10–11, 23,
77–8, 131, 143, 161, 163, 181, 216;
Letter to Herodotus 22; physics 22;
theology 23, 143; ethics 246, 43,
hedonic orientation 143; compared to
Stoics 27; atomism 43; imprint on
Enlightenment; instrumental value of
virtue 131; theology 143; friendship
144; sage 163
Epicurean view 143; Marxian conception
61; and environmental goods 130;
Stoic virtue 144; and non-material
values 156; well-lived life 161
ethics/ethical: 3; and economics 5;
ancient Greek 7; pluralism 11; theories
96; compared to Buddhism 118n25
eudaimonia: 7; compared to utility 13–14;
Hellenistic view of 31; Stoic view 27;
87–88, 107, 14, 182
extended producer responsibility 137

fatalism 28
Feuerbach, Ludwig: 57; materialism and
humanism 57; Young Hegelians 57
Fischer, Irving 173
Freakonomics 12n2
free choice/will *see also* fatalism: 28, 101
freedom: and reason 36, 59, 109; 176
n14; well-being and agency 86;
positive 73–4, 180
friendship: 13; as a source of happiness
24; as highest pleasure 78

gambling/gaming: 11, 161:
state-sponsored 162
Garden, The 21, 55, 78, 133
Gardner, Eliot 99
Gassendi, Pierre 43
Gay, Peter 42
Gibbon, Edward 43
"good, the": 4, 75; for a social animal
80–81; and Plato 15–16; Aristotle'
understanding of 17, 59; Stoic
understanding of 27; and virtue 144
Gnosticism 36
Great Depression 6, 173, 182
Greeks: philosophy 5, 7; democratic
institutions 6; economies 6; city states 6,
30, 35; language and culture 35;
influence on Marx 56; well-lived life 13
Green, O.H. 147
greenhouse gases 136
gross domestic product 127
Gymnosophists 29

happiness: 24, 55; and consumption
172–173
Head Start/Early Head Start 169
health care: 149; end-of-life 11, 149;
palliative care and hospice 142, 150–2
hedonic/hedonism: 7, 142; calculus 11,
12n1; Epicurean 23; Mill on
Epicurean 53–4; ethical 89n8;
research 131
Hellenistic: period 5–6; empire 161
Hellenistic philosophy/ethics: 6, 7–10, 12,
154, 162; compared to classical Greek
philosophy 30–31; environmental
ethics 130; death and mortality 142,
153–154
Hierocles 50–1
Hirschman, Albert 74, 79, 181
Hobbes, Thomas 44, 81, 84, 117n13, 164;
on consumption tax
homo economicus 62n7, 72–73
Hughes, J. Donald 123–4
human flourishing: 13, 30, 107;
environmental requirements for 137;
autonomy and 155; and virtue 179;
policies for 181
humanism 39
Hume, David 42, 44, 6, 74, 81, 84
Hursthouse, Rosalind 79–80, 90n11,
118n24
Hutcheson, Frances: 42, 45; attack on
Mandeville 45; Stoic influence 46

impressions: *katalepic* vs. non-*katalepic*
105–7
impulses: as emotions 105; *eupatheiai* 106
indifferents: Stoic 106

Jaeger, Werner 35, 37
James, William 117
Jesus: as a Stoic model 39; and
Hellenistic doctrines 62n2
Jevons, Stanley 4, 69
John, the apostle 35–6
Justice: 4, 25, 162; ancient notions of 84;
Epicurean account of 162, contractual
theory of 162; social 163; Stoic theory
165; virtue-based theories 165
Justin Martyr 36

Kaldor, Nicholas 173
Kant, Immanuel 81, 117n13
Keynes, John Maynard: 12, 182n1, n2;
on the "good life" 31n1
Kopczuk, Wojciech 146–8

Leopold, Aldo 129
Lipsius, Justin 39, 43
Locke, John 44, 81
logical positivism 69
logos 23, 27, 36, 75, 108–9, 180
Long, A.A.: defense of Epicurus 25–6;
84–5, 165; on Stoic fatalism 108–9;
human and non-human nature 132
Lucretius: 32n9, 41; origins of the
state 44
Lycurgus 154

Mandeville, Bernard: 45–46; *Fable of the
Bees* 45
Marc Antony 5
Marginalist Revolution 3–5, 69
Marcus Aurelius 63n22
Marx, Karl: 3, 9, 47, 56–61, 81; as a
moral philosopher 56; influence of
Epicurus, Democritus 56–8;
materialism 57; compared to Aristotle
on the commodity and value 58–9;
freedom 60; *species being* 60;
alienation 61
Maurer, Christian 46
Meade, James 173
Medicare 157
Medieval Schoolmen 42
Menger, Carl 4, 69
meta-preferences 79
methodological individualism 69
Middle Ages 39
Mill, James 3, 9, 52
Mill, John Stuart: 3, 8–9, 47, 52–6, 181;
criticism of Bentham; praise for
Epicurean outlook; Stoic inspiration
53; on higher and lower pleasures
54–5; expert opinion 55; Aristotle's
influence 55–6; training in Platonic
dialectics 56; natural rights 111; on
consumption tax 173–4
Mitis, Phillip 163–164, 175n1
Montesquieu 43
moral philosophy: 3, 5; relativism/
objectivism 11; of Shaftesbury 44–5;
sentimentalism 62n14
moral responsibility 109–10
Munger, Michael 135–6
Murphy, Kevin 97–9

National Institute of Alcohol Abuse and
Alcoholism 101
nature: importance for Epicurus 23; in
accordance/conformity with 26–8

(Stoicism) 123, 131–3; follow 40, 89,
90n12; as a machine (Smith) 48; as a
basis for ethics 79–1, 123; as a
theological notion 132; intrinsic value
of 129, 139n5
natural law: Epicurus 23; 84
naturalism: of Stoics 28, 124; ethical
79–81, 90n11, Aristotelian 87
neoclassical economics: 5, 9–11, 72;
normative presuppositions and
behavioral assumptions 5, 156; as a
science 67; divorce from moral
philosophy 61; student training in
62n7; individualist ethos of 85; Solow
as 126; growth model 174, 175n12
neo-stoicism 82
neurobiology 100, 103
Newton, Isaac 81
Nichomachean Ethics 3
Nixon, Richard 112
Nussbaum, Martha: 62n11, 85–8;
capabilities approach 86, 118n24, 162,
167; on relevance of Aristotle 86;
Stoicism and its limits 88–90, 90n17,
n18, 167; 175n7

Occam's razor 89n1
oikeiōsis: Stoic concept 10, 162;
compared to Smith's *self interest* 50–1;
compared to Marx's alienation 61;
social 84, 124–5, 164, 181; and justice
164–5; economic aspect 165
oikonomikè 5
Organization for Economic Cooperation
and Development 112
Origin 37

Parfit, Derek 165
Patient Self-Determination Act 150
Paul, the apostle 35–6
perfect competition: assumptions of 4;
model 179
Petrarcch, Francesco 39; criticism of
Seneca 62n4
physician-assisted suicide 142, 157n9
phronēsis ("practical reasoning") 75–6;
and virtue 76
Pico, Gianfrancesco 41
Plato: 5, 7–8, 37; dialogs 14, 30, 89n8; on
the just society 16; 15–17; *see also*
Socrates; and education 16, 166
pleasure: Epicurean concept 10, 13, 77;
naturalistic account of 40
pollution rights 138

positivism: 67; logical 69, 71
praxis 59
precautionary principle 139n8
psychology 100
public finance: 11, 160–1; ethics of 161
public philosophy 12
public policy: end of life 12; ethics of
96–7; pragmatism 110; eating
disorders 114–115; and virtue 175
Pyrrho 29
Pythagoras 166

Raimondi, Cosma 40
Randell Jr., John Herman 35, 38
rational/reason: 9; as the human *telos* 18;
"thinness" of economic conception
67–9, 145–6; and ethics 75; moral 77;
see also right reason and rationality
rationality: 72–75; bounded/procedural/
broad 72, 77, 98; reflective 73, 78–9;
Stoic conception 76–7, 145;
Epicureanism 77–8; ancient and
modern compared 78–9; practical 82,
87; addiction 97–9; fear and Stoic
rejection of 148
Rawls, John 83
recycling: economics and ethics 135–8; as
a moral issue 136; and public policy
137
Renaissance: 38–41; humanism 43
revealed choice theory: 74; rational
choice utilitarianism 9, 72, 74, 78, 95,
97, 99, 107, 128; reductionist
tendency of 74
right reason 27, 76, 89, 105, 107, 137,
156, 175
rights and liberties 83–4
Rolston III., Holmes 129
Roman Empire 6–7, 30
Rostovtzeff, Michael 5–6
Rousseau, Jean Jacques 164

St. Augustine 41
sage 9, 28, 39–40, 76, 105–6, 123, 133,
145, 155
Salutati, Zabarella 39
Sandler, Ronald 128
Sceptics/skepticism: 28–9, 41; as a threat
to the Church 42
Seidman, Laurence 173
self-command 107
self-interest: 26; and virtue 45; and Smith 50
Sen, Amartya: 85; capabilities approach
85–6, 118n24, 162

Seneca 39, 41, 125, 132, 145
Sextus Empiricus 41
Shaftesbury 44–5
Simpson, John 45
Skog, Ole-Jorgen 98
slaves/slavery 16, 30, 88, 117n1, 133
Slemrod, Joel 146–8
Smith, Adam: 3, 8, 42, 47, 68, 131;
    Wealth of Nations 47; ethics 48;
    Theory of Moral Sentiments 47–51;
    impartial spectator 47; Stoic influence
    48–51; high regard for Stoic doctrines
    62n15; "father" of modern economics
    68; market exchange gains 180
social contract theory 44
social science 11, 75
Socrates: 7–8, 14–15; method 8; moral
    courage 8; compared to Plato 14;
    death of 155, 158n12
Solow, Robert: 126, 131, 139n4;
    sustainability 126–7; growth model
    176n13
Sophists 16
species being 181
Sphaerus 177n10
Spinoza 73
Stephens, William O. 124
Stoics/stoicism: 7–8, 10–11, 26–8; ethics
    28, 81, 110–11; wise man or sage 27,
    133, 148, 179; and Christianity 39;
    passions vs. affections 46; importance of
    88; and addiction 104–5; epistemology
    105; "right reason" 105; "character-
    building" philosophy 106; fatalism 108;
    virtues 123, 161; cosmopolitanism 50,
    125; impartiality, reciprocity, solidarity
    134; indifferents (externals) 145;
    outlook on death 145, 147–8; on suicide
    145; theory of justice 164
substance abuse cues 99–100, 102–4, 114
Sugden, Robert 83, 178–81
suicide: Epicurean rejection of 41;
    Smith's rejection of Stoic doctrine
    49; Stoic outlook 145, physician-
    assisted (PSA) 145; arguments against
    151–2; legalization 153; rational v.
    regular 155
Supreme Court of the United States 151
sustainable: as an economic issue 126;
    environment as an ethical issue
    126, 133
swerve 22, 26,32n12, 57

Taxes: 11, 160; Pigouvian 96; sin taxes
    160–2, 170–2; on consumption 173–4
telos: human 17, 59–60, 180; of nature
    124; market 178–9
Theory of Moral Sentiments, A 3, 8
Thoreau, Henry 129
Tragedy of the Commons 139n2

US Census Bureau 158n13
US Department of Health and Human
    Services 158n10
United States Department of Agriculture
    115, 118n22
USA Tax 173
Utilitarianism: 4, 7, 13, 69, 96, 165;
    rational choice utilitarianism (RCU) 9,
    68: criticism of 7172; classical 52–4;
    and economics 178; *see also* Mill,
    Bentham
utility: 7, *see also* pleasure; maximization
    5, 10, 83, 131; 13–14, 69, 143, 146; as
    happiness 126

virtue: 7, 13; versus good 27; as the only
    good 39; and public finance 11; public
    45–6; Mill's conception of 54; as a
    disposition 76; instrumental value of
    77; as an element in choice 79; Stoic
    110; and public finance 161; and
    policy 178; role in economics 178–1;
    as a good 181
virtuous state 11
Voltaire 43

Walras, Leon 4, 69
war on drugs 112–113
Wealth of Nations, The 3, 47
welfare: 7; economics 68, 77; social 69,
    85, 131; theory 95, 130–1;
    maximization 97–8
wildness/wilderness: 129–130; and
    welfare 129
wise person: (*see also* sage) Platonic 15;
    Epicurean 23–4; Stoic 27–8
Wolff, Jonathan 167
World Health Organization 101
World War I 6

Xenophon 52

Zeller, Edward 77–8
Zeno 26, 81, 125

For Product Safety Concerns and Information please contact our EU
representative GPSR@taylorandfrancis.com
Taylor & Francis Verlag GmbH, Kaufingerstraße 24, 80331 München, Germany

www.ingramcontent.com/pod-product-compliance
Ingram Content Group UK Ltd.
Pitfield, Milton Keynes, MK11 3LW, UK
UKHW020952180425
457613UK00019B/640